Yoga inVision 12

I0132704

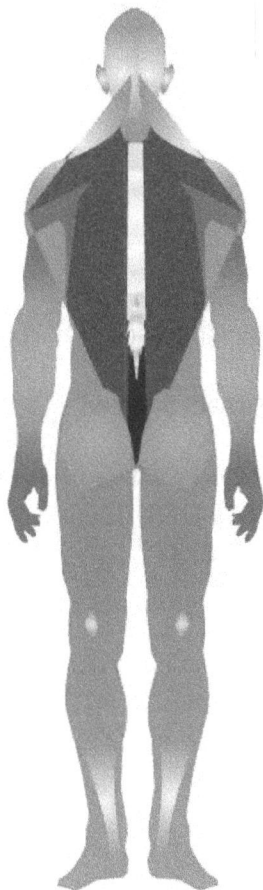

Michael Beloved

Illustrations: Author
Correspondence:
Michael Beloved
19311 SW 30th Street
Miramar FL 33029
USA
Email: axisnexus@gmail.com
                michaelbelovedbooks@gmail.com

Mi-Beloved

Table of Contents

INTRODUCTION

This is the twelfth of the Yoga inVision series. It relates experiences and practices done in 2012-2013. These give beginners ideas of the physical, psychological and spiritual experiences one may have when doing asana postures, pranayama breath-infusion and *pratyahar* sensual energy withdrawal. Beyond that is higher yoga, which Patañjali named the *samyama* procedures. He defined *samyama* as a combination of *dharana* deliberate focus, *dhyana* spontaneous focus and *samadhi* continuous spontaneous focus. During practice, these progress one into the other. If one is expert at *pratyahar* sensual energy withdrawal, one may graduate to *dharana* which is deliberate focus of the attention to a higher concentration force or person. As soon as one masters *dharana* one may slip into *dhyana* which is an effortless focus on a higher concentration force or person. Once you practice *dhyana*, *samadhi* happens as the continuous effortless focus on a higher concentration force or person.

Many persons on a spiritual path feel that they can construct a process as they advance. This idea denotes failure. After all, if the supernatural and spiritual environment, is not already there, no one can create it now. It is either there or it is not. For instance, if one intends to moves to a different country, then of course one will fail if the country intended does not exist. It has to be there prior. Similarly, what you aim for as spiritual life, must be there already, or one will find that the aspiration is incorrect. This is why I speak of a concentration force or person. I could have said concentration person or divine person, or God. I did not because I do not know how anyone's spiritual path will develop.

One may leave an island in the safest boat and still the vessel may sink. One should keep one's mind open and be willing to work with fate. In spiritual development, there is providence too. What one desires to have one may not achieve. What one wishes to see may never appear.

These Yoga inVision journals show how sporadic my course of yoga was. This is after years of practice. It gives some idea of what to expect. Once you get through the lower yoga practice, you will see advancement in a more stable way but it may be incremental, accruing little by little, with bright flashes here and there.

Part 1

Head Infusion Practice

Breath infusion session was very good this afternoon. Near the end of the practice, I worked on the back of the head and then on the frontal part. Practice usually begins with focus on getting the gross body out of sluggishness. Once it awakens, I focus on various parts of the trunk and the lower extremities which are the thighs, legs and feet. Circulation in the extremities is problematic. This gets worse as a body ages. This body is sixty-one years of age, it is an uphill battle with the encroaching authority of time, asserting itself daily, taking more territory, stating that it will soon take the entire body and deprive its usage.

After feeling that I worked enough on the extremities, I focused on the trunk. Some years ago, I did battle with the pubic area. Due to years of effort, and help from yoga gurus, I got a small victory over that area. After infusing the lower extremities and the trunk, I usually work on the neck and then on the head.

Today I did some practice for Tibeti Yogi who instructed that I infuse the lower back of the brain. Yogeshwarananda advised that once I satisfied this requirement, I should bore a channel up the back of the head from the lower brain around the back top of the head to the frontal part of the brain. There are nadi energy channels there. He instructed that I blast them to be sure that they are operative and not clogged.

After that I moved to the front to do a practice which Yogesh introduced. In doing that practice, I noticed that the energy moved up at a slant angle on the exhales. This means that as the forceful exhales went out of the nostrils, the infused energy from the inhales went up.

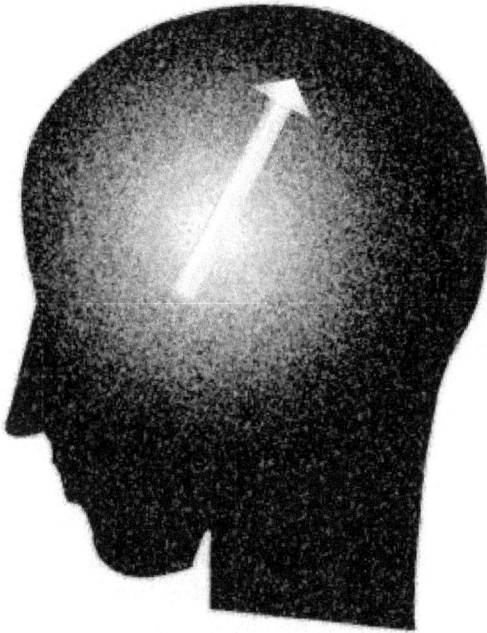

Constipated Yogis

Students should be wary about medications which have constipation as a possible side effect. Many persons take pain killers, sleep aids, stimulants and other kundalini-adjusting medications, prescription or non-prescription.

This is counterproductive to both kundalini yoga and meditation. Many persons who meditate and who use these medications do not understand the effects on their perception. These substances produce ignorance of psychic phenomena which is fine if you desire no distinction and clarity in the psychic and spiritual levels of existence. If possible, students should cease these medications; otherwise they will develop more psychic insensitivity.

Constipation tells one that the base chakra does not function properly. Taking medications to get rid of constipation does nothing to improve the conditions of the chakra, even though superficially on the physical side, those medications may result in evacuation. The *agnisara* practice assist in eliminating constipation. It helps to get the base chakra to be active without it being under the influence of the chemicals in medications.

Always stop to ask yourself if you will have a stockpile of these medications after you leave the physical body for good? Will a doctor write a prescription on the astral side? Will there be an astral pharmacy which can provide drugs?

One's problems will not be over just by losing the physical body. Do not be naive to think that the subtle body will change its habits merely because it loses a physical form.

What about how your new embryo will form in the mother's uterus. Will it form with a constipation tendency?

Some of what the physical body does has no impact on the subtle one but that which does, should be taken into account.

Whatever method one uses, be sure that it has no negative consequences in the long range.

Long range means in terms of affecting the subtle body in a negative way which you will carry to the afterlife and to the next physical body.

Recently within the last ten years, I observed infants who are constipated as babies. Why is this? Previously the condition in infancy was runny stools. In fact, people used to be alarmed. They would mistake that for diarrhea. Now it is the opposite. Is it possible that these are conditions of ill-health are carried over from the previous life?

Suppose I pass from a body which was addicted to morphine, because in elderly years that became necessary, will my subtle body carry that addiction to the next life, so that in that life I will become an infant addict?

If I lean on herbal treatments instead of actually dealing with the cause of the constipation, will those herbs be available to me in the afterlife, if my subtle body mimics what afflicted the dying physical body? Will I retain unwanted tendencies into the next life?

Meditation or Yoga

Yoga is defined by Patanjali as being inclusive of meditation. He wrote that yoga has eight parts. Of the eight he gave meditation as the three advanced parts made into one sequential practice.

Patanjali listed the eight parts.

- *yama* behavioral restraints
- *niyama* approved behaviors
- *asana* postures
- *pranayama* breath infusion
- *pratyahar* sensual energy withdrawal
- *dharana* effortful linkage to a higher reality
- *dhyana* effortless linkage to a higher reality
- *samadhi* continuous effortless linkage to a higher reality

For meditation, Patanjali gave a Sanskrit term which is *samyama*.
He listed the 6th, 7th and 8th stages combined as one meditation.

Certainly, there are many definitions for yoga but Patanjali is accepted because many yogis quote from or refer to his text, the *Yoga Sutras*. Since I translated and wrote two commentaries on that book, I am familiar with his meanings.

In the West, yoga is tagged as the 3rd part of classical yoga, which is asana postures.

King Kundalini

Exercise session was great this afternoon with some work done on the pubic floor and neck. The neck is a troublesome area where the energy flow between the trunk of the subtle body and the head of it, is constricted. The way the kundalini formatted the system of energy distribution in the body, the head serves the interest of kundalini. The kundalini for its part is interested in survival, exploitation and reproduction. As such the brain as the stooge of kundalini invests its main energies to procure forms for kundalini to survive in and enjoy, then to beget forms for kundalini to secure its passages back into the environments of its exploitive interest.

In kundalini yoga the idea is to break this tendency of kundalini. Part of the process is to remove the constructions in the neck. If that is done, energy flows from the trunk of the body through the neck and into the head. This breaks kundalini's grip on the psyche.

Kundalini is like a king who has a strong reserve army. To defeat this king one has to disband his warriors. Once he is weakened, he can be subjugated. The main warrior force of kundalini is the sex hormones in the body. If a student yogi can distribute that energy through the psyche and stop it from pooling in the groin area, the conquest of kundalini is assured.

The breath infusion session should be more than a matter of absorbing, compressing it into the blood stream in the lung and then distributing it. As this happens other events occur. Those are related to psychic perception and knowledge about the layout in the psyche.

When I sat to meditate, I could not focus as required. There were disturbance energies which prevented deep meditation. However, I reached naad sound and naad light. It was sporadic. This is because of a bit of bad luck where certain associations which are hostile to yoga practice, reached me.

There is good and bad weather. There are good sessions of meditation and some which are not progressive. A yogi should practice regardless.

Yogis and Sexual Indulgence

Someone called this afternoon and discussed the incidence of sexual indulgence as it is related to yoga practice.

It is like this: There was this seaworthy ship. At least that is what the crewmen and captain considered it to be. Somehow it sprung aleak. The captain and crew began to wonder about their lives. They were seasoned sailors but the situation was terrible. They understood that they were in a precarious position.

The captain for his part was sorry about the situation but he could not change it. They were in the middle of ocean, far away from land. He gave the order to release the life rafts.

For some days they lay adrift in two rafts staying close to each other, and feeling that things were not so bad. Even if they never spotted a seaworthy ship, they knew that eventually ocean currents beach the flotsam. Even if it took some days or weeks, those life rafts would be cast to land.

It so happened that this was not to be. Suddenly a vicious storm arose. The waves were so large that the lifeboats flooded and sank. Those crewmen, at least the pessimistic ones felt that they were done. One fellow felt a shark pulling at his pants. He began to call for help.

The others looked at him without pity. They knew that the chances of his and even their own survival was nil.

Everybody should try to understand that in yoga practice, it is every man for himself. This is not a course where one person saves others. In this situation asking for help from other crewmen is ludicrous. One sinking sailor cannot assist another. I can look over and see the trouble you are in but that does not mean that I can rescue you or that I am in a better position.

As great a person as Jesus Christ, or so the good book states, said that if God would help him, he would help others. He said, "If I am rescued, I will save others."

It depended on empowerment by the deity he relied on. Even for him helping others was based on other factors.

I sympathize with any elderly person who does serious yoga and meditation and who still carries obligations for sexual indulgence. But it is not that I can do anything to assist anyone. Getting myself out of it requires severe exertion. The way this physical nature is slanted, most students who endeavor to sanitize their social sexual acts are doomed to failure. This does not mean they should stop endeavoring. In fact, that is all the more reason why they should never give up.

There comes a point in a student yogi's life when he/she should make the decision to fight to the bitter end, even if it is obvious that one will not overcome the passionate energy. It is a good lesson about being arrogant.

Thinking that one can overcome this cosmic ocean passion and lust, is a case of severe intoxication. As soon as one sobers, one will realize that one is a straw in the cosmic passionate energies. Then one will do as all good yogis do which is to hide from those energies. When large predators roam, small animals are wise to remain hidden.

Interest Energy in Yoga Practice

One essential feature of spiritual practice is interest.

That is the instinctual interest is in the subtle body. This is not planned interest. Planned interest is the least of problems. That can be controlled. If an interest is dependent on my planning it, it is no problem in yoga

Instinctual interests which are not planned, which one is conscious of or not conscious of, are the ones which should be discovered, checked on with great scrutiny and altered for the advancement of practice, for pleasing the yoga guru.

A yogi does not deny that he has this instinctual interest. He does not take on a self-power, self-control posture, where he feels that he mastered everything and he can sit for thirty minutes and be in the absolute. He admits that he struggles to control the interests. They are not illusions. These energies direct us and cause us to act impulsively. They exercise authority over us.

We see them as energy with real power to cause us to take many haphazard births from here till the end of time. Since the interests are real, we face them like warriors who must fight for their lives.

When one does the postures with the breath infusion, one can recognize these interest energies. At times when one does a certain posture, and the infused energy enters a particular part of the body, one will notice that some psychic shaft of light or a psychic frequency of energy moves from one part of the psyche to another. These are interest energies. Usually they surface in the mind as a forceful inquiry into something or as a forceful attraction to something. These energies are in the psyche, living there like when one lives in a city which has such a large population that one can meet persons whom one never met before if one walks down a busy street.

Some interest energies which live in the psyche are unknown to the self. One never saw them. In fact, energies remain hidden like enemy spies who live in a city and are not discovered.

One set of interest energies is in various parts of the brain. These operate the senses, especially the hearing and visual sense. They pursue things in the physical environment at their leisure. These can move the body against one's will. These can stop the body dead in its tracks even if one wants to move it forward.

There are other places where interest energies hide, like in the chest of the subtle body, in the breasts of women, in the intestines, in the pubic area, in the thighs and genitals.

Postures can help one to discover these energies and to allow one to know their functions. Who do these energies serve? According to Tantra, each energy is controlled by a supernatural person called a devata or deva in Sanskrit. Supposedly, these supernatural entities use one's body at one's expense.

Imagine if you have a car. Someone comes when you sleep or even when you are awake; takes the car, drives it until the gas is consumed and leaves it at the other end of the city. You are called by the traffic department saying that your car is impounded, you must pay a fine and towing fee to repossessed it. The entities who control the interest energies in the psyche are similar.

In yoga, if one is lucky and if one effectively surcharges the subtle form with energizing astral energy, one may see a supernatural person leaving a place in the psyche in disgust. He or she can no longer stay in the psyche because one removed the interest energy which concerned that supernatural person.

Breath Infusion / Head

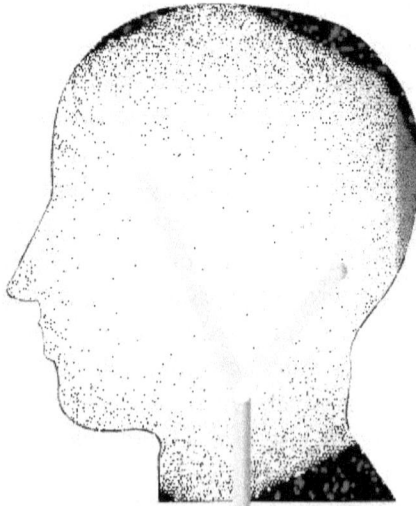

This diagram is breath infusion in the head. Some of the heavy dense astral energy is still on the edges and in part of the neck. Ideally, before the head is treated with breath infusion, the trunk, neck and lower extremities like the thighs, legs and feet should be compacted with light weight astral energy.

However, some attempts to do this may be met with partial success. The student must persist with the practice day after day, twice per day if permissible but once per day minimum.

Corresponding parts

Yogesh gave these diagrams.

In this diagram, the yogi senses a particular part in the lower extremities (1) which corresponds to another part in the trunk (2) which in turn corresponds to another part in the head (3).

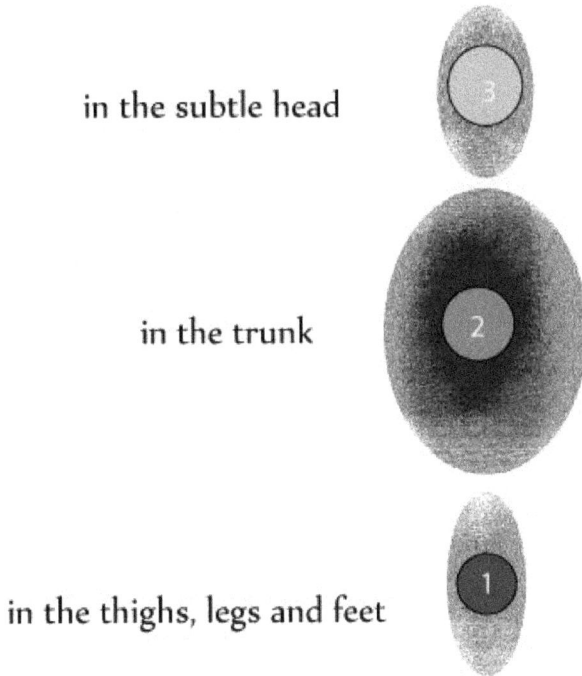

in the subtle head

in the trunk

in the thighs, legs and feet

In this diagram, the yogi senses a particular part in the trunk (1) which in turn corresponds to another part in the head (2).

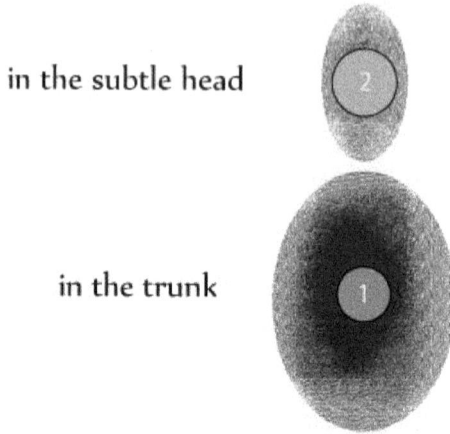

in the subtle head

in the trunk

In this diagram the yogi senses a particular part in the head.

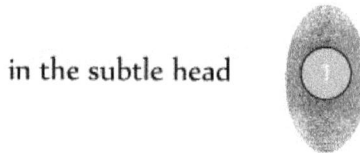

in the subtle head

In these diagrams one sees that when there is a special part of the subtle body which is detected in the lower extremities like the thighs, legs and feet, there is another corresponding part which is felt in the trunk, and there is yet another corresponding part which is felt in the head.

When there is a part which felt is in the trunk, there will be a corresponding part which is felt in the head.

And when there is a part which is felt in the head, one should focus on that part alone. The head is the most important sensing area but the other parts of the subtle body should also be explored, infused with breath energy, and purged of sluggish heavy astral force.

Attentiveness is Necessary in Yoga Practice

Yoga exercises, which means asana postures and breath infusion techniques, are inefficient if one is distracted during practice. The same holds for meditation sessions. If there is a distraction, the student should proceed with the practice but with the understanding that there will not be full effects.

We cannot control everything. We certainly cannot pass through a life in a body without disturbances. Nature will not permit. One should push ahead with practice even if there are disturbances but with the honest view that the practice will not be as effective.

There is also the factor of students. As soon as one learns a little yoga, one usually attracts students. This is a mistake but it cannot be avoided in every case. Over the years, I met many people, who teach yoga and who know little or nothing about yoga kriya or Patanjali. Yet these persons pose as teachers. Some of them even have certification from institutions; something that I lack in every respect.

However, students are a distraction, and a very serious one too. A teacher inevitably is drawn into various social complications which occur in the life of his/her student. Even though many teachers pretend that they can handle any or all karmic reactions which are rolled out in the fate of such students, the association affects the teacher's practice.

When I started an ashram some years ago around 1974, it was trouble and complication from start to finish. Fortunately for me, I took a hint from that and reduced teaching. But I met many people who are total dunderheads when it comes to mystic perception. Some do not take Krishna seriously. Still they declare that they are teachers.

Those who are lucky will remain as students for the rest of the present life, and will not be distracted to become teachers especially of a yoga system which it took God to explain in the *Bhagavad Gita*.

People even in the Buddhism run with the idea that what Buddha did any person can do but they fail to note that the yogis who did gruesome austerities with Buddha when he began to meditate in isolation, when he stopped eating, were told by Buddha that he was the only person who knew anything about enlightenment and that it was him alone out of those people present in the world at the time, who knew anything about it in real terms.

These guys thought that Buddha was just another yogi, but Buddha corrected them and stated that he was the special person and that there would be no one like him in the human race for thousands of years.

I just do not see how one can know this and arrive at ridiculous conclusions about what one can achieve.

In India, Buddha is rated as an incarnation of Vishnu, not as an ordinary entity who attained liberation. Hindus do not like Buddhism for two primary reasons. Reason number one is that Buddha did not promote deity worship which is innate in Hindu culture. Reason number two is that he advocated celibacy and encouraged young men not to get married. Hindu culture includes arranged marriages and rituals to deities. Buddha did not support that. Instead of telling young men to marry, he told them to do *tathagata* which is to go *(gata)* out of *(tatha)* the worldly way of living which is epitomized by family responsibility.

It is amazing that Buddhism became popular in the West where celibacy is rejected for the most part.

Buddha did gruesome austerities and was attentive to the practice, so attentive that it was noticed by the devatas of Hinduism, persons like Brahma who Buddha said came and spoke to him. These are supernatural beings who observe and monitor human history.

Neck Problems

The brain, lungs, heart and spine are the most important physical aspects in yoga. The rate of breathing during practice is directly related to the beat of the heart. In fact, during rapid breathing, the heart changes beats to confirm to the rate of breathing.

I focused on the neck. As the body ages the neck moves forward as if something pushed it away from the back of the body. The neck shifts forward as the body ages. It is interesting that while the body forms in the womb, it forms with a curved spine which gradually straightens to some extent. The spine is never a straight system. It is always curved. The question is how one can deter this natural curving as the body ages.

Tibeti Yogi told me that one should keep the spine as straight as possible. One should slow this curving action by doing neck exercises. He introduced the neck wiggle which is when one finishes a segment of breath infusion and one feels the energy moving through the trunk into the neck. One wiggles the neck side to side to facilitate the energy to pass freely. This wiggling is a physical action but it is also a subtle motion affecting the subtle body. The subtle form is interspaced in the physical system. Actions which are physical may take place in the astral body as well, as that body mimics many physical motions.

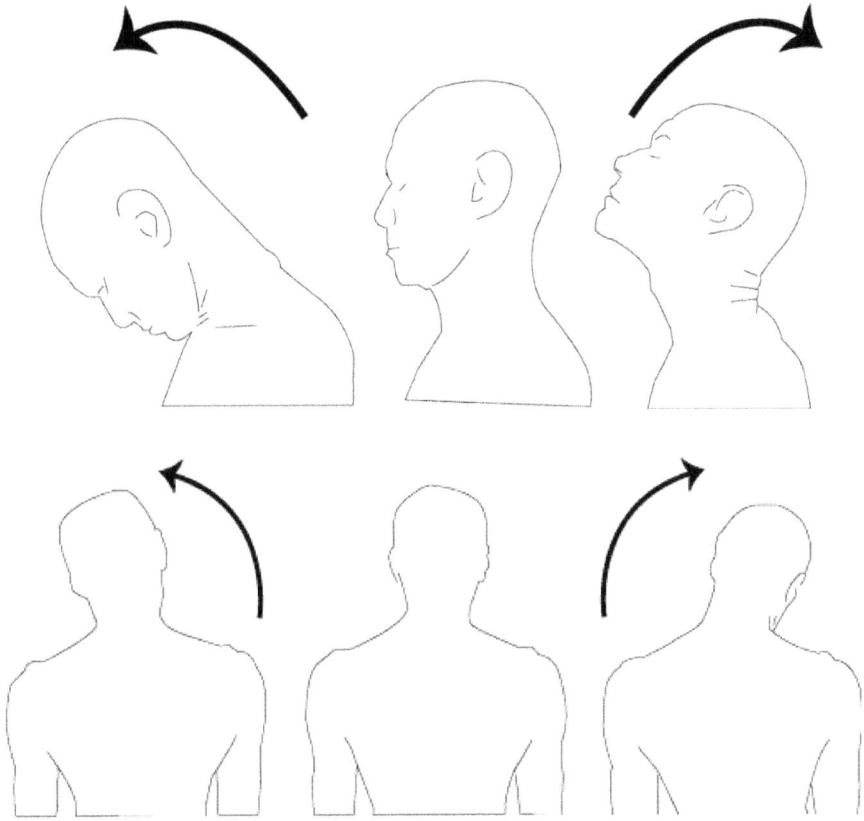

Give Credit to Teachers

Today during breath infusion, I took stock of my impetus for practice. This is a review of yoga gurus and the specific assistance rendered by each. This is time for appreciations to those persons. I have no void, oneness or now-ness to thank for my progression but only yoga gurus, inspirations and discoveries. I am a person not a void. I am not a oneness of everything. All along I dealt with persons. I took assistance from others.

The three practices or kriyas which I focused on this morning were introduced by Yogi Bhajan, Swami Rama, Tibeti Yogi and Yogeshwarananda.

Yogi Bhajan gave the general procedures for breath infusion using *bhastrika* and *kapalabhati* rapid breathing.

Swami Rama stressed the *agnisara* process. I did this process for years now. There was a time when for two years, I did this daily. The elementary part of this process was shown by Arthur Beverford in the California. I saw it in books but he showed physically how it was done. He was good at it.

Once I met the Indra deity in the astral world. For some reason this deity explained the success of siddhas in getting beyond the lower astral heavens which he regulates. He said that to pass those regions one has to conquer the navel chakra. This means mastery of the *agnisara* process.

However, it is not as simple as it sounds. Conquest of the navel includes conquest of the sexual hormone system and conquest of the lower extremities like the thighs, legs and feet. This is a tall order for any student yogi.

Tibeti Yogi stressed cleaning the subtle thighs, legs and feet but that involves a complete change in design of the front sexual region of the subtle body.

Yogeshwarananda gave a process for curbing the intellect for the purpose of developing inner *brahmrandra*. Student yogis may experience a burst outward from the top of the head when kundalini rises into the head. That is not the same practice. Yogeshwarananda speaks about a burst inward in the head of the subtle body from the top downwards.

Anatomy Changes / Subtle body

For a yoga siddha body, the anatomical construction of the form is slightly different to that of an ordinary subtle body. An ordinary subtle body is the one we currently use in dreams and astral projection. This body seems to be a replica of the physical form but it is made of psychological stuff rather than physical substance. With an ordinary subtle body there is no hope for anything but repeated rebirth. This is because of the construction of the form. Its anatomical parts require physical support.

For a yoga siddha form it is not a matter of hopes or of guru favor. It is a matter of changing the anatomical parts of the subtle body. Who will do that? If one is comfortable with the human body and with the subtle body which is interspaced in it in the form of subtle feelings and emotions, why make an effort to change that?

Tibeti Yogi sent information which arrived while I did the afternoon session of the breath infusion. This was an explanation of the changes made in a subtle body of a family person so that he/she creates a yoga siddha form in the astral world. The change takes place through certain mystic practices.

In the subtle body there is a *kanda* bulb which serves as a reservoir for reproductive energies. The counterpart of this in a physical body is the genital/reproduction apparatus either in the male or female.

At first in kundalini yoga practice, the student is not concerned with this *kanda* bulb. The student focuses initially on getting kundalini to rise into the head without regard to the sexual apparatus. Later however, the student must pay attention to the sexual apparatus in the effort to cause the sexual energy to be linked back to the kundalini so that it too can come into the head of the subtle body. But all of this is preliminary and does not make for a yoga siddha form.

Tibeti's message was this:

A person who is familiar with sexual expression in terms of sexual linkage of bodies, has a design in the subtle body which is different to that required for a yoga siddha form. There are higher astral heavens where the inhabitants are also concerned with sexual expression in this way, but they are not siddhas.

In the siddha body, those sexual expression designs are conspicuous by their absence, so that there is no kanda or sexual reservoir. There is no attraction like that. Hence, no resistance is required.

A yoga siddha body looks like any other subtle body, except that it is brighter in terms of the light which emanates from it. Within it the construction is different to other subtle bodies.

On the earth, in a human body, a child of eight or nine years of old does not have to resist the sex urge. The construction of the body causes it to be so that there is no urge to resist even in the presence of sexual exposure. There may be curiosity but there is no genuine sexual interest in the infants and toddlers. Similarly, when the subtle body of a student changes as directed, it loses its sexual interest.

Instead of having a kanda bulb which holds a reservoir of subtle hormonal energy for sexual enjoyment usage, there is no bulb there. The design of that place is such that there is no place to hold such energy. There are no other organs in the form which are dedicated to producing subtle sexual hormones.

A student yogi who was a celibate in youth and who remained a celibate, a swami, that person if in past lives he was a sincere yogi celibate, will not be bothered with sexual energy. However, that is rarely the case. In most cases, those who take the sannyasis or swami status do so superficially. It appears externally that they are celibate but in fact they are not because their bodies generate and store sexual hormones

These energies agitate them from within their minds and feelings. Eventually they engage in sex and are disgraced for breaking vows.

One can pull the tubes and spread them at the bottom of the trunk of the subtle body so that no energy is stored for sexual purposes. The kanda bulb itself is destroyed and the storage tendency is removed from the subtle form. That would begin the deconstruction of a regular subtle body and its conversion into a yoga siddha form.

Yoga siddha forms are not bestowed by the yoga guru or by the deity. They are attained by mystic practice of the student himself or herself. The guru or deity provides the instructions on how to deconstruct the subtle body, to redesign it.

Sex Energy Up-Rise

See the diagram with the sex *kanda*. This was done last year and was a kriya which was given by Swami Atmananda in the astral world. He is the guru of Tibeti Yogi. In this instruction there is allowance for the *kanda* bulb and how to deal with it. This may give some idea of how there is progression in these practices.

Atmananda's Kriya: July 24, 2010
kundalini response to sex energy up-rise

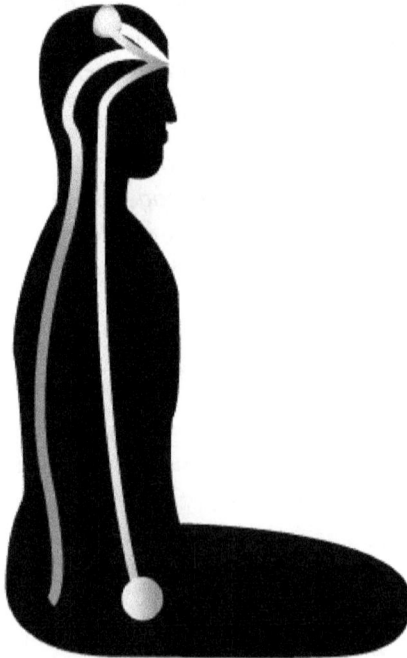

Practice:

- Raise kundalini from sexual energy *kanda* in the subtle body.
- Do not raise it from the base chakra.
- Do bhastrika rapid breathing for at least 50 counts.
- Hold energy at brow chakra while drawing it back to crown.
- Energy will try to disappate at brow chakra.
- Mentally prevent it from doing so.
- Be sure to hold the coreSelf in naad sound while this takes place.
- Naad is the anchor zone.
- Kundalini will rise in unison with the sex energy rise.
- Kundalini is magnetically attracted to sex energy.

Optic Thread Energy

During exercises this afternoon, I noticed an optic thread energy which ran from the sense of identity to the back of the subtle eyeballs. This was a single strand of energy which astrally was a thread of white-yellow light.

When I became aware of this, I sensed a thread which ran through the psyche down through the front part of the thighs and into the knees.

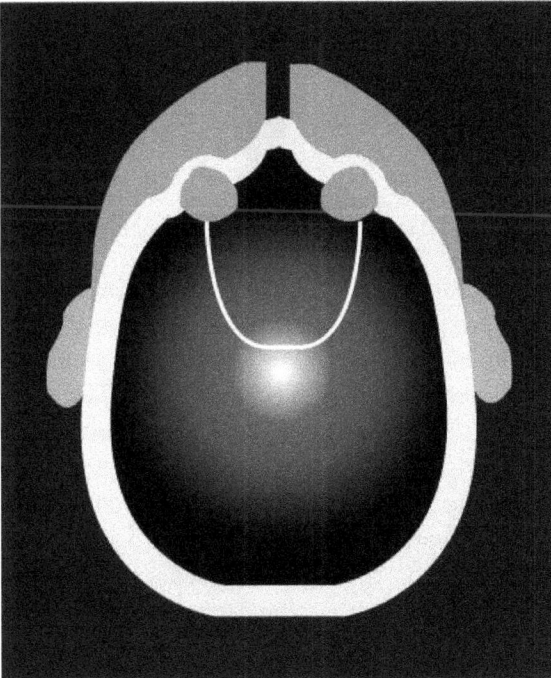

This is similar to the medians and channels in Chinese acupuncture, except that these are subtle transits. This occurred because of a highly infused subtle body. In this way, a yogi discovers the nadis one by one and can have faith in the yogic lore which describes these subtle channels.

Yogic lore are stories about the siddhas which are mentioned in Sanskrit literature. Some stories are dismissed as myths. Some are regarded as allegories, to be used for figurative and symbolic applications.

These attitudes towards these tales can harm a student yogi, robbing the person of the ability to contact siddhas on the supernatural plane.

For instance, there is a story in the *Mahabharata* of Hanuman where it says that Bhima, Arjuna's elder brother, met Hanuman and was in contest with him. It states there that Bhima could not lift even the tail of Hanuman, who is a monkey-man. It is also written that Hanuman will remain alive for the duration of the present era.

Many persons of scientific persuasion feel that this is hyperbole or myth. There is another story in the *Mahabharata* that *Ashwatthama*, an able but criminal warrior who was cursed by Krishna to be a wanderer on the astral planes, is still alive in the Himalayas.

There is yet another story about Babaji, how he can be seen in the Himalayas.

What should one make of these tales? The best attitude is to take these stories at face value, which means to hear or read of them and then to leave the mind open for evidence. This is better than assuming a scientific bent of mind and dismissing these stories as being imaginative, allegoric or symbolic.

Some students tie themselves up with the chains of disbelief. They have an opinion that the books from India were either tampered with or were written long after they were aurally composed by a Vedic rishi. With this in mind, they approach Sanskrit literature as dubious.

Blaming Muktananda

During breath infusion this morning, I got a message from Tibeti Yogi which said that he would not return since I practiced the processes, he showed me. These kriyas are methods of getting to hidden, *hard to reach* places in the subtle body, for removing polluted energy which lingers in those parts.

This is great for him since it means that he is relieved from having to remain on a lower level for the purpose of introducing others to these methods. As I practice these methods and see their effectiveness I could teach with confidence. The only thing is that a student has to reach a certain stage before he/she could make use of these procedures.

Before I finished the session, which was from 4.30 am to 5.30 am, the guy who became known as Adi Da Samraj appeared. He wanted to go over some criticisms which he had about Muktananda. His complaint is that initially when he met Muktananda the Swami advertised himself as a person who was chosen to give *shaktipat darshan*. Adi Da's main contention was that the Swami did not teach the yoga austerities which the same Swami practiced some years prior. He only displayed his *shaktipat darshan* trick.

Shaktipat darshan means that by glancing at the disciple a yoga guru transmits an infusion energy into the psyche of a disciple. The word *darshan* is Sanskrit for glancing or viewing. *Shaktipat* is Sanskrit for transmission (path) of power *(shakti).*

Is this a valid complaint?

Adi Da blames Swami Muktananda for Adi Da's mistakes in creating a cult around himself where he began to do the same thing Muktananda did, which was to walk among the disciples (devotees) and glance at them to transmit infusion energies which was supposed to give them instant enlightenment.

I neither supported nor contended the statements of Adi Da. The poor guy amassed some terrible karma by misleading people and telling them how he was an *avatar* and that by following him they would attain enlightenment. Now he faces the misery of the whole thing. In the astral world some disciples harass him. They say he is a guru fraud.

Muktananda did not permit Adi Da to do this. Adi Da acted on his own. He acted against the wishes of Muktananda who advised him not to do this. Muktananda performed the standard austerities of yoga in his youth and was submitted to Nityananda Dada, who was one of the greatest of the modern yogis in India. Muktananda acted as he was authorized but Adi Da did not understand why Nityananda gave so much authority and infusion power to Muktananda.

Kundalini Selfishness

Vishnudevananda discussed the incidence of selfishness, regarding how it sponsors the retention of sexual fluids just for sexual intercourse. He said this:

> It is all about holding a certain quality of sexual fluids to beget bodies. That is the overall mission of nature. What has a yogi to do with this? Does he intend to beget children? Otherwise why should his body retain the fluids, build up the resulting lusty charge and then have to be expelled to create more complications.

> If one does not intent to raise a family what is the issue or concern with sex. But regardless, the system, the kundalini, is habituated to the reservation and accumulation and then expression of sexual hormones. Therefore, since that is the natural design, the yogi has to do something to distribute that energy as fast as it is accumulated.

> Selfishness is the nature of kundalini because that is how it survives but if you are no longer interested in this physical creature existence, survival has no relevance because your subtle body will not die within 100 years. What is the need for begetting? Every student yogi should carefully consider this.

Yogi and the Bird / Vishnudevananda

During breath infusion and also during the meditation that followed, Vishnudevananda (Vish-noo-day-waa-nan-da) was present. I sensed his presence about ten minutes after I began the practice. It is an interesting name because sorted into the individual words this is the meanings:

vishnu - God Vishnu

deva - God

ananda – spiritual happiness

Translated it means one who has spiritual happiness because of being in connection with the God Vishnu.

Vishnudevananda doing a pose before his guru Swami Shivananda

I have not seen this Swami for months. He did help me with some asana postures some years ago. He did a translation and commentary of the *Hatha*

Yoga Pradipika, which shows that he was not a fake yogi. He practiced many of the delicate kriyas which are used in the Nath sampradaya lineage which comes from Gorakshnath.

This Swami was cool headed. He advocated peace in the Middle East but like so many other socially-concerned liberators, the Middle East ignored his pacifist sentiments.

He spoke of the value of doing asana postures and pranayama practice to discover and then to clear the nadi tubes in the subtle body. He feels that this is a necessary step in the quest for practicing trance states. He said that since kundalini created those nadis, kundalini knows where they are. Thus, if one infuses kundalini and causes it to move, it will show the yogi where those passages are, even the tiny ones which cannot be seen with ordinary perception and which require super-sensory sight.

This idea of the swami is indirectly confirmed by verses from the Anu Gita.

स जीवः सर्वगात्राणि गर्भस्याविश्य भागशः

दधाति चेतसा सद्यः प्राणस्थानेष्ववस्थितः

ततः स्पन्दयतेऽङ्गानि स गर्भश्चेतनान्वितः

sa jīvaḥ sarvagātrāṇi garbhasyāviśya bhāgaśaḥ
dadhāti cetasā sadyaḥ prāṇasthāneṣvavasthitaḥ
tataḥ spandayate'ṅgāni sa garbhaścetanānvitaḥ

sa – that; jīvaḥ - energy of individual spirit; sarva – all; gātrāṇi – limbs; garbhasya – of the fetus; āviśya – entering, diffused into; bhāgaśaḥ - part by part, every part; dadhāti – resides; cetasā - composite consciousness; sadyaḥ - presently; prāṇa – breath energy; sthāneṣv = sthāneṣu – of locations; avasthitaḥ - stationed, resided; - tataḥ - then; spandayate – moves; 'ṅgāni = aṅgāni = limbs; sa – it; garbhaś = garbhaḥ = fetus; cetanā – consciousness; anvitaḥ - conditioned

The individual spirit's energy is diffused into every part of every limb of the fetus. It accepts the body's composite consciousness. It simultaneously resides in all locations where there is distribution of breath energy in the body. Then the fetus being conditioned by consciousness, moves its limbs. (Anu Gita 3.7)

यथा हि लोहनिष्यन्दो निषिक्तो बिम्बविग्रहम्

उपैति तद्वज्जानीहि गर्भे जीवप्रवेशनम्

yathā hi lohaniṣyando niṣikto bimbavigraham
upaiti tadvajjānīhi garbhe jīvapraveśanam

yathā – as; hi – indeed; loha – iron; niṣyando - molten; niṣikto = niṣiktah = poured; bimba – image, mold; vigraham – form; upaiti – can, obtain; tadvaj = tatvat = for that; jānīhi – know; garbhe – in the womb; jīva – individual spirit; praveśanam - enter

As molten iron which is poured into a mold, takes the form of it, so you should know that as being similar to how the individual spirit enters the womb. (Anu Gita 3.8)

लोहपिण्डं यथा वह्निः प्रविशत्यभितापयन्

तथा त्वमपि जानीहि गर्भे जीवोपपादनम्

lohapiṇḍaṁ yathā vahniḥ praviśatyabhitāpayan
tathā tvamapi jānīhi garbhe jīvopapādanam.

loha – iron; piṇḍaṁ - ball; yathā – as; vahniḥ - fire; praviśaty = praviśati = penetrates; abhitāpayan – heating; tathā – so; tvam – you; api – so; jānīhi – comprehend; garbhe – in the fetus; jīvopapādanam – presence of the soul

As fire penetrates a ball of iron, heating it, so you should comprehend the presence of a soul in a fetus. (Anu Gita 3.9)

यथा च दीपः शरणं दीप्यमानः प्रकाशयेत्

एवमेव शरीराणि प्रकाशयति चेतना

yathā ca dīpaḥ śaraṇaṁ dīpyamānaḥ prakāśayet
evameva śarīrāṇi prakāśayati cetanā (3.10)

yathā – as; ca – and; dīpaḥ - lamp; śaraṇaṁ - house; dīpyamānaḥ - blazing; prakāśayet – illuminates; evam – thus; eva – so; śarīrāṇi - bodies; prakāśayati – gives feelings; cetanā - consciousness

As a blazing lamp illuminates a house, so consciousness gives feelings to bodies. (Anu Gita 3.10)

I took the opportunity to ask the Swami about the process used by a yogi to exit the body at the time of death. He did not think much of the question. He said this.

> One should do long samadhis. This is after one mastered kundalini by the restraining power of pranayama practice. Samadhi *before mastering kundalini is nonsense. It is just a mental state of some sort and has nothing to do with the accomplishments of yoga.*

> *You do the practice seriously as compared to years ago when we used to meet astrally. If you continue this, it will progress into longer meditations. When you shift into trance absorption, the body will be left here. You will tour higher dimensions and higher states of consciousness.*

> Samadhi *without clear sensory perception is blind man samadhi.*

> *After doing daylong* samadhi *for a time, one gets a sense of geography of the various realms. One contacts siddhas and deities. What is the question about exiting the body? Once you have the connections on the outside, what does it matter how you get there?*

> *A yogi should fly out as soon as the body is near its end. There will be a time, you will see it. But then do not stall for a second just fly out. I will be there to greet you. There will be some other yogi friends. But be sure to fly out.*

> *The question is: How can one be sure to do that? The answer is that one must practice the* samadhis *but be sure to practice sincerely. Do not be a con. Do not settle for less. Make no effort to change yoga into something that suits you. Change oneself to suit yoga. Do it as it was done by the ancient teachers. And good luck!*

> *The individual spirit is a source of energy, a primal source. Can it use itself effectively? Can it distribute its power in its interest? Having power or being power, has little to do with using that power and especially with the efficient use of it.*

> *Nature has this way about it where it does not package everything with everything or stated more clearly, where it parcels itself so that one part of itself is deprived of the other part of itself, so that some single parts do not have all composites. Until we can find a self which has primal energy and which also have the super-intelligence and super-power to manage that energy, we must have reservations.*

Kundalini and the Astral Body

I used to astral project regularly when I used a child's body in South America. Especially on Saturdays, sometimes we, kids, took naps. Then I would astral project but when I would come back into the physical body the astral one would sometimes not synchronize properly. I would struggle inside the physical form to get it to stand or move any which way. Obviously, the major factor is the lifeForce, which the yogis call kundalini. That is the principle which must operate this properly.

The astral body runs mostly on the basis of the lifeForce. The individual spirit with its primal energy is a side feature in this. It is a necessary feature but still it is a side feature, just like the battery in a car. The battery is there for starting the motor and some other auxiliary concerns but it is not the main power. In the subtle body the main power is the kundalini.

One can do what one likes with the individual spirit and its primal energy but if one does not take care of the kundalini one will get nowhere. This is because the subtle body is operated by the kundalini. When one leaves this body and one develops as another one, it is the kundalini which will do that not the coreSelf. One will have to tag along like a child who is pulled through a street by holding its mother's dress but the main pulling is done by the kundalini. The planning for the next body is done by the kundalini.

I am not saying that the self does not have to be present or that it has no importance. In fact, it has all importance, but only as a primal energy source which has to be converted. This conversion principle makes the kundalini prominent because it takes the power of the self and converts it into various kinds of energy. It also mixes that self power with various grades of energy depending on what level the psyche is on.

When the astral body separates from the physical system, the individual self leaves the physical one but still the physical body continues to exist in a living form though it is in sleep or comatose.

How is that? That is because the kundalini stays behind in the physical body. Death means that the kundalini left the physical system in full. Death does not mean that the individual spirit has left the physical body. It is the departure of the kundalini that causes death.

The energization of the subtle body when it is separated from the physical one, is directly related to how much energy the kundalini can transmit through space to the subtle form. If it transmits very little energy, the person will astral project but he will have no recall because the memory in the subtle body will be disabled due to a lack of energy.

The astral body cannot use any higher energy from any higher dimension if that body is not in the proper condition which relies on the condition of the lifeForce.

It does happen sometimes that there is an exception to this but that happens when a yoga guru or deity pulls one into a higher dimension on the basis of that deity's spiritual or supernatural power, not otherwise.

Usually when one goes to a higher dimension it is because of an energization of kundalini on this side of the border first of all. If the astral body is made fit, the person will go to a higher place and can utilize those environments. Making the astral body fit has more to do with elevating the kundalini than any other discipline.

When the astral body is separated from a living physical form, the kundalini which stays behind in the physical form sends energy in a pulse signal (so called silver cord) to the subtle body. That is how the subtle body is connected.

Once death occurs, this system of transmission ceases. The kundalini will be housed only in the astral form, at least until it fuses into a parent and uses the genetic materials in the parent body for creating another embryo.

Subtle Body Detection

Mind or mental and emotional energy are the basis for the formation of the physical form, just as the mental idea in the mind of an architect is the basis for the construction of a physical building. The relationship is such that the mind is the bridge between the self and the physical body. In this case the word mind is the equivalent of the words, subtle body.

Mind is a composite part of the subtle body such that the subtle body has within it the mind, the lifeForce and the spiritual self. This subtle body is the basis for the formation of the physical form. So long as the physical form lives, it is ever linked to the subtle one.

When the subtle body is vacated from the physical body, the physical system is understood to be different to the psychological energy which enlivened it, which collectively is called the subtle body. The feelings which we feel in the physical body are from the subtle body.

In yoga, if one is focused within the body and if one keeps the attention within it, one may realize the subtle parts of the energy.

Studying the subtle body is a two-part process. The first part is to realize oneself objectively in dreams. The second part is to sort the subtle energy in the waking state while doing asana postures, pranayama practice and meditation. It is a task for the self to realize itself as being the force which is essential for there to be a living body.

The energy of the subtle body is required for the operation of the physical one. If the subtle body withdraws totally from the physical one, that physical form is pronounced as being dead. If in giving energy to the physical body, the subtle one becomes drained, exhausted or fully utilized, there will be no psychic awareness.

To operate the psychic part of the subtle body one has to reserve a certain percentage of energy for that subtle form. If the energy is consumed on the physical side of life, there will be a shutdown of the psychic components of the subtle body. The result of this is:

- no dream recall
- no telepathic ability
- no clairvoyance
- no awareness of astral projection when it takes place
- realization of aroused kundalini only as sexual climax

If the physical body is fit, that may be utilized for more materialistic activities which will not help with developing the psychic perception in the subtle body. The physical body's fitness only helps if the person is trained to give the minimum energy to the healthy physical system.

There are many people who have a healthy physical body and still we see that they have absolutely no faith in psychic perception and consider it to be mental fantasy.

The point is that one needs efficient distribution of energy from the subtle body to the physical one. If one achieves that, the conserved energy would boost psychic perception, providing more objective awareness during dreaming, astral projection and meditation.

If someone's practice is little, he will have little ability to sort this during the normal events of the day. Remember that in the *Bhagavad Gita,* a similar situation arose, where Arjuna was baffled on how to act on the battlefield of *Kurukshetra*. In fact, if you read the *Bhagavad Gita* casually, you would never know that Arjuna was a proficient and well-trained yogi who mastered *samadhi* practice to such an extent that he kept his body motionless in samadhi for months in the Himalayas, while he toured in his subtle body in astral dimensions.

Bhagavad Gita is really about Krishna showing Arjuna how to apply yoga expertise to social living. That is so difficult as an accomplishment, that Krishna, a person who declared himself as the Supreme Person, said that only he could teach it. He said it was his system of yoga.

Muktananda on Drugs

During breath infusion, Muktananda came on the astral side. He reminisced on the initial years when he first came to America. The main thing, he said, concerned the yogically-unprepared persons who came to him. He said this.

Fate has a sense of humor. When I first got here, I was surrounded by free love people, the hippies. These were people with absolutely no background in yoga, at least in the present life. Perhaps these persons did yoga in previous lives.

You can imagine that yoga begins with yama and niyama which are don'ts and dos. These people had no idea of that. They were in the process of deleting the don'ts and dos which were imposed on them in the culture of their birth.

Yoga begins with: "Do not do this. Do this." These persons were callous to social restraint. How was I to turn them into yogis?

You can see my predicament. If you are born Christian and reject that religion, what is the possibility that you will accept rules from any other religious system? Yoga of course as Patanjali defined it does mention Ishwar, the Mahapurusha, Supreme Person, but he does not stipulate that as a religion. Still, yoga functioned in India alongside religion. In fact, yoga was assisted by religion. Religion was assisted by yoga.

But here providence threw me into a situation where I was challenged to make yogis out of bhogis. What is a bhogi? That is a person who is hedonistic, who is a pleasure seeker.

That is on the social side. On the transcendental side, we gain spiritual experiences through austerity in higher yoga, but there is a group of yogis who smoke ganja. That is how they get transcendental experiences. This method of using aushadi *is mentioned in Patanjali and also by Krishna to Uddhava, even though neither of them recommended it.*

Aushadi *is Sanskrit for herbs.*

So yes, these people were into aushadyananda *or bliss (ananda) acquired through taking drugs (aushadi). I was kriyananda or bliss (ananda) acquired through mystic process (kriya). How does the teacher move these students from drug-induced transit consciousness to meditation-caused transit consciousness?*

Once someone attains spiritual happiness and supernatural perception though drugs, he will be disinclined to follow through with Patanjali ashtanga *yoga. Why do those austerities, sitting in weird poses, breathing in special and unnatural ways for something which one can achieve by popping LSD and injecting cocaine?*

Desires in Yoga

Desires need to be controlled. First one should be aware of the desires. Then evaluate their worth. Some desires are worth the effort. Others are not worth it unless fate will sponsor those and carry the larger part of their expense.

Here is an example of a desire of mine which fate was reluctant to sponsor. This is not a desire which I am attached to but it is a desire in my psyche, something that was in the psyche and remains in the psyche no matter what I do.

This is the desire to be well-off. For about two years in this life, this desire was fulfilled. This happened suddenly when my body was fifteen years of age. At that time, I lived in Guyana in poverty-stricken conditions. Then suddenly the father of the body arranged its passage to Trinidad. This is a father who was completely neglectful towards raising this body in its infancy and adolescence.

At that time, the father had ample salary as a marine pilot in Trinidad. He rented a palatial house and lived with my step mother and step sister. Before this I lived in a one room house in which three adults and two children (including myself) resided. When I got to Trinidad, I was offered a room. I could not attend high school because I was an immigrant. Still there was a servant's quarter which was a small cottage. I used that to do self-studies.

That was the time in this life when fate decreed to permit me to be well-off. That was the beginning and ending of such a fate so far in this life. After that I never was inclined to work hard for living well-off. It made no sense. It is not that I am a humble person. Nor is it that I am attached to poverty.

The truth of the matter is that even though that desire to be well-off is in my psyche, I am not interested in fulfilling it at my expense, nor at the expense of exploiting or using others to make money. In the higher dimensions of the astral world there is so much opulence that poverty is absent. In such places one is well-off without effort. This is the reason why I will not exploit the resources of the earth or the human beings or any other species on earth, to be well-off. I prefer to endeavor in yoga to attain the state of a celestial being who lives in a world where opulence is available without the need to exploit anything.

Yogi fails to make notations

During breath infusion this morning, near the end of it, Yogeshwarananda appeared. He praised Tibeti Yogi for giving me the process for conquest of the thighs, knees, legs and feet. I was just about to stop the session, when he reminded me that I did not do the lotus sequence which he showed some time ago. Previously he insisted that these postures be done daily and that I should be sure to sit in a tight lotus at least for twenty minutes daily.

Here are postures which show some poses which Yogesh wants me to practice daily. These relate to the full lotus position:

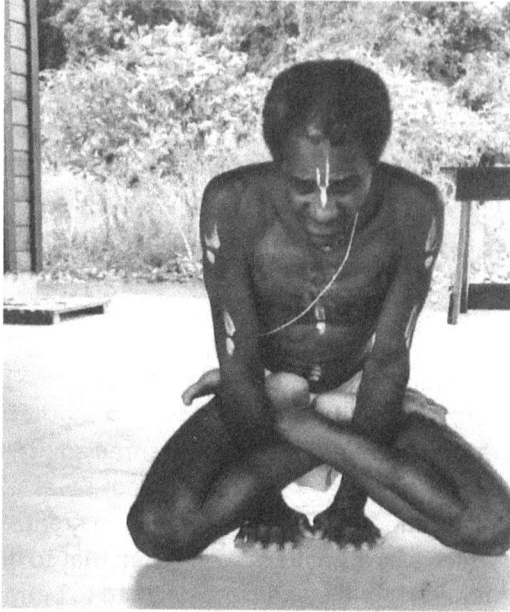

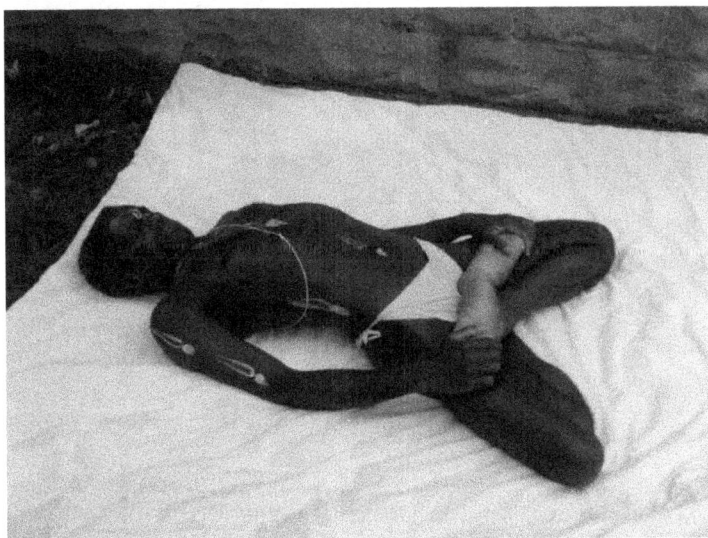

Perineum Stub Kundalini

This session was a bit different with more focus on the base of the trunk and the thighs of the subtle body. This happened because of the influence of Tibeti Yogi. Never lose sight of who renders assistance in yoga. Always acknowledge assistance. Do not run way with the no-personality obsession where one appraises the self of the self and that of another.

Tibeti yogi showed a passage through which light travels to the knee. This passage which travels from the perineum through the thighs begins as a stub of light, like a torch in darkness. When this stub is infused sufficiently, it sends out shrieks of light through the thigh. These flash out like pin shrieks of lightning.

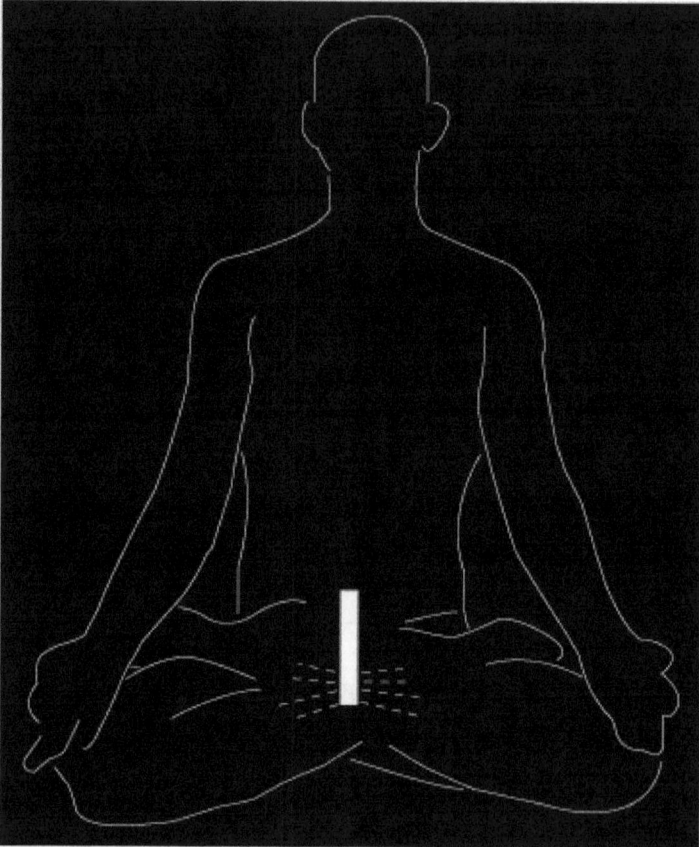

Even though I saw a movie yesterday, and looked at forty minutes of television, a practice which is detrimental to meditation practice, when I sat to meditate, I simmered down quickly. There was naad sound below the neck. That is a low location for naad. This was because of the intense infusion in the lower part of the trunk of the body. This relocation of naad sound is good. It is an indicator that the practice is organic, varying daily.

Part 2

Sex Pleasure

During practice this morning, Tibeti Yogi passed some energy whereby I would help anyone who is celibate through the life of the body, who did not have sexual needs. Of course, finding such students is near impossible because hardly a soul is interested in a full life of celibacy. Because the sex chakra is open, the few persons who have no interest, cannot maintain celibacy. They have no idea how to close or deactivate the chakra. The efforts to do this usually end in abject failure.

Still I got this ability to help anyone who is celibate or is capable of full life celibacy. I have children. Usually householders do not have the potency to instruct others about celibacy. Perhaps because only a few yogis qualify to teach this, Tibeti was instructed to pass the energy to me.

On the basic desire and whim, one cannot remain as a celibate for life. One must be supported by a great yogi. The support may be direct or indirect. If it is direct, then one would be in direct touch with that person, otherwise one would get the energy of a proxy agent. I will serve as such a proxy. I traced the energy which Tibeti gave me through Yogeshwaranand and terminating in his guru Swami Atmananda. Atmananda is no longer available on the astral planes.

Before this energy of full celibate life was passed to me, Tibeti Yogi showed a specific technique which targets the perineum area. For the last three days he instructed but I failed to report it, because I did not have enough information. Some methods are so abstract that to report on them would be unfair. Usually I must do such kriyas for a time to get a handle on them, to see them psychically. Then I report.

Mostly I like to see the effects before I report. If the process is subtle, I wait until I have increased psychic perception. Then I report.

I remember when I was studied math in Trinidad in 1966. I went to this teacher (Mr. Morain) every two weeks. He told me not to come on a daily basis. I was to do the examples in the books, mostly Algebra, Geometry and Additional Math. I would go to him. I would show him the examples which were baffling. He would show me how to move from where I was to the level required to understand those problems.

It is similar to that in yoga, where as one practices, even with books, one must sometimes reach an advanced teacher and take instructions on particular problems which arise. Assistance is necessary.

Imagine that I did this practice for forty years, and mostly on a daily basis and still some people who want to learn this think that they can tell me something about it, even though they practiced for two, four or ten years. Even after forty years, I am still a student to certain yogis like Tibeti.

To him, I must take a student's posture if I desire to learn. Anyway, he first showed a wiggle practice where when one sits on the pubic floor of the body, one does infusion into the pubic area, especially the pubic bones and the reproductive apparatus. Then one stops and compresses the infused energy, and as one does that one wiggles from side to side on the bottom so that one's attention shifts from left to right to left continuously. This causes something to happen in the perineum area.

On the first day when I did this, Tibeti spoke of it but I did not experience what he described. In cases like this one does not lose faith. One does the practice with full faith, knowing that in time one will experience and understand. On the first and second days, I did not experience what Tibeti explained.

He said that the energy will shoot out and move in a scattered way like tiny icicle or like macro-bolts of lightning. In retrospect I understand now why I could not detect that. It was because my mental reference for the experience was sexual experience. I used the sexual climax experience as a reference. It is not that I did this deliberately. I did not but this was how my psyche used the information. Once a person takes a body and then it reaches sexual maturity and carnal knowledge is gained, that person becomes stigmatized with sexual climax as the ultimate pleasure reference. Even if a person denies this, the denial will have no practical application because the psyche will still have that as its pleasure reference.

I moved away from the sexual pleasure reference, the way a boat moves from a pier. Still, it is a reference. Eventually it will no longer be there as a reference. Then the more subtle psyche experiences will have amply register, just as it does in the experience of Tibeti Yogi.

On the third day he explained what to do during the exercises to wiggle the perineum area by rocking the body from side to side while focusing on each side down on the bottom of the pubic floor. This morning I felt micro-lightning bolts. I realized that they occurred at the same place from which the sexual climax arose and is expressed in sexual experience.

This place is a hidden place, which kundalini targets during sexual affairs. It becomes visible in terms of intense pleasure after the physical body reaches puberty. Then it only is recalled as a memory and becomes visible anytime there is sexual stimulation, which develops into sexual climax, where there is a pleasure explosion at the perineum area.

On the siddha level, this place is visible as a tiny sliver of bright energy in the perineum area. I asked Tibeti about students who are sexually involved? They experienced the sexual climax. Their psyche is addicted to it. How can they reach this stage where it is no longer a vulgar need and they lose track of its bliss sensation?

Tibeti laughed and said this:

In my present state, I do not know how that would be achieved. This much I know. I was once in that condition but now that is a distant history, like if it was galaxies away. I cannot perceive it. I no longer have the information or memory of it. Thus, I am never haunted as they are. In our case, we are first shown what happens when one attempts to have sexual intercourse on Satyaloka. Then one fades away from that place and finds oneself in the lower astral plane, where one sees many scenes of creatures who have physical bodies having sexual intercourse. One is shown how their lives develop as physical beings and where they would transit at death.

When one falls to the lower astral planes, one is attracted to new parents. One enters into the psyche of a parent and goes into trance in the process. One's objectivity is suspended. Suddenly one realizes oneself as a baby. One is put into circumstances which are crafted by fate, so that one can fulfill the desire for vulgar sex. You are aware of King Mahabhisha whose history is in the Mahabharata. That is a description of the same event, because it happens even to some of the supernatural controllers.

We are shown this. Then we decide to abandon those needs or to fulfill them. I think it is reasonable that if you were about to commit a crIme which has a gruesome tortuous death as the penalty, that itself may deter you, even though a compulsive person may have no restraint even if he is told of the outcome.

No one in his right mind will go to a lower plane with the prospect of remaining there for millions of years helplessly and irrationally transmigrating.

Whatever will be will be! If someone is not convinced that there is a range of experiences which are available on the lower planes, that insensitive person will not anticipate the horrors.

For us, sex is the forbidden fruit because it is the sure way to descend. We aspire to go up. For that we self-deprive. We avoid the slipways which would take us into physical life.

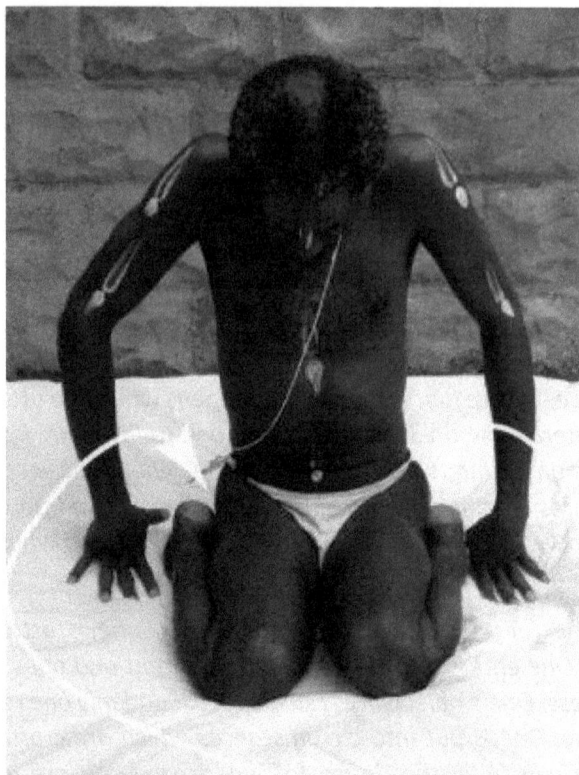

body on pelvic floor, wiggle bottom from side to side,
keep focused on perineum area
do this after a breath infusion where infused energy
becomes saturated in lower pelvic area at perineum

Lifetime Practice

During breath infusion this morning, Swami Rama appeared. He was his usual *happy go lucky*, carefree self. He smiled broadly; his subtle body being filled with diffused light. He praised the *agnisara* practice of stomach pumps with various types of coordinate breathing, saying that for a person who must go through the death of a body, the *agnisara* practice is the sure cure for easy transition away from the physical form. He said this.

"Of all practices of yoga, I feel that in relation to going through the death of a body, the agnisara practice, if mastered beforehand, would give a definite advantage. At least a student should do it during his yoga session daily for ten minutes. People will cry about this. They only want to do one or two churls of the stomach. That is not enough. If your body must die

and you do not know under what condition it will perish, then why not do this practice if it will give you the upper hand? Tell me why they cannot practice this for ten minutes per day. It is a sure guarantee to help with the transition because it frees one from the binding point which is the navel area. Anyway, tell them I recommended this."

During the session about twenty minutes into it, there was astral chatter. A friend, who does *Brahmakumari* method of *atmayoga*, came in his astral body. Near the end of the exercise session when I vanished my subtle body from the perception of my friend, Yogeshwarananda appeared. He was happy about something. I do not know what it is. He said this.

"Be sure that you keep doing these kriyas and the breath infusion until the very end of the body. Do not do as the others did which is to cease this, and sit to meditate as if you are an advanced yogi going into samadhi *all the time. Do not con people. So long as this body can do these postures, keep doing this practice. I will appreciate your compliance with this."*

Sex and the Siddhas

Someone contacted me mentally about sex life, regarding if it can be the cause of a loss of spiritual progress or if it would deter spiritual attainments in yoga siddha accomplishment.

To be truthful about this, sex life has nothing to do with siddha attainment. It depends on what one aspires for. If one is into sex life, then do not bother with the siddha life. Siddha life is for people who are done with physical social life. In other words, one is done with it because one went through it in many lives. One exhausted the need for it.

If one still feels the need to be a husband or father, one should not bother with the siddha life. It is best then to perfect the life of responsibility as a father and husband. When the time comes where that life is no longer fulfilling, when one matures through it, one may aspire for siddha life. Even then one will be hesitant because as soon as one develops the parenting skill, one has that sense of mastery. Then it is difficult to relax it.

People who go to the higher astral heavens and who still have the need for sexual indulgence; return to the physical world to satisfy those desires. Why?

Because that is how the physical nature operates with that kind of desire energy. There are stories in the Puranas. These are incidences which actually happened. There is a story about the deity, the sun god, *Savita*, the person whom brahmins attend with prayers three times per day. Once his wife named *Samjna* wanted to leave him. She arranged to have her shadow take her place in the dimension they were in. Because she was a supernatural being, her shadow was a living woman. This shadow woman's name was *Chhaya*. It took some time but the sun god got to understand that his wife left and that he was with a substitute.

He left that dimension and searched for *Samjna*. He wanted to be with her. Because he was the sun deity, none of the dimension below his zone were off limits to him. He could penetrate any place. He found her on the earth but *Samjna* when she detected that he tracked her, took the form of a mare. She felt that as a mare he would not recognize her but he did. He took the form of a stallion, approached her and had intercourse. Even though he is the deity, still because he came to a lower plane and assumed a lower form, his affection for his wife converted into sexual intercourse.

This story seems like a myth but it is valuable in showing that even a deity like the sun god can be brought down to the physical plane just by the fact of conjugal attraction. If someone is attached to any person for sex, then if that person goes to a higher place, the attached one will desire to go there. If that person goes to a lower place, the attached one will desire to go there. Sex is such a feature that someone will risk has entire existence and imperil the self for it. One may become a hog if it is necessary. In whatever situation the attractive person is placed by providence, the attached one will attempt to enter that level of existence. When one does so one will manifest the desire there by the rule of involvement on that level.

My body is sixty-one years of age. I meet many men my age and older. Some still desire sex. Sex is powerful such that even when the body is elderly, one continues to crave it. One feels that one can get fulfillment and satisfaction or conclusion of pleasure from it. This means that it will outlive old age and death of the physical body and will continue to harass for fulfillment even in the hereafter.

There is a story about a celestial woman named *Urvashee* (oor-vuh-shee). This woman was no ordinary person. She was in fact a supernatural person, a goddess from another world. Somehow, she came to the earth and took a body here, just as sometimes we find that a beautiful and irresistible woman becomes recognized globally by acting in movies or by being born in a royal family. This woman *Urvashee* was that kind of woman whom if she walked on a street, nearly every man would desire her.

Urvashee got in touch with a king named *Pururavaa*. They began living together but there was a hitch in the nuptial agreement, where if her pets, two lambs, were ever stolen, she would leave and never return. Once some celestial people from the dimension where she was a native decided that they had to get her to return to that astral place. They stole her lambs in the middle of the night. She called for *Pururavaa* to save them. Unfortunately for him.

When he got out of bed, he was naked. The celestial people were far away with the lambs. In any event, *Urvashee* cursed him. She said, "Since you expose yourself when we are not in the mood for intercourse and since you allowed my pets to be taken, I am done with you." She left him.

The guy went crazy. He looked for her in every place. He could not find her. She left and slipped into another dimension. Once however when there was a religious festival in India, when many mystic yogis came from seclusion in the Himalayas, *Urvashee* came there with other celestial people. *Pururavaa* saw her. He went out of his mind when he located her. He ran to her and begged her to stay with him. She agreed but instead of staying with him she substituted a celestial woman who had the power to be a copy of *Urvashee*. *Pururavaa* was happy about this but after a while he got to realize that there was something different in the way this substitute woman had intercourse. Then he sent that substitute away.

Again, another time he met *Urvashee*. He complained about her neglect of him. When he passed from his body, he went to the dimension where she was a native. He lived there for many years. This was a horrible thing in the eyes of the siddhas and great yogis, so much so that Uddhava questioned Lord Krishna about it in the *Uddhava Gita*. Uddhava wanted to know how it was that a devotee of Krishna like *Pururavaa* was allowed to be taken away by an enchantress. Uddhava asked why Krishna did not rescue *Pururavaa* from the goddess.

This means that it is not easy to give up sex life. It is a native aspect of this existence. The idea of getting away from it is more or less a fantasy. You can imagine what it is to the siddhas so that Uddhava pleaded to Krishna about what happened. He asked Krishna why he allowed for the goddess to control *Pururavaa*.

Siddha life has nothing to do with sex desire. It is not that anybody is saying there should be no sex desire but if someone wants to be a siddha then he must forego that desire. If one is attracted to a companion and that person takes a lower form, one will descend with that person just for sexual union. Actually, the pleasure of sex is intense in the other species of life as well. One may not miss the human form if one descends into a form which gives more sexual facility and especially if one is free from social pressures like morality.

Yogi investigates the Psyche

Tibeti Yogi stressed what he called the full inner pratyahar practice. Pratyahar is the fifth stage of yoga. Some people do not practice it. Many people sit to meditate who have not spent a few years with just pratyahar. Some meditate and pretend that they know what pratyahar is, as if it is a simple achievement.

In any case Tibeti Yogi piloted me to a terminal pratyahar practice which involves withdrawing the inquiry interest of psyche. Nature's convention is that the psyche should be focused into the external environment of the physical world. Yesterday I found some insect larvae squirming on a kitchen counter. These fellows had just eaten themselves through the walls of a papaya. Now they inquired about the environment.

Their mission: massive exploitation through eating

First the mother laid them as tiny eggs on the skin of the papaya. They punctured the helpless fruit which could not defend itself. They entered and ate their way to the hollow inside. All the while their bodies matured. At a certain stage they were inspired to eat and dig their way out of the fruit. With the exploitive business done, their mission of penetration complete and their successful escape completed, they emerged but found themselves on a Formica counter which was manufactured by another set of exploiters, the human beings. This was not their objective. They were supposed to be on earth with vegetation under which they could crawl and hide to pass through the pupa stage.

Pratyahar? They were not interested in that.

In the human form one can consider that one's inquiry interest is invested needlessly and at a loss in the physical environment. There is a degree of mastership of the environment as is proven by human scientific achievement, but still it is a loss because a body only lasts for about one hundred years.

Pratyahar is when that interest-energy which we put into the physical world, is withdrawn from it and is contained in the psyche of the self. Later when one reaches a higher stage, a person like Tibeti Yogi introduces the idea of expressing that interest in the psyche itself.

Tibeti Yogi showed how some inquiry energy was held in reservation for further investigation in the physical world. This energy once it was successfully withdrawn from the physical world, remained in the head of my subtle body in a silence, like a grenade which was not activated, because the pin was not pulled to trigger detonation. Some years ago, I did some pratyahar practice and withdrew this energy which used to pry and investigate items for exploitation. Much of what I did to achieve that was explained in chapter one of the *Meditation Pictorial* book.

Tibeti Yogi pointed to the inquiry energy in the head of the psyche, as if to say, "What will you do with that? That is trouble. Get rid of that. Use that up. The thing sits there but it will eventually explode if you do not dissipate it properly.

He pointed to the thighs, legs and feet. He said, "Expend it there. Let it investigate that. Use it there."

He used the analogy of a train which was driven into the main depot in a city. The idea of a train system is to have a main depot from which the trains depart. They spread through the city along tracks. Each morning they depart. Then they return and are parked in the depot until the afternoon rush hour. Then they again go out. They seek various parts of the city and investigate those tracks on a daily basis. In the same way the sensual energy goes out of the body through the various senses like the eyes, skin and ear. These energies go out and procure information and then return into the psyche with information which is collected by the appropriate sense organs.

Initially in pratyahar the student retracts the sensual energy. This is like instructing the train operators to stop all trains and reverse the motion so that the trains back into the main terminal. Then those operators are asked to turn off the engines. The trains will then stay in the main terminal.

In this rather advanced pratyahar, operators are again asked to start the engines and to drive the trains further into the terminals. This depot is large. It has subterranean passages; a vast network is within the terminal itself but this was unknown to the train operators. Now they are instructed to drive the trains within the terminal itself.

There is a mystic world within the psyche. One should investigate it with as much enthusiasm or more, as one had before when one was involved in creature existence exploiting in the physical world.

In Buddha's time, someone was asked to go from the married life, to become a *tathaagataa*, one who went *(agataa)* out of *(tatha)* (pronunciation tut-ha) family life to become a monk *(bhikshu)*.

When Buddha returned to his home town, many males suddenly got the idea that they should leave the householder life. Some who were on the verge of getting married, had doubts. Buddha did not give the positive side of life. He gave the negative pessimistic view explaining that it pans out in trauma.

One elderly man who had a family decided to leave the clan and go with Buddha to the forest to meditate from then onwards. He told his son to go with him but the young man said that there was work to be done and that when the chores were completed in the years to come, he would leave the family. The old man corrected him, "Who do you tell of the work getting done. I worked all my life. The work never finished. Why do you think that for you the work will be done? It will never be done. It never got finished for my father nor for his father. It will not be finished for you either."

Duty is ongoing in the physical world. Maintenance of this, and maintenance of that, will continue. In the simpler less-sophisticated societies one sees this more clearly, like when I used a child's body in Guyana in the 1960s. I noticed how an old man would have a job. He would dutifully come home to his family every afternoon. Some old geezers did not drink and enjoy.

Some went to church and were sober, being ideal family men. Their wives and children looked up to them and loved them. They provided everything as much as they could afford by their means of livelihood.

Then suddenly there would be a message that Mr. Jones or Mr. Edwards was dead. People would run about to inquire how he died. Somebody would say,

"But he greeted me this morning. He looked healthy."

Somebody else would say,

"I heard that he had hypertension but it was under control."

Somebody else would say,

"I wonder if his wife will get the pension."

Like that the man serviced duties until his body dropped dead. Duties will continue. There will never be a time when they will be finished. The first illusion is to think that later a hard-working man will cultivate spiritual life. Physical nature will remember one as the person who failed to incorporate spiritual interest into his daily life. Later, when one thinks one can do it, nature will spoil the situation in such a way that one cannot practice.

Babaji requested and I think I explained this in his commentaries in the *Kriya Yoga Bhagavad Gita,* that even though it is risky, and is facilitating to expanded materialistic attitude, yogis should enter the family life. His idea is that from youth, one should learn the kriya yoga system from a reliable guru. Then one should have children, discharge the obligation to the ancestors by giving bodies, but all the while keeping the kriya practice. Then later when the children reach maturity, one should accelerate the practice.

A word of advice

Family life and community service should be closely monitored. One should budget one's energy just as one would budget money. We should monitor and regulate energy distribution to family and country. If one fail to do so, the plan to rein it in later, will prove to be a failure.

The most important thing in life is not money, it is psychological energy. This is usually known under the titles of emotions and thinking energy. Both should be tightly budgeted so that the family and community expenditures do not consume every bit of it. All the way through the family life, some self-energy should be reserved for spiritual practice.

Yogi's Address

Due to the influence of Tibeti Yogi, a new event occurred which in a way seals my effort to attain a yoga siddha body, at least at departure from this physical system if not before. That is the conquest of the thighs, legs, feet, arms, forearms and hands. These extremities are hard to reach places which if left to their own devices will remain in a polluted state.

The main concern of a yogi is the subtle body. It does not matter what state one reaches in meditation, if the subtle body is not elevated before death or thereafter in the gap between taking another body, the yogi will be linked to a lower astral plane as the psychological address.

Even though some people pretend that they are detached from the body, that it has no impact on their realization, still their address is the physical body. They are mostly in denial and delusion. Patanjali gave a hint about the saturation of the subtle body with the energy from the level the yogi wants to attain.

जात्यन्तरपरिणामः प्रकृत्यापूरात् ॥२॥
jātyantara pariṇāmaḥ prakṛtyāpūrāt

jātyantara = jāti – category + antara – other, another; pariṇāmaḥ – transformation; prakṛiti – subtle material nature; āpūrāt – due to filling up or saturation.

The transformation from one category to another is by the saturation of the subtle material nature. (Yoga Sutras 4.2)

Where will the subtle body be in the interim stage between leaving one physical system and getting another? One should have no fantasies about not getting a body. That is hardly likely because nature provides support for getting a body. It is not concerned with not getting a body.

In the interim state where will one be? In which environment? That is the least one should clarify to oneself before being evicted from the physical form.

One may think that one is the mind, which really means that one is the subtle head. Or one may think that one is the emotions, which means the chest of the subtle body. But I state that one must carry the whole psychology at the time of death, not just the preferred part of the identity.

As such one would do the self a favor to clean all parts of the psyche. A clean head or chest which is bogged down by other parts which carry polluted energy will cause failure after leaving the body. One will be disappointed as one will not achieve the goal.

Tibeti Yogi gave instructions in the past two weeks which caused strides in my practice. These were simply actions on the subtle plane and on the physical level and yet, previously I overlooked these techniques. This happens that when one focuses on a certain aspect of the practice, one overlooks another feature which may be relevant. Help from a greater yogi is necessary for success.

Yogi / Sexual Intercourse

I have information from Tibeti Yogi. This has to do with why kundalini puts the observing self out of commission on some occasions when it rises through the spine into the head. Incidentally, it does rise through the body, through the neck and then enters the head. In sexual climax experience kundalini does not rise into the head usually. Usually in that circumstance, it becomes awakened and then it jumps to the sexual intercourse chakra and then leaps again to another small chakra which fires the last bit of pleasure energy which is so intense.

How does kundalini affect the head or mind during intercourse if it does not rise up the spine? It does so by attracting the intellect from the head down into the body. That attraction is felt as if the mind is full of pleasure. In addition, in the case of people who practice tantric sex or the Chinese system of chi sex, they may on occasion cause kundalini to go in the two directions, up into the head and down through the sexual organs.

There is *Kama Sutra* and there is *Yoga Sutra*. If one wants to have sexual success one should study Vatsyayana's *Kama Sutra*. That leads in one direction. If one wants success in spiritual life, one should follow the *Yoga Sutras*.

Once a student draws out the energy from the sexual intercourse chakra and the energy is no longer moving into that area, the knowledge about sex dries up day after day until a time comes, where that person loses the idea of sexual pleasure altogether. He/she becomes like a child before puberty where there is no conception of sexual pleasure.

The system in India for lifelong celibates is such that they do not have to study the movements of kundalini through the sex organ chakra. They have to deal with the sex chakra on the spine but not with the sex organ chakra which is totally different. However, yogis who have a family must settle with the sex organ chakra. This is because so long as there is an opening of the sex organ chakra, closing it becomes a major feat.

Those who remain without sexual experience through their lives do not have to deal with the problems of a sex organ chakra, but that is only if they are totally sincere in the effort and have made no sexual encounters on the astral planes. Once a sannyasi has sexual encounters on the astral plane, his celibate life is finished.

It is important that if someone will be a lifelong celibate, he should remain under the protection of a great celibate master or of a great family man yoga guru who is an expert in the control of kundalini.

Tibeti Yogi explained that the kundalini a person is endowed with is designed for all the lifeForce needs of that person, as he/she transmigrates through the physical creation. This means that if this force is not distributed evenly through the subtle body, if it accumulates in one part and is deprived of access to other parts, it will produce an imbalance.

This will cause that if it is aroused it will max out and affect something here or there. In the case of it rising into the brain specifically, if it enters the brain without being shared with other parts of the psyche, the observer self may lose perception or may go into bliss or unconsciousness energy and lose perception and self-consciousness.

"One must learn," he said, "how to make kundalini be distributed in all parts of the psyche from the toes to the finger tips and not just into the head of the subtle body."

Kundalini's natural impulse is to accumulate for sex expression. It will require a superhuman effort to adjust this tendency which is the natural way in these physical creations.

Yogi Who Killed Others

I was in a crazy astral realm last night but at about 4.30 am, I found myself back on this side with a memory of an instruction which I got from Yogeshwarananda during the night. Somehow, I entered a cross world where people are allowed to reformulate their frustrations and resolve these in the astral. These are places for psychotic people but then again, most human beings are just that and so are the entities in most of the other species.

In this world many people want to settle disputes. Many controversies are purely of a social nature, mostly having to do with physical existence. You can imagine how mad that is because a body only lasts for about seventy years which in comparison to the length of existence of the universe is miniscule. Almost every human being considers itself to be valuable, important and indispensable. That is the wonder of nature that it gave pride to something that is insignificant.

While using a child's body in South America I observed three household visitors; ants, lizards and spiders. It was always a wonder how a spider which is less than one quarter of an inch, would stand its ground over what it considered to be its territory. Some philosophers speak negatively of fear. They feel that fear disfigures the profile of the self. Those tiger spiders were so fearless as to be stupid in not being able to estimate what their power and energy really was.

The ants are a different observation. They made trails to the kitchen counter. They use the trails and take anything which they gain access to. They are not interested in salt, just sugar, food crumbs, meat, fish, eggs and the like. They never moved over for anybody. It was theirs as far as they were concerned. If one interfered, they stung the person.

There were two types of lizards. One, a gecko, had the ability to change skin tone according to the surface it was on. Somehow their perception of an external environment caused their minds to influence the skin color.

The geckos would crawl on a ceiling or crawl up a wall and then eat insects like mosquitoes, and moths. We lived in a small one room house with one dull light bulb which was the total appliance. The lizards came out at night, near the bulb, flick their tongues and ate moths. For them electricity was the solution to the food problem. They had no idea who created the bulbs or the current which went through it.

We had green lizards. These did not have the mystic power to change skin tone. These did not come out at night. They rarely entered the house. They remained on the outside and kept their distance from human beings.

As children we would do wicked things like hold a lizard by its tail. That is a no no, because the tail sometimes snapped off. It will remain there while the lizard skittered away. It still had lifeForce in it. It would wriggle from side to side for a while. We had no idea that this action caused suffering to the lizard.

We had black ants which we called running ants. These always moved quickly like the workers in New York City at Grand Central Station during the rush hour. These ants never moved at a slow place. Fittingly they loved sugar.

Sometimes I would find their nest under a board. I would lift the board and expose their nest to light. They would move quickly to relocate their broods of larvae. Talk about no opinion. I had no idea that this was like the act of taking away every residence of every person in a human city and even throwing the newborn babies out of their cribs.

There is one other thing I want to mention which is especially wicked. The gecko lizards laid eggs in walls and crevices. These eggs were about one quarter inch. Sometimes I would find one of these. Then I would wonder what was in it. I would then crack the shell. Need I say more?

Once I saw a baby lizard crack its own shell and emerge from it. In this way I got to understand how that operation was completed. I then connected that to the incidence of hens sit on eggs and then have chickens produced as a result.

These were some of the criminal acts I did as a child. This happened because of lack of parental supervision. My father was busy drinking liquor, gambling and working on ships. My mother was miles away up a river working for a company which mined bauxite.

Once when I was in a forest area in South America, I came upon a large tarantula. These are the types which catch even humming birds. The creature jumped at me. I was agile enough to jump back before it could reach me. I don't know what its intentions were but I left in a hurry. Once however there was a jungle spider on a path and I was about to step on it, when a voice in my head said,

"Can you make it? If you cannot make it, do not kill it. Have you any idea how many millions of years it would take you to make something like that. How much time would you require to make even one limb? Do not kill a life form willfully or I will have your head for it."

Yogi and the Ladies

During breath infusion session this afternoon, Tibeti Yogi appeared. He said this, "I saw your friends this morning." He spoke of some ladies whom I was with during the night in the astral world. These are ladies who use physical bodies which are older than mine. These are relatives. Along with these ladies, I sit on death row waiting to be evicted by fate from this astral residence which is the physical body.

There was more meaning however in Tibeti's remark, in the sense that he is a sannyasi renunciant. Rules of the order do not permit the monks to mix with females. To make matters worse, once the sannyasi leaves the body, the prohibitions tighten even more, since such association is the most rapid way to become an embryo, where one comes out in nine months crying as someone's baby, without no spiritual promise, in a family in which one must get a decent job, make a decent livelihood, drive a decent car, and do whatever is necessary for the family, forgetting yoga and spiritual life.

Since I am not a celibate monk, the danger of this is always present with me. The added danger of being with female relatives in the astral world is not sensational. A fisherman's hands are resistant to the jabs and stabs of the sharp fins of fish, while others are afraid of even the sight of a needle point.

When I sat to meditate, Tibeti Yogi gave an instruction which was to pull down the super consciousness.

This is the practice of pulling the infused energy in the head of the subtle body into the lower trunk and then further into the thighs, legs and feet. The idea is that for a yoga siddha form the entire subtle form, not just the head of it, must be saturated with super consciousness.

First, I established connection with naad which was in the back of the head. Then I pulled the energy. It was resistant to this.

Yogi takes a Flesh-Eating Body

Sometimes I get the feeling that someone expects me to report on the daily practice and meditation experience. It is true that something happens daily even though it may be an occurrence of no significance. Just as someone may think I should file a report, initially I thought that others too would file reports. That idea produced disappointment. Someone may feel that the standard of reporting is too high.

During practice today I worked on the legs and feet. This is done because of the interest of and instructions received from Tibeti Yogi. To tell the truth, even though I did breath infusion practice for about thirty-eight years in this body, still I did not focus on the legs and feet. I did initially when I began to do asanas formally under the training of Arthur Beverford in the Philippines.

Since I used a body which was from a family of non-yogis who had no interest in anything like yoga or reincarnation, it was tough going initially. I grew up eating flesh, fish, eggs and such items which are against the dietary rules for yogis. These foods make for a sturdy body but they are not conducive to yoga postures, where loose limbs are an asset. With such a body, I could not do the lotus initially.

When I met Beverford, I recalled past lives in India as a yogi. I desperately wanted to resume the yoga profile.

Beverford was not a strict vegetarian. I got no support from him with that, even though he contributed other important aspects, like the proper way to do the asanas, brow chakra centering, meditation, and also some literature which was written by Rishi Singh Gherwal, his yoga guru who was deceased.

I tried everything I could to get my body to change so that I could do lotus. I studied the anatomy of the thighs and legs. I realized that so long as these areas were taut and stiff, the lotus posture would not be possible. After about six months of doing a bouncing down exercise, which I invented, I sat in lotus but it was uncomfortable.

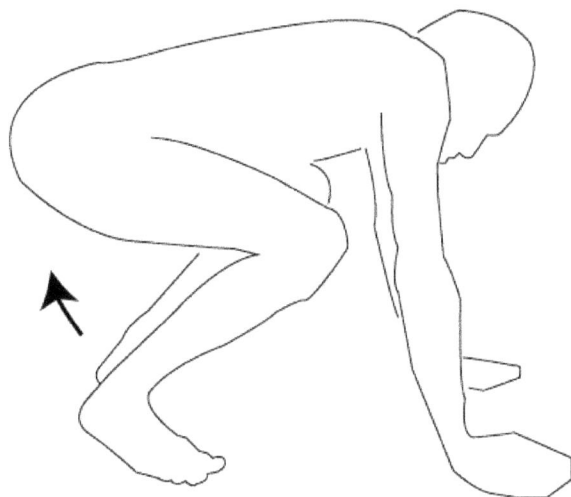

inhale as buttocks rise

exhale as buttocks
slam down

After that when I finally got the muscles in the thighs and legs to relax
and I could sit in lotus with relative ease, I no longer focused directly on the

thighs and feet. Actually, initially the student cannot focus on anything but the gut area, the sex energy area, the base chakra area, the spine and the third eye. That is it.

Later after I got serious with myself regarding celibacy, I was confronted with the fact that the pubic area cannot be conquered so long as the thighs are not reformed. Strong healthy thighs make for good sex but that puts a damper on the amount of energy kundalini could send or contribute to the sushumna central spinal passage and the brain.

With help from Yogi Bhajan and Swami Shivananda, I again turned my attention to the thighs but I did not award much importance to the legs as Tibeti Yogi emphasized. Getting help from proficient yogis is a must for rapid development in these practices. If you are alone and are not open to more advanced souls, the progress will not be steady because by yourself you would not be inspired into certain techniques which others mastered and which you require for progression.

Seeing Energy in the Subtle Body

This morning near the completion of postures and breathing, I had two inter-related experiences in the subtle body.

While seated, after a round of breathing and with locks applied, there was a golden, cool heat on the pelvic floor, in the approximate shape of a 2" x 4" x ¼" flat rectangle. The 2" sides were at the back and front of the body, with the shape sitting flat on the pelvic floor, just as a ceramic tile lays flat on a surface. As I observed the cool heat on the pelvic floor, I was vaguely aware of a similar sensation in the center of the mind space.

After doing the next round of breathing and application of locks, an agitated mist filled the pelvic cage. It was ball-shaped, misty, like clouds swirling or like a pile of dust stirred by wind. This misty sphere moved up through the sushumna channel and into the psyche. As it moved up the sushumna, because of the size, it filled sushumna and spread outside of it too. When it entered the head space, I was no longer aware of it. But I felt a burning energy at the sides and back sides of the neck and lower head.

Previously, I would have said that I felt these things, but would not say that I actually saw them. However, the shapes and movement of energy were seen. I saw the ball-shaped misty energy and the heat on the pelvic floor was registered as an image in the mind, comparable to an image of a flat bar of gold. The meditation which followed was not of strong focus.

Psychic perception must be developed. It needs to do so in its own way, even if that means vision without eyeballs. As soon as one frees oneself from the idea that perception has to be physical, one may develop various kinds of sight. One should have an open mind in this regard and not be skeptical of everything which is not physical.

Interestingly, the mental function of imagination is done in the same location as the mental function of sense perception. The same mental faculty which imagines, also formulates parallel matching and very functional copies of the reality which is the physical world.

The imagination faculty in the mind is a magic psychic instrument which can create matching copies of the realities it encounters.

People may criticize the mind's ability to copy and reproduce reality and then show it to the individual. This attitude is steeped in ignorance and arrogance. It is a veiled way of denying the fact that the mind with its imaginative powers proves to be quite useful and functional.

The mind is a crystal ball device. The question is: How accurate is it? Disbelieving in it, not accepting each of its conclusions and constructions cannot happen in fact. Nobody can live like that. It is really a matter of calibrating it, of knowing its deviation

Thus, with the imaginative mind, that is what you must do for psychic perception. There is also another type of perception which I call pranaVision. That is different to the imagination orb perception.

In pranaVision one sees through energy. That can be accepted on this basis: Say for instance if I tell you to look at a heater. Obviously, you will use your eyes to do so. But the eyes are a specific physical apparatus which has proven to be reliable to such a degree that planes are flying in the air and not crashing into each other. However, suppose I told you to see the heater with your skin. How is that done?

Then of course the perception is tactile. In the human form tactile perception is not as acute as say in the unicellular species. But still you could put your skin against a heater and give some idea of its temperature. Tactile perception is perception. pranaVision is similar. One sees through a membrane of energy.

Energy has membranes. Many trillions of membranes exist between here and there. In the psyche there are membranes. One can see through these just the same as a unicellular organism can see through its skin.

To use these perceptions, one must be open-minded to this information. One should practice meditation regularly and over time this will develop.

Yogi and the Non-Persons

This morning, breath infusion practice was without much sensation but with clarified energy in the lower trunk, thighs and the top part of the legs. Tibeti Yogi did not come. This is his program for the clarification of the thighs, legs and feet, something he insisted on as being a meaningful part of the yoga siddha body attainment.

Once a yogi picks up a physical format, an embryo, from some parent somewhere on planet earth, the problem begins to get the subtle body to become detached from its physical copy. The subtle body is synchronized to the level of the physical form, hence the need to elevate it.

You can imagine my difficulty with this, if at 60+ years of age I still endeavor to elevate the subtle body away from the lowering effects of the physical form.

However, my interest is the subtle body. When all is said and done, every person has the physical body as the astral address. Why speculate on a fantastic state of consciousness at death, when one dies every night when one sleeps in wonderland with no objective consciousness. Begin where one is in the ignorance of sleep. Figure that before regarding super-consciousness.

Master astral projection first. Study the psychic situation, how nature controls it, how one has little or no access to it. Do not fantasize about control at the time of death. On a daily basis nature restricts the use of these utilities. It keeps one out in the dark of deep sleep and ignorance every night during a span of unconsciousness of the physical system.

During the practice Muktananda appeared. He praised the Tibetans for their yoga. He said this.

Gone are the days when Indians were the masters of yoga. Now yoga means fixing diseases and making an attractive physical body. It means getting rid of obesity. But that is not yoga. That is not what it was originally intended for.

Even the asuras, the hostile sorceress in India, wanted to master yoga to gain control of the supernatural realms. Yoga concerns the supernatural, not the natural, the subtle body not the physical one. What has it to do with beauty of a physical form?

But higher yoga is even different. That means one is concerned with the energy in the psyche. But if one has no psyche, why bother with it. If one is nothing, or if one will merge into nothing then why waste time doing meditation. For meditation, you have to be something that will be something more sublime by the process of yoga. Only that makes sense.

I have a Guru. I love him. This is why I completed the austerities. He is someone. He is not a void. He is a person. I saw deities. Yes, it is personal. The only thing impersonal about it is the escape from identifying the self as a physical body. One must take help from higher yogis. That is necessary. Do not approach them as if they are none persons.

What do you think namaste means? We do not say namaste to a cloud, to energy. We say it to a person. We mean it sincerely.

Someone found someone greater and he is embarrassed? He does not like the idea? He thinks that perhaps he will become that greater self.

Namaste to someone who is great. Find some shelter. I found that in my Guru, Baba Nityananda. Krishna is Bhagavan, not you. What do you think Bhagavan means? Great yogis call him Bhagavan but it is not because they feel they are his equivalent. Figure that.

Yogi Thigh-Leg Infusion

This morning during breath infusion practice, Tibeti Yogi was present for fifteen minutes. Then he left. He wanted to discuss details about breath infusion into the thighs, legs and feet. He feels that this is important.

His main point was that at the knee there is a lock-off, where energy is not easily transferred from the thigh to the leg. He said that to break this constriction, the yogi must get the thigh completely relieved of the pressure which is caused by polluted subtle energy. Here is what he said.

When the thigh is infused with fresh pranic force, and when this is done with the lower trunk of the subtle body being filled with astral light, something happens where the dark polluted force in the legs increase in pressure. Then it blows.

It blows so that the valve like structure at the knee joint which keeps the legs segregated from the thighs suddenly opens. The polluted energy flows into the thighs. It comes in like a black-grey smoke and spreads through the thighs. When this happens during breath infusion, the yogi should keep pumping fresh energy into the thighs. This will result in the extraction and elimination of the dark energy. A yoga siddha body is not possible unless all parts of the subtle body are consistently filled with energizing subtle energy.

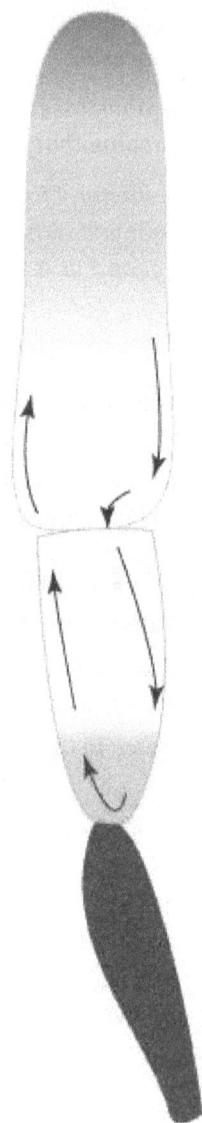

trunk side-view

energy-infused thigh

polluted leg

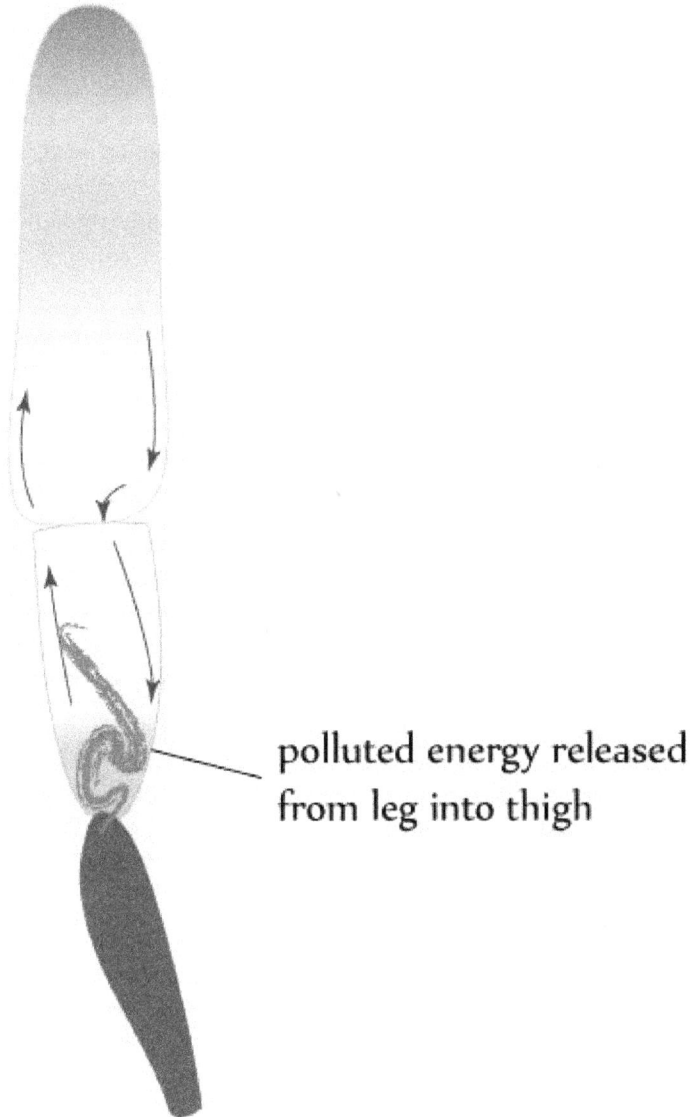

polluted energy released
from leg into thigh

Diffusion Kriya

Tibeti Yogi explained what happens when the breath infusion enters the second phase of practice, which is where there is no lower astral energy in it. During the first stage, the student's effort is to infuse fresh subtle energy and to force out the used heavy astral force.

This is done repeatedly day after day with no end in sight for when this will not be required. However, at a certain point, the psyche retains more of the fresh energy. It has less and less negative energy to discharge. Then the student enters the second stage, where on the inhale, fresh energy is pulled into the psyche, and on the exhale, it is distributed to *hard to reach* places.

This is in contrast to the first stage where the fresh energy is pulled in during the inhale and stale polluted astral force is pulled out or drawn from the subtle body.

The formation of the yoga siddha astral body begins when the yogi is consistently doing this second stage practice of breath infusion and breath distribution. No longer is the yogi required to focus on pulling out or extracting old, stale, heavy astral force. The attention which was used for that effort previously is applied to energy distribution to *hard to reach* areas.

Yogi Tests Yoga Siddha Form

Due to recent progress with conquering the lower part of the trunk of the body, including the *hard to reach* thighs, legs and feet, I noticed a dramatic shift in who can reach me in the astral world when my subtle body is at the high end of the practice, when it is infused to the highest by breath infusion.

This report should be encouraging for those persons who use this rapid breathing *bhastrika* process and who hope to attain a yoga siddha body.

This test was run by me early today while doing practice. This was a test to see if the subtle body could be infused to such an extent that it would disappear completely from the lower astral worlds where people who have little interest in yoga, can usually reach me. The importance of these people is that their association is focused into the physical world, in this gross existence, even when they are departed from a body, which means really that if I maintain association with them, it will of necessity cause me to again come out in the physical world as the son of a human or animal.

The only way out of this is to disappear from the lower astral levels, so that these persons lose track of one's existence or forgets that one exists in the first place. If this happens, the yogi will not receive help calls from these persons.

Usually when I do breath infusion, I endeavor until I reach the level where one of my gurus becomes perceptible. For instance, I usually make contact with a person like Yogeshwarananda or Yogi Bhajan. As soon as I make contact, that gives me the idea of which level I attained. It is like an altimeter in an aircraft, according to the reading the pilot can tell how the aircraft ascends. The pilot knows well that he cannot accept his intuition about heights. The intuition is faulty. The pilot checks by reading the altimeter. A yogi checks by the contact he makes with a departed or living advanced yogin.

Usually I know when the infusion is complete. I gage by the yogi I reach during the session.

In this special test however, I checked to see which of the materialistic persons whom I am usually in touch with, got out of my range of consciousness, where I could not reach that person and the person, as well, could not contact me, and in fact, forgot about me since my existence was subtracted from the range of consciousness.

I did this twice to be sure. The first time I noticed that a person who reached me for practice in the astral world, disappeared and did not remember anything about being with me. Then I allowed the infused energy to lapse so that the vibration in my astral body was lowered. Then I was again in touch with that person. The person continued association and even wanted to do some practice but I noticed that the person had no recall that I disappeared about four minutes prior.

Then I infused again, and again I disappeared. This test proves that the subtle body reached a stage where it could be in a yoga siddha configuration without any pulling and tugging from anyone in the lower astral places. This is a milestone for me as a yogi.

It happens because of conquest of the lower part of the subtle body, removing all dense astral energy from those locations. This is accomplished due to the help from five yoga gurus, namely, Tibeti Yogi, Yogeshwarananda, Yogi Bhajan, Rishi Singh Gherwal and Swami Rama.

There were others who assisted with special techniques from time to time, persons like Swami Muktananda and a Shakyamuni Buddha deity in South Korea. To these persons, I am obligated for assistance rendered.

The success with this must be consistent and not just something that happens once. It should not be like those experiences people have when they become conscious while their bodies are in surgery. They experience a supernatural light or an apparition of Jesus Christ or God. A *once in a while* experience is no guarantee that this would occur consistently after death of the physical system.

My experience of a heavenly world during an astral projection or a sudden apparition of a deity at the time of death is no guarantee that the experience will continue. It may be a flash, for a second or even for a day, and then I may again be on the normal level. That does not make the experience an illusion but it does mean that for me it is not permanent. It means that for me my subtle form could not synchronize in that higher dimension for long.

Here is an example. Those persons whom I escaped from on the previous day when I reported that my subtle body successfully disappeared from them, again appeared this morning during meditation. When they did so, only one person came at first. This person came with a higher energy than before.

The person's psyche decided that it was best to approach from a higher plane of behavior. But as soon as there was perception of my subtle body, the person's energy dropped to a lower level, and then others who were on that level perceived my subtle form.

This is the reverse of what happened yesterday. A yogi has to be clear on the psychic plane so as to identify and dismiss illusions and misconceptions. Aspirations and high hopes about practice, make-belief, positive thinking and visualization, have no place in this advanced yoga. For this only the bare psychic reality need be considered.

If I escape from someone on a lower plane, the person may note that. Then the person's psyche may adopt a scheme to attain a higher plane of consciousness just for the purpose of communicating with my subtle form. Once that connection is made, the person's psyche may then lower itself and I may be lowered along with it.

Hence what I reported yesterday as success was only a partial success. Getting to a higher plane, staying on that level and then going even higher is a difficult achievement if it is to be done in a permanent way.

If the breath infusion is successful to at least about 90%, the yogi has a good chance of staying with the siddhas, but even then, there is likelihood of coming down to the lower levels because of the loophole of compassion for entities who struggle to get out of the physical world.

On the higher planets, there are sound vortexes and visual perception vortexes which expose a yogi to what happens in the physical world. There are psychic signals coming from this earthly planet, from astral hells, from the adjacent astral dimensions. This energy rises in the astral dimensions and reaches higher zones from time to time. Sometimes a student yogi, who achieved the siddha stage, hears or sees the conditions of others on the lower levels.

This student becomes involved in an effort to help those distressed persons. Then he/she may descend to the lower plane, take a body and then discover that the people who sent the distress signals are atheistic or do not believe in higher personalities. Such beliefs make it near impossible to assist such people. The yogi learns a lesson, so that when he again regains a foothold on the siddha level, he does not answer the distress signals.

Some of these signals come through special vortexes in the psyche of a yogi. When this happens even if the yogi is on a higher plane with siddhas, he/she may be forcibly drawn to a lower level and may through that transit become stuck on a lower plane and not transit upwards.

For instance, in my own situation, I have so far avoided fame. My plan is to become famous after leaving the body. This is because fame is a sure way to fail in yoga due to the multiple associations which fame brings. But let us say that I can leave this body successfully and not be famous while I have it. Even then if I know one person who sends a distress signal while I reside on a higher plane hereafter, that one appeal could be the cause of my return to lower levels. By that I may resume the dreary course of these physical transmigrations.

There are many phony students who adopt yoga practice. They ask for instruction but have no intention of ever adopting yoga as a full-time pursuit in the way which Patanjali or Krishna described. These persons are a danger to a teacher. The energy exchange with such persons may be enough to cause a yogi to remain in these lower dimensions perpetually.

When yogis are with Babaji on the higher astral planes, they are prohibited from responding to the distress signals, if they respond, they immediately disappear from that higher plane and find themselves in lower astral places from which the calls originated.

Babaji's attitude is that if you are his student, you cannot be a teacher for anyone. It is either that you are a student or you are not. This approach of his is a safety net for the yogis who take shelter under his guidance.

With Lord Shiva one is better off, because he does not accept anyone as his student. You can be his sexually immature son, like if he is a father and you are a son. Then because you are without sex experience, the configuration of your subtle body is such that it has no sexual maturity symptoms, no sex drive only gender configuration.

That is super protection because then you will never hear a single distress call from lower planes. Read in the Puranas about the four Kumaras, who are juvenile sons of Brahma.

If one does not get protection from a deity or yoga guru like Babaji, it will be impossible to remain on higher plane permanently. It is impossible to do so without this higher assistance.

Breath infusion is a big slice of the spiritual practice but it is not everything. In fact, spiritual practice for success is a very complicated mix of austerities and restrictions. One must complete all of it. Breath infusion will give one the insight and get one to understand the status of the subtle form before passing from the body. It is important but there are other considerations which need be regarded.

If after death, the yogi still has to do the same infusion process he did when he used the last physical body it means that he has not attained a yoga siddha form. In a yoga siddha form, there is no need to do these practices. Such a form remains permanently infused with the right type of astral energy. It maintains itself there.

If after passing, a yogi does not attain such a form, he should use the astral form that he has and infuse it in an effort to permanently shift it to the yoga siddha level. If he fails at doing that his best option will be to keep practicing with other failed yogis and then find an opportunity for rebirth according to his karmic merits. Of course, that is risky but what choice would he have?

Getting distress calls from people on lower astral levels may be directly or indirectly connected to sexual intercourse because everything in the physical world is centered around sex energy. Sexual involvement is the means of getting another body. Once you get a body, sex may lose its importance in terms of your desire to manifest physically but until you get that body, sex has all importance because it is the only way to get a physical body.

Generally, however, distress calls are calls for relief from the inconveniences of physical existence. It is the reason why people get down on their knees and pray to imagined or real deities.

The way it is set up; if a person calls a real deity, usually that distress call is intercepted by some other person, who is not the deity but who is an agent of that supernatural person.

Once the subtle body takes on a yoga siddha configuration as its permanent demeanor, its permanent status, no further yoga practice is necessary. Then the yogi lives in the higher heavenly world or that person may go to the spiritual territories in total. That is another environment. To get some idea of this, we should locate those places or in the meantime, accept the descriptions in the Vedic scriptures. For instance, in the *Bhagavad Gita,* Krishna told Arjuna about those places.

अव्यक्ताद्व्यक्तयः सर्वाः

प्रभवन्त्यहरागमे ।

रात्र्यागमे प्रलीयन्ते

तत्रैवाव्यक्तसंज्ञके ॥८.१८॥

avyaktādvyaktayaḥ sarvāḥ
prabhavantyaharāgame
rātryāgame pralīyante
tatraivāvyaktasaṁjñake

avyaktād = avyaktāt — from the invisible world; vyaktayaḥ — the visible world; sarvāḥ — all; prabhavanty = prabhavanti — they are produced; aharāgame — at the beginning of Brahma's day; rātryāgame — at the beginning of Brahma's night; pralīyante — they

are reverted back; tatraivāvyaktasaṁjñake = tatra — at the time + eva
— indeed + avyakta — invisible world + saṁjñake — is understood
as

When the day of Creator Brahmā begins, all this visible world is produced
from the invisible world. When his night comes, the manifested energies
are reverted back into the invisible world. (Bhagavad Gita 8.18)

भूतग्रामः स एवायं
भूत्वा भूत्वा प्रलीयते ।
रात्र्यागमेऽवशः पार्थ
प्रभवत्यहरागमे ॥८.१९॥

bhūtagrāmaḥ sa evāyaṁ
bhūtvā bhūtvā pralīyate
rātryāgame'vaśaḥ pārtha
prabhavatyaharāgame

bhūtagrāmaḥ — multitude of beings; sa = saḥ — this; evāyam = eva
— indeed + ayam — this; bhūtvā bhūtvā — repeatedly manifesting;
pralīyate — is shifted out of visibility; rātryāgame — at the arrival of
Brahma's night; 'vaśaḥ = avaśaḥ — happening naturally; pārtha — O
son of Pṛthā; prabhavaty = prabhavati — it comes into existence;
aharāgame — on the onset of Brahma's day

O son of Pṛthā, this multitude of beings which is repeatedly manifested, is
naturally shifted out of visibility at the arrival of each of Brahmā's nights.
It again comes into existence at the onset of Brahmā's day. (Bhagavad Gita
8.19)

परस्तस्मात्तु भावोऽन्यो
ऽव्यक्तोऽव्यक्तात्सनातनः ।
यः स सर्वेषु भूतेषु
नश्यत्सु न विनश्यति ॥८.२०॥

parastasmāttu bhāvo'nyo
'vyakto'vyaktātsanātanaḥ
yaḥ sa sarveṣu bhūteṣu

naśyatsu na vinaśyati

paraḥ — high; tasmāt — than this; tu — but; bhāvo = bhāvaḥ — existence; 'nyo = anyaḥ — another; 'vyakto = avyaktaḥ — invisible; 'vyaktāt = avyaktāt — than the unmanifest state of the dissolvable creation; sanātanaḥ — primeval; yaḥ = which; sa = saḥ — it; sarveṣu — in all; bhūteṣu — in creation; naśyatsu — in the disintegration; na — not; vinaśyati — is disintegrated

But higher than this, there is another invisible existence, which is higher than the primeval unmanifested states of this dissolvable creation. When all these creatures are disintegrated, that is not affected. (Bhagavad Gita 8.20)

अव्यक्तोऽक्षर इत्युक्तस्
तमाहुः परमां गतिम् ।
यं प्राप्य न निवर्तन्ते
तद्धाम परमं मम ॥८.२१॥

avyakto'kṣara ityuktas
tamāhuḥ paramāṁ gatim
yaṁ prāpya na nivartante
taddhāma paramaṁ mama

avyakto = avyaktaḥ — invisible world; 'kṣara = akṣara — unalterable; ity = iti — thus; uktaḥ — is declared; tam — it; āhuḥ — authorities say; paramām — supreme; gatim — objective; yam — which; prāpya — attaining; na — not; nivartante — return here; tad — that; dhāma — residence; paramam — supreme; mama — My

That invisible world is unalterable, so it is declared. The authorities say that it is the supreme objective. Attaining that, they do not return here. That place is My supreme residence. (Bhagavad Gita 8.21)

Notice that even though many people feel that the primeval unmanifested state of this creation is the ultimate or the absolute, and they aspire for that, Krishna says there is an environment which is higher than that.

The only way one can guarantee that one will not return to these lower planes of existence is if one uses a subtle body which has no content that relates to these levels. If the subtle body retains content having to do with these planes of existence, it is always a probability that one will return.

To be sure, I add that a yoga siddha form is not a spiritual form but it is the form which is the precursor of the spiritual form. It is the form in which one becomes quarantined from the lower astral planes, in preparation for going to the world which Krishna described which is beyond the primeval unmanifested state of this dissolvable creation.

Those whose objective is to merge into the primeval unmanifested state of this dissolvable creation, may if they are determined enough, reach that level of existence but they will not be allowed to stay there for long. Ask any of these persons, including the yoga masters who attained that state like Ramana Maharshi, if they can explain how they got into the physical creation as singled-out individual entities in the first place. Of course, Ramana is now deceased. But if you know any masters who now use a physical body, ask that person.

Unless someone can prove that he/she was the cause of the divergence from the primeval unmanifested state, then any idea about controlling his/her existence so as to remain in that stage in oneness, is absurd.

Yogeshwarananda was an Arya Samajist by religion. These are people who do not believe in a deity. They feel that the ultimate is an absolute energy. In fact, Yogesh translated part of the Vedas under the title of *Essential Colorlessness of Absolute,* just to verify that idea. And yet, when questioned closely about remaining in the absolute, he honestly admitted that no one can say that they can permanently do that because in the first place, that person would have to explain how he got differentiated out of that oneness initially.

The whole idea of remaining in oneness is totally absurd. Krishna dumped it in a statement where he told Arjuna that once a person existed, there is no turning back to merged existence ever. That is not going to happen permanently. What will happen is that the person will be segregated when fate allows or decrees and will be merged or will lose the sense of separate I-ness when fate sees fit.

When the universe crashes, we are out of it, unless we transferred to a higher dimension. When the universe begins again and there are suitable environments in the process of its development, we will find ourselves to be individuals again. That is its process.

To get a yoga siddha body, one must endeavor. If one is successful, the next step is to get a spiritual form. This is where one must realize that it is not possible to assume that unless one has a relationship with a deity from the spiritual environments.

In the next verse of the *Bhagavad Gita* following what I quoted before, Krishna mentioned that in no uncertain terms.

पुरुषः स परः पार्थ

भक्त्या लभ्यस्त्वनन्यया ।

यस्यान्तःस्थानि भूतानि

येन सर्वमिदं ततम् ॥८.२२॥

puruṣaḥ sa paraḥ pārtha
bhaktyā labhyastvananyayā
yasyāntaḥsthāni bhūtāni
yena sarvamidaṁ tatam

puruṣaḥ — person; sa = saḥ — this; paraḥ — supreme; pārtha — O son of Pṛthā; bhaktyā — by a devotional relationship; labhyaḥ — attainable; tv = tu — but; ananyayā — not by any other; yasyāntaḥsthāni = yasya — of which + antaḥsthāni — existing within; bhūtāni — beings; yena — by which; sarvam — all; idam — this; tatam — energized

That Supreme Person, O son of Pṛthā, is attainable through a devotional relationship and not by any other means. Within His influence, all beings exist. By Him, all the universe is energized. (Bhagavad Gita 8.22)

To avoid having to deal with the deities, some yogis attain what is called the brahman effulgence, brahmananda. Look at this chart.

Spiritual Cosmology

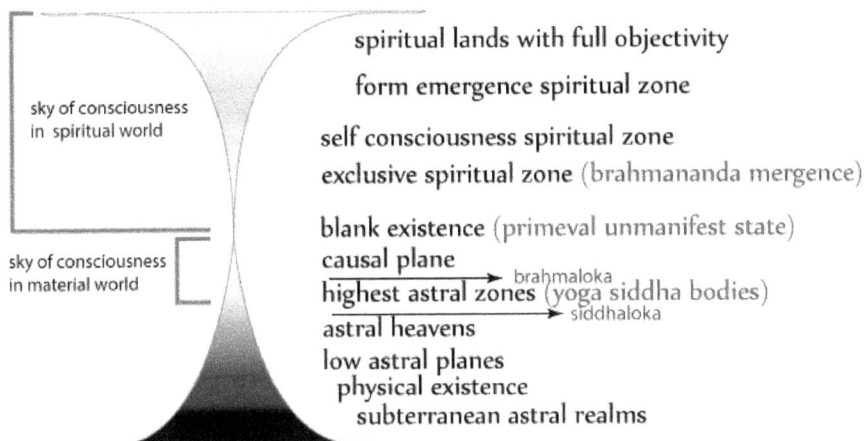

sky of consciousness in spiritual world

sky of consciousness in material world

spiritual lands with full objectivity

form emergence spiritual zone

self consciousness spiritual zone

exclusive spiritual zone (brahmananda mergence)

blank existence (primeval unmanifest state)

causal plane

highest astral zones (yoga siddha bodies) → brahmaloka → siddhaloka

astral heavens

low astral planes

physical existence

subterranean astral realms

Just as on this side of existence one gets a form based on relationship with someone as a father and mother, so on the spiritual side one converts as a spiritual form based on a relationship with a deity from that sort of world.

There are two skies of consciousness; one is on this side of the existential divide. The other is the other side in full. On this side the sky of consciousness begins on the supernatural level where the highest deities like Brahma, Buddha and such divine beings have their residences and under-control domains.

Above the level where they are, there is the causal plane, which is a zone in which individuality is suppressed so that one's willpower is de-activated. Slight pre-thoughts occur there but they never develop into anything because they cannot be transformed into willpower. This causal plane has the essence of everything which occurs in the physical world, but as a non-expressed concentrated energy. This is a nice place to be, a place where great yogis sometimes spend millions of years in absorption. Without an active intellect, such study is totally in the realm of subjectivity which makes it extremely abstract. Yogeshwarananda has just recently spent many years in the causal plane, but about it, he is completely silent.

A serious yogi foregoes this physical existence and all the social benefits it offers, and its challenges. He goes to the causal plane where those distinct forms are no more. The yogi does this, for the reason of seeing how he/she was held spellbound by desires.

Patanjali issued an alert which says that hope and desire energies are eternal. This is an alert to prevent student yogis from thinking that their hope and desire energies can be terminated. That will not happen because those energies came from the causal plane which a limited spirit, even as a yogi, cannot alter in the least. Still, it becomes necessary at some stage of practice to confront desires, to root them out. It is at that stage that a yogi gets interested in researching what the causal plane is about.

Beyond the causal plane there is a blank area such that if you went there, your sense of individuality, your sense of self, everything, would vanish. Yogis, who enter that plane, find that when they go there, they lose track of themselves. Then according to how far they progressed, they find themselves again on a lower plane. Unless a yogi gets pre-trained in how to pass through this place, he cannot successfully get through this area because the will to do so and his motive for doing so, his power to act, will be lost as soon as he enters this plane.

This may be compared to say, when the pilot of an aircraft loses his sense of direction because of erratic movements of the craft and foggy weather. If he has no instruments, there is disaster. He will crash and either get hurt or crash and die and finds himself in some other existence.

Yogeshwarananda is of the view that one cannot tell what is beyond this plane from this side of existence. In the *Srimad Bhagavatam* there is a story about Arjuna who is said to have gone through this place. Once when Arjuna took a vow to protect a brahmin's children, Arjuna was unable to fulfill the promise. Then, as a matter of pride he pledged to kill his body. At the time if a prince made a vow in public and did not fulfill it, he had to commit suicide.

A brahmin lost children one after the other, due to death in childbirth. This brahmin went to complain to the king Ugrasena. In those days there was a superstition that untimely death was caused by the actions of the ruler of the country.

Anyway, the brahim got disgusted and said that the Yadu family were unqualified rulers. When he said that Arjuna was with the Yadus. He was related to them.

Arjuna told the brahmin that he was a prince from another ruling family, the Kauravas, and that he would protect the brahmin's wife from another still birth incidence.

It so happened that the next child died as well. Arjuna was disgraced. He did everything he could including chanting mantras, doing rituals, putting spells on weapons, using mystic yoga methods which he learnt. In any case, fate struck. Arjuna was to commit suicide but Krishna told Arjuna not to do it. Arjuna then said he had to because he failed to protect the child and his reputation was at stake.

Krishna then took Arjuna to meet the person who was the cause of the death of the child. Since that person was a deity in the spiritual world, Krishna took Arjuna through this place, the place of nothingness, the location of absence. There is a description of it in the Srimad Bhagavatam.

You can cross this place successfully if you have the grace of a deity from the spiritual side; otherwise you cannot because your existence does not carry within it the required propulsion energy to push through this place into the spiritual sky.

Notice the word spiritual, because the sky of consciousness which is on this side of the existential divide is the supernatural sky of consciousness.

If you attempt to enter the supernatural sky, you will go blank for a period of time and then you will again come out in the physical world somewhere. As a piece of Styrofoam cannot remain at the bottom of the sea, so a limited entity cannot remain in this place.

Let us assume however that you do cross this place. Then what will be next? You will enter into the brahman effulgence. You will find that you exist and that is it. Unless one is pulled by a deity from the spiritual places, one will not go beyond this place. Arjuna went through this place. It was a blinding light.

This place is called *sat* in the *Upanishads* and in the *Bhagavad Gita*. *Sat* translated in that usage means the Reality. That which is.

In the Upanishads there is the mantra which is

Tat Twam Asi

Which means that you *(twam)* are *(asi)* that which *is (tat)*, or that you are from this place. This is your point of origin in so far as location goes. But when were you located there?

To know that one must retrogress in time, to the time before the coreSelf began transmigrating in these physical worlds?

Gautama Buddha went to this place. He also noted his trillions of transmigrations after initially coming out of this place. He noted that in this place there is no separated individuality. There is no cultural self, nothing. He then promoted *anatma*, non-self, no-identity. In this place all the selves are neutral existences all compacted together as glaring specks of spiritual light.

One of the special things which Yogi Bhajan gave was the process of breath infusion to raise kundalini. During that practice, the student sometimes gets propelled into this place where there is sheer spiritual light and spiritual pleasure energy. This gives the yogi experience about the nature of this place. It is said to be nirguna which means without *(nir)* qualities or attributes *(guna)* which are found in the physical world.

The sky of consciousness is a general term covering many levels of existence. To think that it is only one place is fallacious but initially one should think like that or the course of yoga can seem very complicated, which may discourage little minds.

Part 3

Air Conditioning and Yoga

I came to the conclusion that cold air causes the digestive system and evacuation process to operate slowly. This means that if one lives in a building which has air conditioning, the intestinal system will take much more time for digestion. The evacuation process will be longer.

There may be no flaw in that but for yoga quicker digestion and faster excretion is preferred. The more the lifeForce is involved in these activities in the gut of the human being, the more it will be disinclined to send energy into the head of the subtle body for meditation practice.

To offset these advantages one may, if one lives in an AC environment, use hot or very warm water or liquid whenever a liquid is required. I conducted an experiment recently and found that if warm water is used, the digestive and excretory systems act in a lively way otherwise they drag at a slow pace. This causes more energy usage on the physical side, which results in less psychic perception.

I noticed that people usually sleep better in an AC environment. However, this may be because the air is compressed in that environment. For every breath taken, more mass of air is taken into the lung cells. The coolness of the air also causes the vital functions of the body to move at a slower pace. But these advantages are disadvantages in the terms of psychic perception and yogic accomplishment.

I never ran a scientific experiment on this but I would speculate that people who live in tropical climates, process food faster and evacuate waste in a prompter fashion over all. It does not make them any smarter but in terms of yoga, that is a preferred.

Yogi: Family Man or Single?

During breath infusion yesterday afternoon Tibeti asked me about the situation of family men. He wanted to contrast the life of an ascetic who has children and the one who has none. He felt that there may be some hidden aspect in the family life which makes it superior to the celibate bachelor life. He presented the following argument for the family life:

If the ascetic makes a contribution by forming a family, that may be better than the single life as a monk. Gautama Buddha did not like the family life. Every monk who followed him in his time had to avoid or leave aside the family life. In fact, Buddha himself is the example of a person who spurned the family life. He had a lovely wife, concubines and a son. Still he rejected the family life. What flaw did he perceive in it?

I replied:

The astrologer told Buddha's father, that Buddha would be the greatest ascetic or a world conquering monarch. This means that ultimately the family life pans out in political sovereignty as its maximum potential. In both cases as a militant ruler or as an ascetic leader, Buddha was to be the role model for male human beings.

The householder life is a service facility but it is not related to spiritual progression directly. That is its defect. All the same, insincere life as a celibate ascetic is worthless and may even carry the monk to hell. There is no spiritual glory in the married life. There is none in the single ascetic life if the monk does not master celibacy to make the reproductive energy course upwards through the body.

The householder ascetic will stockpile social credits for his future lives, but his course is risky. He cannot put his foot on the earth and say, "I know for sure that what I did will bring fortune in future lives." Therefore, the family life is filled with uncertainty because its effect-energies which are carried over into other lives require supports from fate for their fulfillment. One never knows what fate will do.

Advancement of one family, one clan or even one country cannot be done without the suppression of others. Hence the progression of social status for the family, clan or country causes the formation of resentment of those who are suppressed or denied privileges. That is the bane of family life. Underneath the ancestral trail is a violent passage of exploitation and advantage-taking. Such is this life.

The only advantage I see to the family life is the approval for it by providence. Providence is more responsible for, and less objecting to the family life. The advantage of it is itself its danger because once something is approved by fate, there may be arrogance in its performance. Later when fate withdraws its support, the ascetic will be left to face the ensuing rejection.

With the support of providence, one becomes a great man, a respected and appreciated member of society. With the withdrawal of that support which will happen? Sooner or later, one is left in an abject state of mind, without respect and with feeling of neglect and rejection.

In addition, an ascetic who has children, must clear the psyche of those unwanted features of his life during the family support years. How will he forget the carnal pleasures? How will he rid himself of the repeated need for sexual indulgence? Where will he hide when persons who have no interest in spiritual advancement pursue him?

My conclusion is that even though the married life has benefits, these are offset by the negative aspects which are imposed by fate. Few, if any ascetics, can become liberated while they serve in the family life. In the history of India, the person who lived in the family life and who was a successful ascetic while doing that was Rama the son of Dashratha. But he is a Personality of Godhead, which means that a limited entity cannot match his behavior. Even though he is God, still he faced many challenges. He made ideal decisions by outmaneuvering fate but a limited entity cannot be as successful doing that. Hence, wherever possible, an ascetic should take the single celibate life. If one has superhuman powers and psychic perception, one may successfully traverse the family life. But it is unlikely that an ascetic will master that.

Sexual Energy Withdrawn

Tibeti was present during breath infusion. Because of an encounter I had last night in the astral world, he remained at a distance from my subtle body. I knew the reason. I did not comment on his distance. After forty minutes, he said that he noticed a positive change. I noticed this but since I was used to it, it did not seem remarkable to me.

A female relative who is now deceased came and took sexual energy from my psyche. Usually this loss of energy is negative for a yogi but if the yogi is smart about it and realizes it for what it is, especially realizing that the energy was extracted by the person who deposited it early on when he first got the body, it serves to release the yogi from an obligation. That has a positive effect. This is a case where the yogi's attitude makes the difference.

Tibeti had a celibate body in his last physical life. I use a sexually experienced body. Sexually experienced forms which were used to beget progeny, are inferior forms in so far as the attainment of a yoga siddha form is concerned. Usually a lifelong celibate, a person who has no recent carnal information or experience, has a much easier path if he aspires for a yoga siddha form.

Once there is carnal experience, sexual contact in and with a form, the condition changes. The scene for liberation becomes uncertain. There is a way however to escape this uncertainty.

Tibeti asked about it. I explained:

Some of the energies belong to others. In fact, most of the sexual experience energy belongs to others. These others deposited certain quantities of that energy in the psyche of the student. It only appears that the student owns much of the energy. The fact is that the student owns only a fraction of it.

This particular female relative who is now departed deposited some sexual potency in my subtle body while I was an infant. At that time, it entered my psyche and was converted into an affection desire energy. As soon as my body developed into puberty, it reconverted into sexual energy. Some of that energy was used in the production of children. Some of it was not utilized. That female relative returned to claim the remnant.

Because I have no desire to be in the reproduction scheme again, at least not in this body which is now 60 years of age, I was glad to release it to her. If someone deposits their money in a bank in the hope of getting a benefit like a large interest, then it is only fair that they should withdraw the funds if the bank proceeds to bankruptcy.

Thus, if the student understands that and can identify his portion, his responsibility is for his portion of the sexual investment, not for the greater percentage of it. The other persons will extract their part of it, if the yogi is to be freed. Once the yogi becomes determined to get away from the reproductive process, once the yogi decides that sex pleasure is not the objective, others will come and remove their portions of sex energy which is stored in his psyche.

This is similar to a business enterprise. If the business is to fail, investors, even dear family members, will rush to remove their money. No one will let their funds remain in a sunk enterprise. Any yogi, who becomes serious about liberation from the physical world, is a crashed entrepreneur. People lose faith in such a person. They rush to withdraw their pious credits which were lodged into his existence.

Once a yogi has an interest in developing cultural activities, he becomes famous. People join him and help him with the farce which he perpetrates as a religious, social or spiritual enterprise, but if along the way he gets crazy and decides for isolation and real serious spiritual discipline, people will run away from him.

At that stage, concerned friends and relatives, look on him with pity, thinking how unfortunate it is that he has lost the foothold in cultural development. They see him as a wasted cause. If he becomes neutral and does not attack anyone in the family, they regard him as a retarded person who unfortunately is related to them.

A yogi should never feel that he owns all energy in the psyche. That is never a fact. One should realize that most of the energy in the psyche is from social connections, like the parents, other relatives, and friends.

If one is a sincere yogi, one will be tied to another yogi who is greater. With the help of that person or those greater persons, one will derive resistance energies.

Yogi Who Killed and Ate Crayfish

Tibeti Yogi was with me this morning during breath infusion practice. This lasted an hour, which is a long time for kundalini practice. One may wonder what is the necessity for such a long period of such a forceful practice, as *breath of fire bhastrika* pranayama. There are legends about yogis from antiquity where they did pranayama practice continuously for months, having left aside even eating food.

These are not myths. Tibeti returned to give encouragement and to inform that I would need to energize the *hard to reach* areas of the subtle body. Those areas must be meticulously assaulted until all dense astral energy is removed, being replaced with energizing subtle force.

A great example in this effort, is a female celebrity who is very particular not to leave her penthouse until every last bit of makeup is applied, every hair on her head is set perfectly, all blemishes in her complexion are covered with the desired color tone, every lump of inordinate fat is squeezed into submission with spandex and everything immodest in her behavior is banished for the time being so that the most critical Pope sees it fit to write her a recommendation for entry into heaven.

A yogi can learn how to be particular from such a celebrity, to be tedious, specific and downright fanatical about cleansing every part of the subtle body, to bring it into the status of a yoga siddha form.

Tibeti spoke of the difficulty in getting the shoulders, armpits, arms, forearms and hands of the subtle body into a purified state. During the session, he was in one of my memories, one from the earlier part of this life. He reached an event which happened around 1965. He pulled it out and threw it into the environment. It came out like a scab on the skin which was peeled. He looked at me for an explanation of the circumstances under which that act was committed. He said, "Never mind. It belongs to the parents. let us discard it."

The incidence was one where I used a body which was 14 years of age. The father of the body arranged for me to visit him in Trinidad in an area called San Juan. I used to wander around the area. There were ravines where crayfish lived in the water. Once I caught three crayfish, took them home, killed them, remove their shells and cooked them. These crayfish are a large shrimp species.

The interesting thing is that the name of the place, San Juan, is a name I have not said in years. It is not a name that I recalled in years. After Tibeti tore the scab from my memory, the experience was fresh in my mind. Even the stage of the body I was using at 14 years of age, came back to me vividly. A body at fourteen years is different to a body at sixty. In fact, even the manifestation of personality is different. There is a small core which is the same but otherwise the character is completely different.

When Tibeti showed the experience, he looked deep into my psyche to see if it was my tendency. Once he was sure that it was not, he discarded the memory. He said,

> "This is not yours. It is the parents' tendency. However, these aspects, even though they belong to others, must be removed from the psyche. Once you take a body, you invariably carry undesirable tendencies from the relatives. Locate those aspects. Remove them from the psyche. These will prohibit the development of a siddha body. My duty is to bring this to your attention. Small as this may seem, it could be the cause of your not attaining the siddha form.

Yogi Meets Tibetan Yogis

During practice this morning, fortunately I again made contact with the three Tibetan yogis whom I got in touch with yesterday. This time only one of the yogis spoke to me. He was the leading one. He sent a mental message which would be this in English:

> Swamiji wants you to take my position so that I can be relieved. I was lucky that you got serious with the practice. You reached a stage where you can take my position because through that I can travel on and leave these systems of astral life. The other two with me will stay at this place and maintain their practice until they succeed. There is no need to give them advice. They have in their psyche the completion instructions.

This was in reference to Yogeshwarananda's guru who was known as Atmananda. The swami was not there but his three students practiced in the astral world. These are examples of what is possible if one gets serious and can complete most of the practice but does not reach a siddha yoga status before passing on.

Before he left, the senior yogi whom I am to replace, said that I should do the wiggle method. He noted this:

Generally due to familiarity with sex pleasure, the students cannot get on to the wiggle method. This is because they are stuck with one intense rush of pleasure. As such little kundalinis and little surges of kundalini are of no interest to them. For that matter they do not have the required sensitivity. Use the wiggle method consistently. That is the key.

This wiggle method is a way of moving from side to side and in other ways, especially in the neck area, with stretches to one side and then to another. This procedure causes the release of little amounts of infused energy instead of a big accumulation which may burst out in the head of the subtle body. This concerns purifying the *hard to reach* parts of the subtle form.

Kundalini is paranoid about getting sex pleasure. For that matter the most stubborn thing to get rid of is the need for sex pleasure. So long as kundalini holds out with this desire, spiritual life in terms of getting a yoga siddha form is nil.

When I sat to meditate the senior yogi gave an instruction, which was to remain in naad at the back of the head and then comb through the energy in the front part of the head. This combing action begins at the front and is pulled through the energy in a direction pulling backwards. This causes some very subtle sand-grain size thought-energies to be discovered.

Since these energies were transparent, they seem not to be there but with the combing action, one finds them and can throw them out of the psyche, out of the mind. These are thought energies which are psychic objects which bother a yogi by their presence in the mind.

Usually these yogis have positions they accept on behalf of their yoga gurus or the guru of the guru. In this case that person held a position and maintained his practice but he was prohibited from leaving the position until a replacement was found or until any person would develop spiritually to the extent of qualifying for that position.

Sometimes even though one progressed enough to move to a higher plane, one is prohibited from doing so by a yoga guru and has to stay on a certain level to assist selected students. Later when one student progress, he/she may assume the position and one can move on.

This person had long advanced sufficiently to move up to a higher plane but he had to stay there so that someone would be there to give instructions.

Yogeshwarananda's guru must have considered that I could fill in. He gave instructions for this person to be released from the duty.

Pubic Energy Distribution

During infusion practice, Yogeshwarananda showed a *base of the trunk* astral energy distribution system. Look at this diagram:

The thick horizontal light represents the very bottom of the trunk of the body. The energy is distributed through the trunk base but it spreads into the thighs. This becomes the situation after the lower pubic area is penetrated by the breath infusion energy. Because by nature it is a hormone reservoir, this pubic area has a resistance to such penetration of the infused energy.

When one can change its construction, it acts as a transit area for energy rather than a reservoir. There are some *flat down* poses which help in the effort to change the nature of this area. People who are attached to sexual pleasure will naturally be resistant to these poses and will instinctively dislike the idea of doing these exercises to change the construction of this area in the subtle body.

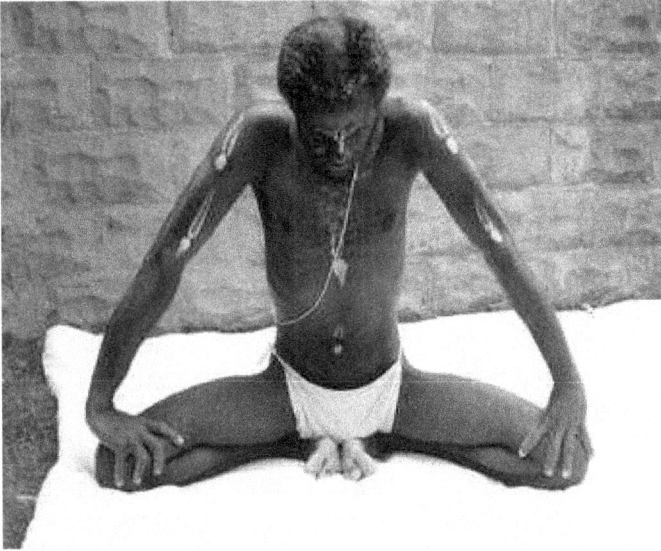

Downward Distribution of Kundalini

This concerns the practice of monitoring and improving the efficiency of the downward distribution of kundalini below the base chakra. The normal concern is to raise kundalini from the base upwards through the spine into the head.

This upward activity is a start in higher yoga, but one must go further. In fact, if one becomes proficient in the upward rise of kundalini from the base to the head, one will over time, discover or be inspired to cause kundalini to surge in other parts of the trunk.

There are left and right side kundalinis. There is front kundalini. These are different directions in which kundalini moves as it rises. The most popular and well-known process is spinal kundalini. Spine kundalini control is a feat in itself but it is the start of the process of subduing the lifeForce.

The subtle body is more than the subtle spine and head. Eventually a student realizes that clarity in the spine and head is not enough. One should achieve clarity in the rest of the subtle body, even in the feet. The natural system is to neglect the feet and *the hard to reach* areas like arm pits, arms, hands, thighs, legs and feet. However, if one strives to reach these areas, over time, trying repeatedly, one will penetrate the dense astral energy which is in these areas. One will displace that energy with new energizing astral force. This makes for a yoga siddha body which is the first step in assuring that one will not take a haphazard transmigration after the death of the body.

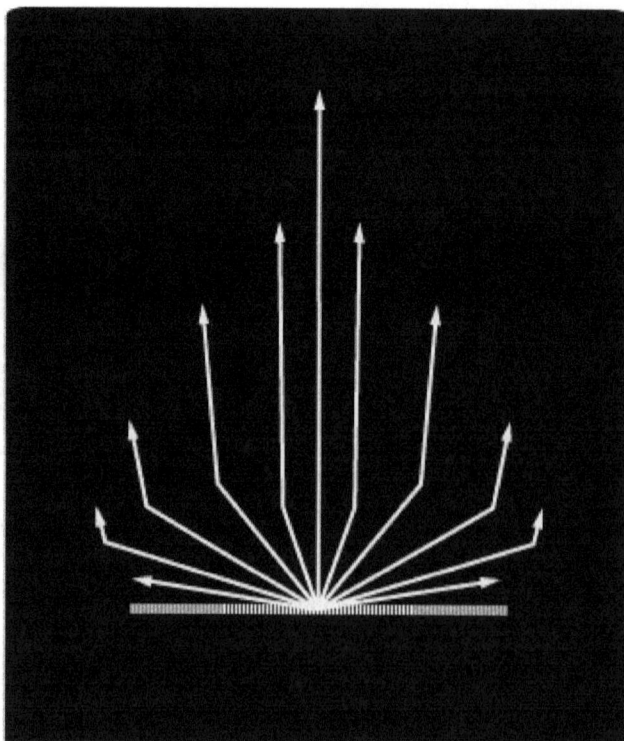

In the diagram, the line at the bottom represents the base chakra and its spread of control at the bottom of the trunk of the subtle body. From there energy rises into the body and spreads around, either efficiently or inefficiently according to the pollution and heavy astral energy in the subtle form.

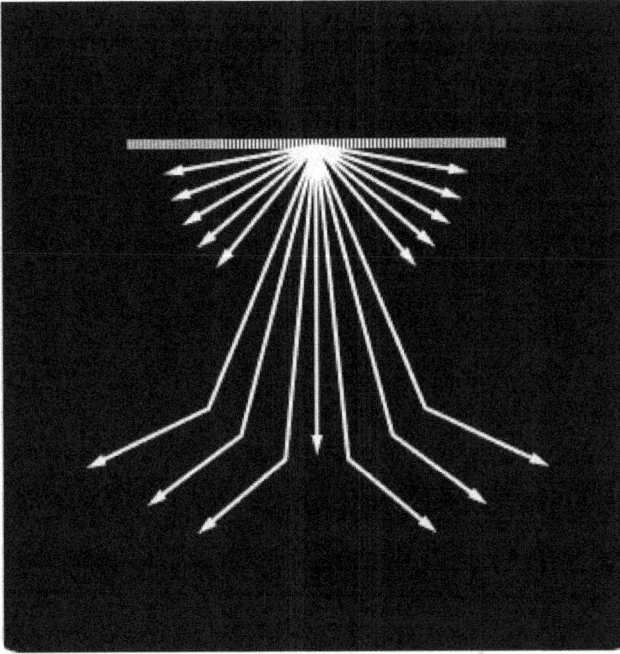

In this diagram, the line at the top represents the same base chakra and its spread of control at the bottom of the trunk of the subtle body. From there the energy spreads downward. It penetrates the thighs, knees, legs, and feet.

This second diagram is the one which is of interest in this practice. A yoga siddha body is one in which all parts of the form have light (as in sun-light) astral energy and no dense astral force which is heavy. Making the subtle spine *(sushumna nadi),* and the subtle head (the mind), become infused with fresh energy from the breath infusion practice does not necessarily cause improvement in the *hard to reach* places of the subtle form.

In this discourse the word mind is the equivalent of the subtle head. The subtle spine is what is called *sushumna nadi* in the hatha yoga books from India. The individual entity is not that subtle body but it resides in that body, just the way a human being resides in a building. Specifically, the coreSelf resides in the head of the subtle body. The kundalini force has the base of the subtle spine as its default residence. The effort in hatha yoga as taught by Yogiraj Gorakshnath was to unseat the kundalini from its default residence.

Yogi Tampers with Karma

One side effect of breath infusion is the efficient passage of karmic energies through the psyche. Karma is the cumulative effect of an action which was committed by the person in a past life. A simple act, like a flirtation with someone forms a karmic energy or a consequence force which may cause either of the persons to take a haphazard rebirth.

Once I act, even mentally, I am automatically tagged for the reaction to the act, regardless of whether I like the reaction or not, regardless of if I remember that I did the act or not. Nature never forgets. Human beings are into forgiving. They do magnanimous acts but nature is not concerned with that. Nature is a mathematical operation.

Because I flirted with someone in a past life, nature arranges a meeting with that person in this life but under totally different circumstances and with my not remembering the original exchange. Even though I do not remember, nature replays the flirtation when I meet the person in this life. From that a relationship may or may not develop. It depends on the facilities nature affords. If I cannot develop the relationship, I feel that I missed something. Nature notes that. It will keep that notation in my subconscious and use it in a future time when I meet that person. In the next encounter I will have a stronger more compelling urge to be with that someone.

The breath infusion can help to thaw these subconscious energies. These are lodged in the psyche. They are hosted in the subtle body. By breath infusion one can cause these energies to move out of the psyche, thus dissolving nature's schemes.

In some cases, however when a yogi tries to breathe out those harbored energies; he/she finds that the energies do not move out of storage. They remain there. This means that the infusion is not sufficient to blast that type of memory. Some memory packs form a heavier astral energy than others. The heaviest ones cannot be removed by a student yogi. He/she does not have the required power and efficiency of infusion to displace them and cause them to be evacuated from the psyche.

You may hear that yoga can destroy unwanted memories but do not think that this means just meditation. Meditation alone cannot do everything. Certain things must be done by some other of the methods of yoga. Remember that yoga has eight parts. In fact, the meditation part consists of either four or three parts according to how one practices. When it is three parts it is called *samyama* by Patanjali which is the highest three stages as a sequential practice.

When it has four parts, it is the four higher stages of yoga. When it is one part it is the final stage of yoga which is *samadhi*.

Many people feel they enter *samadhi* even though they are far away from it. They do concentration, or a mentally neutral practice or a mood-altering process.

Bear in mind that nature keeps two logs of activities. One is filled in the subconscious. This log stays with the self wherever it may go in the physical or astral worlds. This stays in the psyche. This is the rough equivalent of the subconscious in Western psychology. The other log is nature video storage of the action. Both logs are off limits except to advanced yogis.

Others cannot tamper with memories. If he has the required mystic perception, a yogi may enter a memory and see its information, but he cannot alter it.

Swami Rama / *Agnisara*

This morning Swami Rama praised the *agnisara* practice for the use of developing a yoga siddha body. This is a masterful process. In the first place this has to do with freeing the navel chakra which is constricted at the time of the placenta of the mother being inoperative at delivery. During the fetal stage, my navel chakra was open to the world of my mother's psyche but at delivery it closed. It remained closed until I mastered *agnisara* practice.

I as an individual subtle body, fused into my mother's psyche. I looked to her for sustenance. At first when this happened, I was interested in the emotional energy of my mother. Soon after this emotional exchange developed into a physical reality when my sperm body from the father's form became forcibly attracted to the uterine wall of my mother's form. This attraction caused all of my mouth energies to adhere to the uterine wall. Through that place where I adhered, I extracted nutrients from the mother's body.

Why bother with the *agnisara* practice?

The reason is that if the navel chakra in the front of the body (not the one on the spine) is not opened again, it means that no matter what I do or think, I will again recycle effortlessly and without resistance into another mother's body.

Swami Rama gave three diagrams.

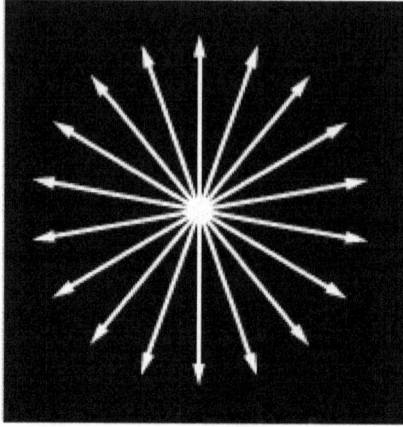

In the diagram, the energy at the navel spreads with a limited range of about 3 inches away from the center of the navel. This is an undesirable condition for those who want to become siddhas. This is the ordinary lay out of the navel chakra in a human being.

In the diagram the lines which go downward are extended into and through the groin. This is a desired condition for yoga but it is not the whole process. In this stage the choke-hold of the navel is somewhat broken. The pubic area (sexual facilities) is under attack from the released energy from the navel chakra.

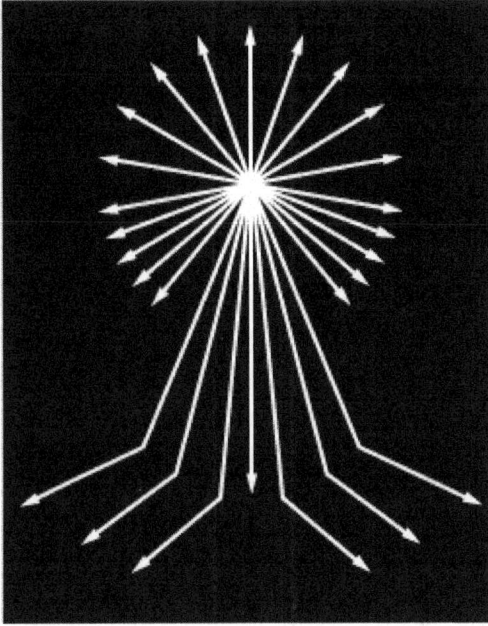

In the diagram the energy passes through the groin area and penetrates into the thigh. This is the beginning of the third stage of conquest of the navel.

Swami Rama was there astrally as I did physical exercises this morning. He said this.

Agnisara *must be mastered. It is best if a student can gain the required proficiency before passing from the physical body. This practice is wonderful. It will cause rapid progress. The student must achieve the groin area break-through. Then it is easy to attack the thighs which are supportive of reproduction and sex desire. With the conquest of the thighs, the student can be a genuine celibate. Without celibacy, there is no chance of transiting through the higher astral regions with the siddhas.*

There are sexual allurements there but for the yogi who mastered agnisara *and who carries that skill in the subtle body, those attractions do not present themselves.*

Kundalini Attitude Change

The longest bone in the body is in the thigh. It is an accessory of the reproductive system. It is dedicated to aiding sexual activities. For those yogis who want to reach the siddha stage, this attitude of the thighs must be changed. They should practice tight stretches and do these with breath infusion so that they extract the old energy from the thighs and install energizing force (subtle air).

If the yogi is successful, there will be a flow of energy as in the diagram. The energy in the trunk courses around the lower part of the body, beginning near the spine and then going around the body in either direction into the thighs, then out of the thighs near the pubic area. Once the energy gets back into the trunk of the body, it courses upwards through the front of the trunk.

When this practice is complete, the yogi will find that as a result, the subtle body has no sexual interest. It will retain a gender configuration as male or female but it will have no interest in genital reception or penetration in a give or take way. It will not abhor sexual penetration but it will not have an interest in it and will not try to procure opportunities for it.

The lack of interest of the subtle body about this will not occur because of a mental decision to forego sex or to pursue celibate lifestyle as required in the moral restraints. It will occur then on the basis of the change in interest in the energy itself. This is not a will power decision. It is not an intellectual decision or enforcement of moral principles. It is a decision by kundalini because of a change in the nature of the energy which the kundalini is provided with.

Student Yogis Resisting the Yoga-gurus

Yogeshwaranand gave diagrams.

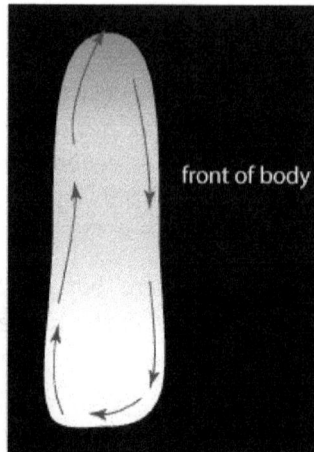

front of body

This is the situation of a student yogi who accomplished a little in the breath infusion practice, where the infused energy goes down through the lungs past the navel, to the groin and then jumps to the kundalini at the base of the spine and courses upwards through the spine into the head.

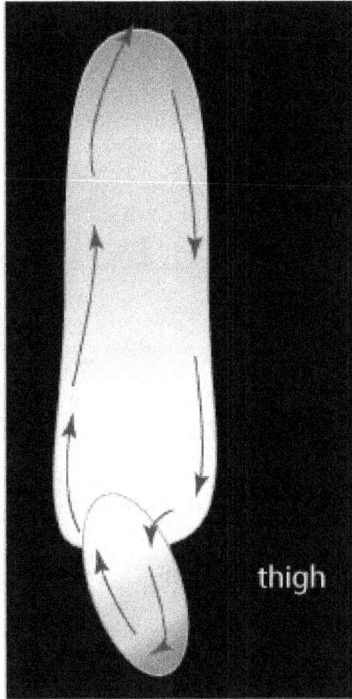

This is the situation of a more advanced yogi, who makes the energy go down through the navel and then into the groin and then into the thighs and then coursing around the thighs it jumps to kundalini and goes up through the spine into the head.

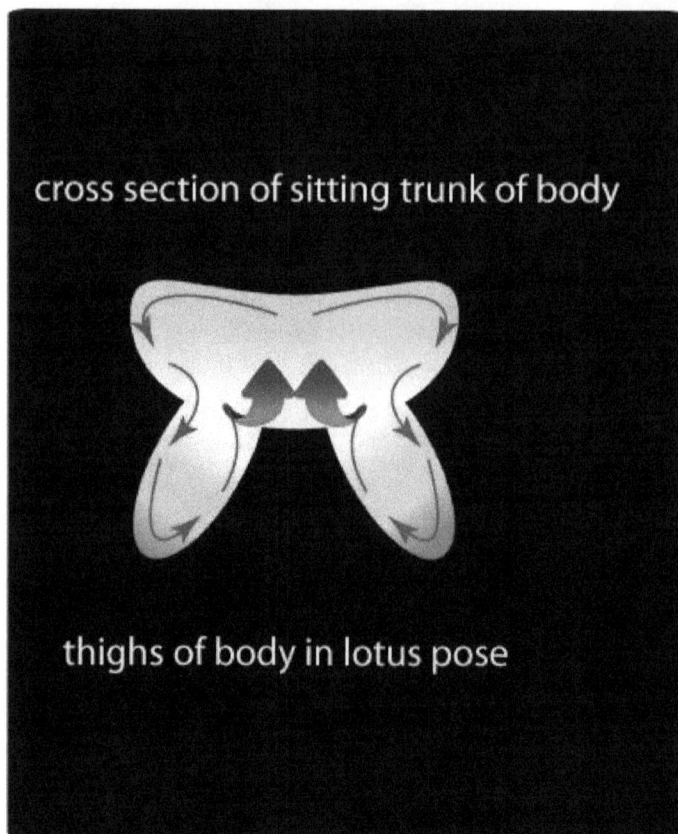

cross section of sitting trunk of body

thighs of body in lotus pose

This is the situation where the energy which is infused by rapid breathing is accumulated in the trunk of the body. Then it infuses into the two thighs as far as the knees.

Initially due to craving for sex pleasure and other means of physical happiness, kundalini yoga is valued for raising kundalini to enjoy the bliss energy which arises from the awakened kundalini. Later when the student matures, there is no need for sex pleasure as the reference.

Physical nature gave the transmigrating individual self the lead on how to procure pleasure especially sex pleasure. Nearly everyone in the world craves it. Over time, that psychosis leaves the mind of the student.

Once the student gets free of the sex pleasure craving, there arises in the nature of the student a certain beneficial submissiveness to yoga-gurus and deities. Otherwise the student keeps on resisting and thinking that he/she knows best.

Two Types of Siddhas

Students of kriya yoga and breath infusion should seriously consider that if they view everyone as being equal, it will be near impossible to take help sincerely from superior souls. If we are all the same and there are no superior souls or even a supreme being, there is no reason to open oneself for help from someone else.

I ask students to abandon atheistic beliefs and the idea that everyone is equal. Do this for the sake of advancement. One must get assistance and be inspired by superiors. If one approaches them with the wrong attitude and with the equality idea foremost in the mind, that disposition will undermine one's ability to benefit from them.

During breath infusion this afternoon, Yogeshwarananda made a statement about siddhas.

> There are two types of siddhas who use physical bodies. One is the siddha who descended from the higher worlds. This is a perfected individual who descends, a kind of avatar, godPerson. The other siddha is the one who ascends which means that he/she came through the mundane evolutionary cycle and attained the status of siddha by the grace of nature's evolutionary push and by self effort under superior guidance. Self effort alone cannot make any person evolve into a siddha. The inspiration to be a siddha comes from the higher levels. One who is inspired by the pushes of the mundane evolutionary cycle cannot become a siddha by that impetus because it does not have within it, perceptions of the absolute world.

> Of the two siddhas, those who descended are greater than those who are ascending through the mundane evolutionary cycle. The technique is to recognize a siddha who descended and not to mistake that person as one who ascends.

> All beings evolve. Even those who descended, evolve. When they descend, they act as if they are required to evolved. Their actions provide fresh impetus for those who must evolve. It is the only way for the superior beings to make contact with the others who evolve. Help must be obtained from the superior beings if an evolving entity is to move beyond physical nature for good. One cannot get this help in a wholesome way if one does not stop to realize the difference and then appreciate the descent of a superior soul.

> There are two reasons why a siddha would descend. One reason is that he is instructed to do so. The second is that his inherent sense of compassion takes control of him. When he sensed that others are on

lower levels, he develops a desire to assist even though he may not be commissioned for this by higher-ups.

Once you are exposed to certain social mediums, your nature may respond to those in a way of neutrality, abhorrence or attraction. If you are attracted, you will transit to those lower worlds regardless of the risk. You will be pulled into those environments.

Once an individual enters a certain lower realm it is near impossible for that person to escape. The social gravity pulls that person into those places and keeps him/her there.

Some siddhas come down because they are requested to by higher gurus or by a deity who is the existential source. In that case one has no choice but to do as suggested. Refusal to comply with the request of either a yoga-guru or a deity is just the same as saying to yourself that one will go to hell. If one damages the relationship with a deity, it means that one sabotaged one's right to stay in the level of existence where that deity predominates.

Refusing to comply with a powerful yoga-guru means being cut off from the techniques which he mastered or created as method of release from lower levels. There was a case however which was an exception where someone disobeyed a yoga guru, got away with it and gained elevation as a result. That person was Yajnavalka. He had a disagreement with his guru but then he worshiped the sun-deity and as a result produced the White Vedas (shukla yajurveda). Vaisampayana was the guru involved. He is mentioned repeatedly in the Mahabharata because the author of that aural text commissioned him as the main person to memorize it.

Yajnavalka was once ordered by his guru to return all knowledge which he was taught. Yajnavalkya mentally vomited it. After that happened, Yajnavalka was annoyed. He silently decided not to take a human guru. This is very similar to the situation today. Many people are cynical and do not think that a human being can be an authority. Yajnavalka was no atheist. He was aware of the deities. He meditated and contacted the sun-deity, who gave him mantras, like the gayatri mantra which is dedicated to the sun-god or Savita:

ॐ भूर् भुवः स्वः ।

तत्सवितुर्वरेण्यं

भर्गो देवस्य धीमहि ।

धियो यो नः प्रचोदयात् ॥

om bhūr bhuvaḥ svaḥ

tat savitur vareṇyaṃ

bhargo devasya dhīmahi

dhiyo yo naḥ prachodayāt

People translate this mantra in novel ways without respect to the fact that after being rejected by Vaisampayana, Yajnavalka got it from the deity, the sunPerson.

Originally Vishvamitra a guru of Rama and Lakshman, was the one who first got the gayatri mantra. It is said that among the people who know the mantra, Yajnavalka was the last student, who was directly taught it by the deity.

Try to understand that freedom has no meaning whatsoever. We talk about it but it has no meaning because we are not in control. When we gain some control it may be for the duration of the body.

Do you know where you will be tomorrow, as to whether you will be king or slave? Can you guarantee where you will be?

In whatever environment one finds oneself, one will have to accept that accommodation and live there for the duration of the body which is suitable for life there. If one finds oneself in the sea, a shark's body is the way to go, but for how long?

Yogis Who Sleep In

Getting up early to meditate during the yogic traditional period which is between 4am and 6am is somewhat unnatural since usually the body wants to sleep at that time. Still that is the best time to meditate because then the minds in the area of the planet where one resides, are mostly involved in sleeping, where ideas, images and the like are mostly shut down, where there is the least static in the telepathic transmission zones.

One great benefit of meditating at that time is that to do it, one has to escape from materialistic astral association. One also escapes from friends who though they are interested in talking about spiritual life, have no interest in doing the yogic austerities which would help to consolidate progress in self-realization. These friends may be pot heads, dope addicts, music freaks, winos, LSD heads, sex maniacs and pleasure addicts, all who are non-conformists as far as the establishment is concerned. These people are cool to be sure, but they do not have the impetus required to pursue a yoga practice in terms of the methods left behind by siddhas like Gorakshnath and Chaurangi.

If a student is serious, he/she will have to escape from all sorts of materialistic and non-materialistic association so as to rise early in the morning to practice. Do not grumble in a corner thinking:

- Who says yoga has to be done early?
- Why the judgment about when it is done?
- What does it matter?
- What does time have to do with it?

Forget those sentiments.

To rise early one must get to bed early. What occupies one's attention so that one cannot get to bed at least by 9.30 pm? There are some people who live in places like New York City. Sometimes they must rise at 5 am to catch the train. These people do this daily, rain or shine. If you ask them to do that on weekends so as to facilitate an early meditation, they turn a cold shoulder. Why is that? Why is there an argument about rising early to meditate but none about rising early to make money? To rise early to meditate one must be in tune with the yogis who practice in that way.

Internal Supernatural Transit

After the physical body dies, there are various ways of going to higher dimensions. This is for those yogis who experience astral projections, who are aware of dream encounters and who study nature's operation of the shifts from sleep to partial consciousness to waking consciousness and to day dream.

The subtle body is impure with many filthy subtle energies within it. This must be altered.

The coreSelf will keep on existing with or without its present identity format, but more likely without that, as we experienced in the infancy and youth of this body, where we could hardly know the isolated identity of the coreSelf without other mental and emotional influences.

The core will keep transiting. It is a question of where it will be and with whom. Even if it is in a spatial existence where it cannot distinguish itself from anything else, it will still be, it will still exist with or without a cultural format of identity.

During practice this afternoon, I had one short visit from a yoga guru who assists me with practice and shows different techniques which he feels I should do during a particular session. There is much to do, just as one as a student on the primary level is given tasks to complete by a teacher. Each day the student is faced with something else to learn.

Yogeshwarananda gave some association during the breath infusion session. His main energy at that time was that he would answer something which was on my mind.

Being that my practice may not be fully consolidated before time closes in on this body, I need a method which would guarantee that I would at least continue the practice after this body is confiscated by time, so that I can develop the subtle body into a yoga siddha form. That is the least achievement a yogi should attain. Anything less than that is unacceptable and spells doom for the yogi, because it means that he will take another body haphazardly, at random, under the chance throw of the dice by inscrutable fate.

That may work out in his favor. It may not. Who knows? Does providence care about one individual? It did not in previous lives. There is no reason to think that it will do what is favorable for the yogi.

Yogeshwarananda made a statement about this. He spoke so quietly, I could barely hear him with psychic ears. He said:

If the student yogi can infuse the subtle body, he/she will meet siddhas on the higher planes. It is not a matter of travelling astrally to higher levels, even though that is possible. A yogi should resort to higher yoga in terms of samyama. *But failing that or if he cannot do that but thinks that he does, he will realize that he failed. Then on a lower level in the afterlife, he may infuse the subtle body and it will shift to higher levels where siddhas can be contacted.*

This practice should begin now while one has a physical form. It is guaranteed for those students who advanced in the ashtanga methods sincerely, just the way Patanjali described or even as Krishna explained in chapter six of Bhagavad Gita.

The path of travelling astrally to the higher levels is not the path for the yogis to take. Those who do ritual ceremonies in India to various demigods, may if they are sincere and if they are lucky, leave a dying physical body and travel to the higher astral realms to meet deities, but that is only if those deities make arrangements for such transit. And why should these supernatural entities make an effort to infuse celestial energy into the subtle body of a dying human being, even one who was religiously occupied?

A yogi should not waste energy or endeavor in ritual acts which are to be converted into astral propulsion of the subtle body after death. The yogi should stick to the internal process of *samyama*. A yogi if he or she is proficient in practice will bypass the ritualistic devotees by the internal method of psyche transit.

Yogi Gurus without Sons

This morning during breath infusion, Yogeshwarananda had me focus on a part of the thigh which is important for reaching the legs and toes. This is the area of tendons near the knee. In a body which is not supple, this area is out of reach of the yogi. As one stretches and relaxes these tendons, this area can be reached.

This, of course, is a physical action in postures but the real concern is the subtle body which is interspaced into the physical one and which is affected when this is done physically.

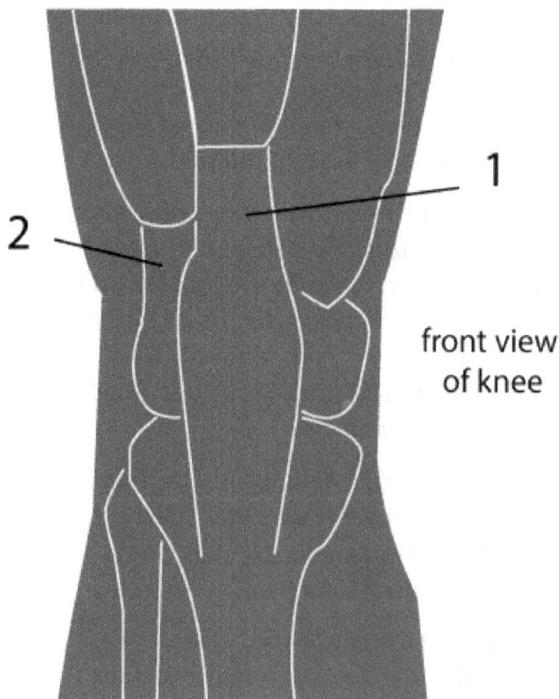

1

2

front view
of knee

In that diagram there are two tendons numbered 1 and 2. This practice targets those tendons especially 1. By stretching one stimulates the bones the tendons are connected to. That in turn causes changes in the blood marrow which is produced by those bones as well as how that marrow is distributed to other parts of the body.

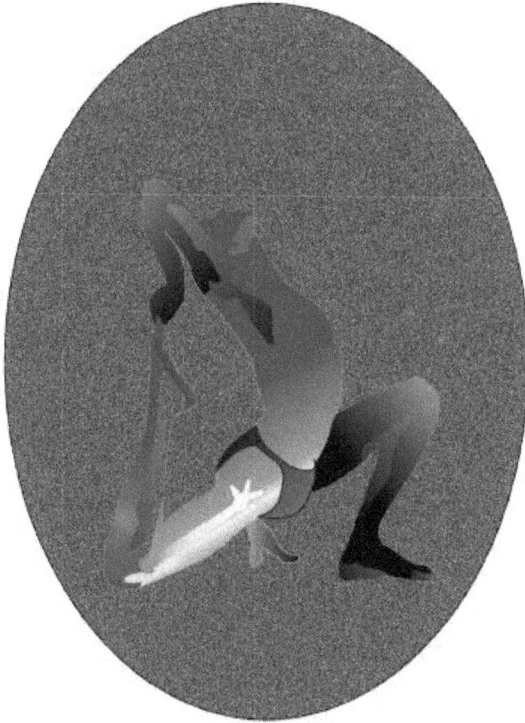

In the subtle body this relates to the quality of pranic energy which is in those parts of the psyche. A yogi cannot afford to be only concerned with the head or with the chakras on the spine. The other parts of the psyche need to be elevated and cleared of heavy astral force as well.

While I did the breath infusion, Yogesh examined aspects in my memory. Once he saw a notation which was of a conversation with Yogi Bhajan, where the yogi admonished me about beginning an ashram. Yogesh looked at it. Then he said,

"Begin an ashram? That is what you want to do. Do not think about this again. Stay close to your yoga gurus. What will happen if every disciple becomes a guru? Then there will gurus but no disciples. Fathers without sons, what is this?"

Yogi who Never Found a Siddha

By sheer good luck, I was in the presence of Yogeshwarananda during the afternoon session of exercises. A student who takes training in breath infusion practice, was absent because of a malfunction in his spine.

The spine is important to a yogi. Both the spine and brain are of utmost importance. In fact, the human body is considered in the Vedic literature to be a special tool which can be used by the self to attain spiritual perception. The *Brahma Sutras* begins with a verse which says *athato brahma jijnasa*, which is to say that now *(athato)* that one has this human form and can read books, one should with enthusiasm, inquire *(jijnasa)* about the spiritual reality *(brahma)*. If I was in an animal form, I could not make the inquiry because the form has no literacy.

Due to the special construction of the human spine and brain, it permits an entity who uses a physical body to pursue spiritual inquiries. In the other species, such pursuit is not possible.

Hence if a yogi's brain or spine is damaged, he/she will be deterred in practice, at least until the physical body meets its end and the yogi is left with only a subtle form. All precautions should be taken to protect the spine and brain. Even a simply act like sitting should not be done carelessly. The spine should be supported even when sitting. A yogi should avoid sitting carelessly without proper back support. Activities like lifting and even doing postures should be done with the awareness that if the spine is damaged, it will have a negative impact on practice.

During the afternoon session Yogeshwaranand again mentioned the postures and breath infusion which have to do with the thighs. He said this,

"Keep the thighs cleared of foul energy and passionate force. That is the key to going with the siddhas. Going with the siddhas means having a subtle body which has a vibrational level which is similar to that of the siddhas. There is a dense astral energy which comes from the lower back part of the subtle body. There is also a passionate force which drops from the reproductive area. These energies are compiled in the thighs where they are infused into the bone marrow and blood in the thighs. This combined energy influences one's desires and life style. It makes a yogi into a hypocrite. He poses as a yogi but he has interest in creature survival. When the body dies, he never finds even a single siddha to associate with."

"He loops around by the natural attraction to sex indulgence. He manifests again as a mammal body. It could be any mammal not just the human."

It is very dangerous for a yogi to take a lower birth, even accidentally. There is no telling when he will again assume a human embryo. By all means one should not get close to any lower species. One should not keep pets if it is possible. The service which one trades with the animals, is itself the route to a lower transmigration for the human pet owner in as much as it is a route for a higher transmigration for the pet.

The route for rebirth is emotions. If one develops emotions towards an animal species, it is likely that one will fuse into the body of an animal after death and be transformed as one of those species. In the same way we take human births. The animals also by being human pets, get access to human births through developing affections for humans. It can go either way. For the animal it is an upgrade. For the human it is a downgrade.

There is the story of Bharat, a king in India, who when he took up the life of a yogi in his elderly years, became attached to a deer calf which lost its mother at the time of its birth. The mother ran away because of fear of a lion that was nearby. Bharat, as a good human being, rescued the deer calf and raised it but he became attached to the animal as a pet as we usually do.

At the time of death, Bharat thought of the deer. He became attracted to the deer families and transformed in the next life into a deer calf. In that deer body, due to the intensity of his practice in the life as a king, he used to go to the ashrams of yogis in the forest, steal their palm leaf books and eat the pages.

In the next birth he took birth as a yogi brahmin. In that birth he completed the yoga austerities through which he was liberated.

The father of Bharat in the life when he took the deer calf as a pet, was Rishabha (Ri-shab-ha) who is rated as an incarnation of God. In that life Bharat had special yoga training in very advanced hatha yoga which is described in the *Bhagavata Purana*. Therefore, King Bharat was not an ordinary yogi. He had connections with divine people, one of whom served as his father in the physical world in that life when he was degraded to a lower species.

There are other instances to show that taking a lower body is risky even for a yogi. In the Mahabharata two ascetics quarreled. They cursed each other. The curses stuck so they took bodies as elephant and tortoise and were in those species for some time. There is a story also about other great yogis who went down to lower species of life and who were left in those species for thousands of years transmigrating.

Buddha told of his lower transmigrations even in aquatic species. All of this is undesirable if one is interested in spiritual life but it is highly adventurous if one is not mature in self-realization.

It is sheer madness to be in any other species except the human one. The mental state of the other forms is devoid of the idea of self-realization.

One becomes obsessed with the activities of that specific species. One's attachments are transferred into that species. One has no idea of anything else.

Anyone who thinks that the human species is just like the other species and has the same capacity for liberation as the other lifeforms is crazy. One should place a high value on humanity and try to at least keep transmigrating as a human being until one can see the passage to the divine world. The tools for attaining divine status do not exist in the lower species.

If one takes a lower body, the truth is that one may be left for dead, which means that no yoga-guru may make an effort to get one out. In that case one will remain in that species and by the grace of the evolutionary thrust of physical nature, one will over time, after many lives, be again ushered as a human embryo.

If, however a yoga guru or deity has special interest in one's development, the person may do something supernatural to get one transferred to human birth or may send someone who will act in a way which causes one to again get a human body.

Even taking a human body is dangerous for a yogi because usually one gets involved with the family of that body. One is compulsive about family status and genetic relation.

In this life, I took this body to write books explaining spirituality. It was a risk. I was directly protected by Swami Shivananda who used to come to me and try to wise me up when I was an infant in Guyana in South America in the formation of this body. Once Lord Krishna directly tried to help me to wise up. I was lucky. The temptation to be of physical use to the family is great. Even in the human body it is dangerous to take these births what to speak about taking an animal form which lacks capacity for spiritual discrimination.

Distracted Yogis

This morning I was back on schedule for practice. By the grace of fate, I escaped from the situation in which my time for eating, and the type of food eaten, were counterproductive. This body I use was born under the auspices of a flesh eating family. It was conceived in an environment that was hostile to *Patanjali's yama* requirement for *ahimsa* {a (non) + *himsa* (killing)}. In childhood this body was not vegetarian, even though fruits and vegetables were part of its diet. This body was omnivorous, eating fish, shrimp, iguana, cow, chicken, sheep, goat, cooked cow's blood, crab, turkey, duck, and geese.

Some of the original cells which formed this body were taken from a father who in the Amazon rain forest ate snake, turtle, labba (large rodent), tapir and who knows what.

That diet is hostile to the yoga.

I got back on track. The practice did not have as much resistance as it had a few days ago when my meals went in a direction which is suitable to persons who do not do yoga, who have no view about reincarnation and who have no aspiration for conscious astral projection or the awareness and maintenance of a subtle body.

After about twenty minutes of practice, I became aware of Muktananda on the astral side of existence. I did infusion into the lower trunk of the body. He directed me in a breath infusion mental thrust in the center of the lower trunk. When the exhale is made forcibly, the yogi may feel a force going downward which hits the membrane of the psyche which is the base floor of the subtle trunk. Then on the inhale that force flattens out and spreads along that base floor.

About ten minutes after Muktananda came. Yogeshwaranand came, looked and disappeared.

Students should always be on the alert not to be distracted during practice. There are external and very obvious distractions like lights and noises from the physical world. Lights are especially troublesome. One may use a blindfold which Yogesh said helps to keep focused on breath infusion and meditation.

There are essentially two types of distractions which afflict the student during breath infusion and during meditation. These are disturbances from the physical world and disturbances from the psychic world. Those from the physical world can be kept at bay by being in physical isolation. But if that is not possible, one can cover the eyes and even the ears with a cloth or bandage. If one practices daily and fails to protect from physical lights and sounds, it is to be understood that one is not desperate for success.

Though physical distractions are the easiest to get rid of, some students fail to deal with it. These may be compared to hard working men who spend their paycheck at a club after working. Instead of saving the money or at least using it constructively for their families, they squander it on alcohol and sexual recreation. They work. No one can criticize them for not being employed but they are stupid in the way they use income.

The other type of distraction is psychic. Once one shuts out the physical distractions, one's problems will begin in earnest because then one has to deal with abstract psychic phenomena. These are in the mind. Some come from outside the mind, penetrate it and take control of it, just the way a virus may enter the nostril, penetrate the mucus membranes and then inflict the body with disease.

Regardless of whether those psychic distractions are self-created or are alien penetrations, their effect is the same in that they distract from practice. What is the sense in doing breath infusion in a certain posture which is supposed to infuse energy into the right thigh, while at the same time, thinking of last night's sex with a partner?

Yogi Who Eats Here and There

If one is interested, if it has meaning or significance, I would explain that reaching siddhas now or hereafter will depend on location in consciousness. First of all, one should get rid of the idea that there is only one level of consciousness in the psychic, supernatural and spiritual dimensions.

When one does breath infusion or even when one meditates and did no breath infusion, one may shift into different levels of consciousness.

To be clear when one does practice, one should be sensitive so that the vagueness and abstractness of the subtle consciousness clears and shows the distinctions.

When I did breath infusion this morning, there was a problem because two days ago, I sabotaged the practice. Due to that it took longer to infuse the subtle body. There was some extra-dense energy in the lower trunk. It was there because of what I ate and when I ate that particular meal.

People feel that anybody can cook for anybody. That is approved in the normal day to day world. When one becomes a yogi however and one is serious about practice, the practice becomes like a dictator who makes stipulations about what to eat, when to eat, and how it should be prepared.

If you break the regulation, your practice suffers and you must work with the subtle body to get it back in order.

After about forty minutes, I got this tap on the shoulder from Muktananda, He said,

"Where were you yesterday? You cannot afford to miss practice. How do you know when that body will drop dead? If you cannot maintain the practice, how will others? Eating here! Eating there! Eating now! Eating then! That is not for yogis."

How about a little math from the elementary level when we used to add this to that?

Food + Air + Ideas = Mood

Or in Sanskrit:

Bhoga + Prana + Chittavritti = Guna

Diet

Due to having to attend a social function yesterday, the breath infusion practice was not as effective. I could be a fake yogi who thinks, believes or even visualizes energy bypassing the denseness which is in the bottom half of the trunk, but who would be fooled by that? Who besides me?

Usually, to facilitate breath infusion practice and the meditation which follows that, I eat speclflc foods and take these foods at certain times. If this system is upset for one reason or the other, the practice is deterred.

I begin my day with the maximum empty stomach at about 4 am. Since at this time the last food which I ate was in the early afternoon of the previous day and the last main meal I ate was in the early morning at about 8am of the previous day, my stomach is fully relaxed from having to process foods. There is no food in the stomach to be processed at 4am.

I do breath infusion and then sit to meditate. This comes to an end soon after 6 am.

I take my main meal at about 8am. That time may vary from day to day but it is usually in the morning hours and never in the afternoon, at least it will be before 10am. That is my main meal.

This primary meal follows immediately after my most important breath infusion/meditation session. This means that it has the most time to be digested within twenty-four hours before the next main meditation session.

I do a second breath infusion session in the afternoon around 5pm but that is the subsidiary session.

I eat light foods in the early afternoon, nothing heavy and never my main meal. During the morning two hours after the main meal, I take three bananas. I usually use these with warm water or milk, which aids in the digestion of these and causes these to move through the digestive track with ease.

The main thing is not so much what one eats but the time of eating. Eat to facilitate the breath infusion which is a huge factor in improving the quality of meditation and also in causing one to have psychic perception.

Right now, we have little faith in psychic perception because we rely heavily on the sure physical senses but that will not help us beyond the life of the present body. At least it will not help until nature can manufacture another physical body for each of us in the womb of the next mother.

Psychic perception will develop rapidly if one were to do the breath infusion. This will give one the required confidence in the afterlife and in the body which one will use hereafter. If there is no confidence in the afterlife, one will have little impetus to prepare for it. That will cause one to lose the present body and then curl again as an unconscious energy in the next mother's womb. The result of that will be another baby form crying for milk when it is born.

Since I attended a function, and did a courtesy of eating a main meal at about 4 pm, the energy from that meal was there as a blockage in the belly region of the physical and the subtle bodies. As a result, the breath infusion was not as effective as it usually is when my main meal is in the morning hours.

I did the breath infusion and did the best I could with it but I noticed that the infused energy was absorbed by the dense energy in the system which was the current state of that food matter.

Somebody may prove that I am not the body and I am not the petty self which ate that late meal but that does not solve the problem of the energy upset which is tagged to that petty self which in turn is tagged to the transcendental self. Question to ask on these occasions is why did the transcendental self not control the petty self which in turn failed to control the social associations which caused that meal to be eaten. If this transcendental self is such a big deal and if the petty self is a nuisance and is unwanted, why is the transcendental self for all it is, unable to control these situations?

I will be back on schedule today. This will not be repeated. It is a great lesson in deviation from yoga practice and in confirming to influences which are not supportive of a rigid breath infusion / meditation habit.

The dichotomy of self into ego self and non-ego absolute godSelf really points a finger at the ineffective and powerless godSelf, which is unable to properly monitor and control the ego self which it blames for its inadequacies. Until the godSelf can get itself in order and control the ego self, what is its value in the practical sense?

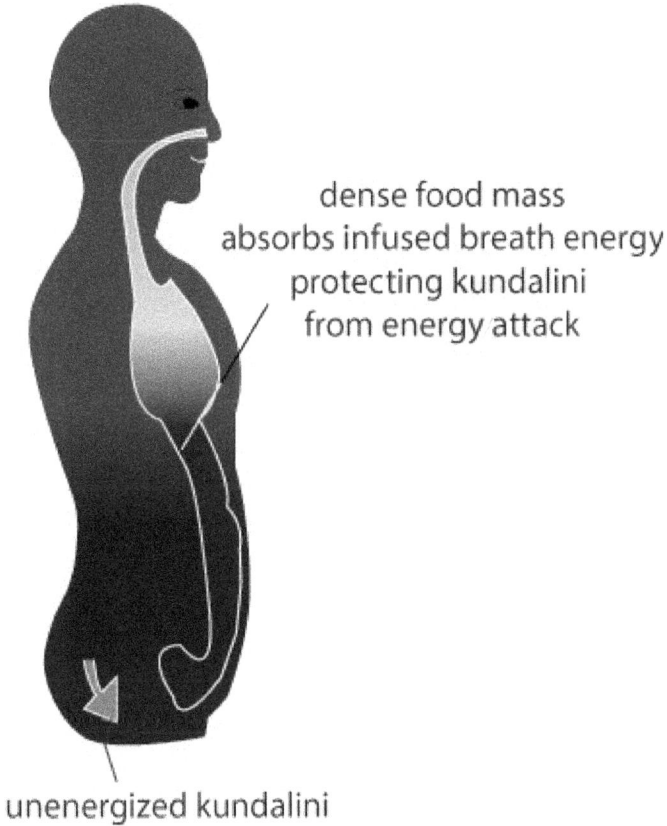

dense food mass
absorbs infused breath energy
protecting kundalini
from energy attack

unenergized kundalini

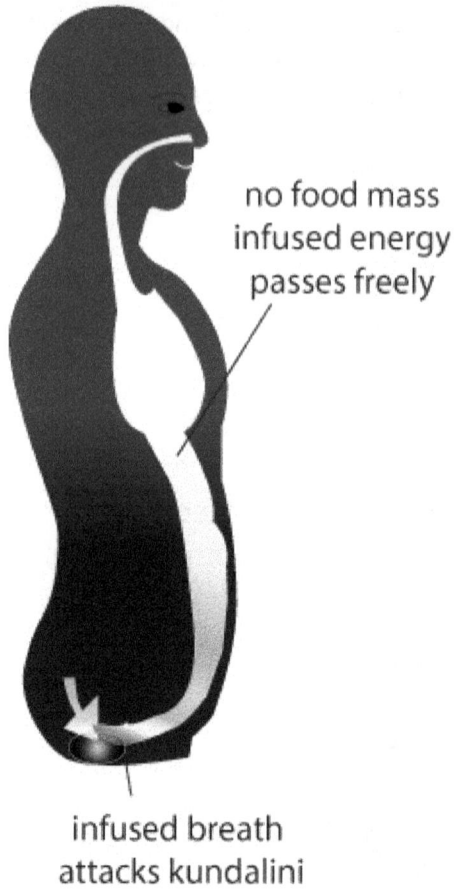

no food mass
infused energy
passes freely

infused breath
attacks kundalini

Part 4

Pressure Lock / Breath Infusion

Breath infusion this morning lasted for an hour. The subtle body was not infused as quickly as on some mornings, when the same amount of energy was put into it.

Ten minutes before the session was over Yogeshwarananda was present. He showed a sitting posture used by some yogis when they do pranayama practice for two hours before going into *samadhi*. These are research *samadhis* to search for, discover or be transited into higher levels of consciousness and also higher dimensional environments.

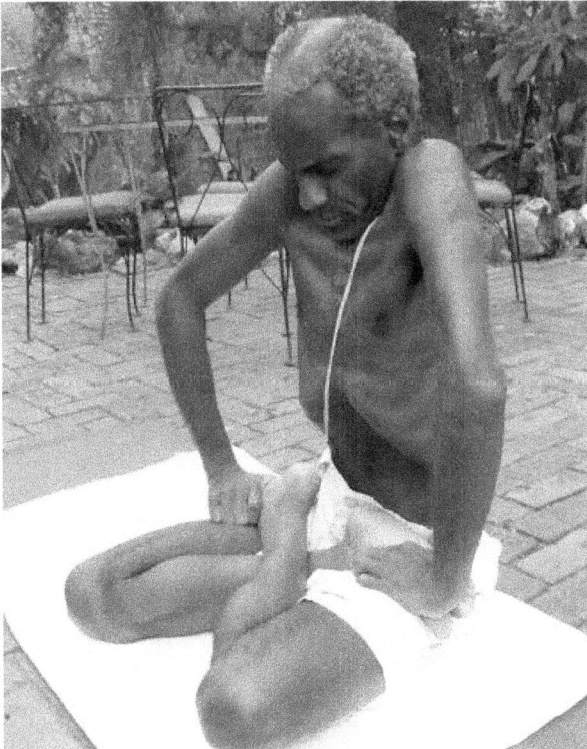

This particular posture is used after doing the tight lotus posture, *padmasana*. After that posture was used during breath infusion and it cuts circulation, there are some related lotus postures and semi-lotus postures which are used. This one in particular is used by yogis who reformed the reproductive system and the evacuation process. The heel of one foot is put under the body and the yogi sits on that heel, while the other foot is folded up on the thigh just as it would be in lotus.

This posture is balanced. The spine assumes a fully upright posture when this posture is assumed. When breath infusion is done in this posture, the energy has a tendency to course down and up on the inside of the trunk of the body. This creates a charge condition there which attracts kundalini.

The stomach and pubic areas are pulled up and back. This lock is applied immediately after doing some rapid breathing and then stopping on an exhale. The infused energy is clamped so that it moves into the spine from the bottom up.

Lowest Part of a Yogi

This morning during breath infusion, the infused energy came up from the base of the trunk on each side under the collar bones. It felt like crushed compacted energy with a tingling sensation like peppermint. It also rose like springs coming up and then vibrating back and forth. This occurred while I did various postures and infused more and more air into the system.

After a while I realized that Muktananda did bhastrika nearby. He did the same postures and focusing within the psyche to direct the energy to different locations.

After ten minutes he showed a *break off the organ* technique which is used by yogis to remove the reproductive urge from their subtle bodies. This urge is troublesome for a yogi who does not want to take an embryo. It is also a problem for those yogis who want to go to an astral place which is called *satyaloka* or *brahmaloka*. In that place there is no support for reproductive organs in the bodies. That place cannot be entered by anyone who has the reproductive capability in the subtle body.

This kriya concerns dissolving the sex kanda which is a small bulb in the in the pubic area of subtle body. This gland sponsors rebirth in a species of life which is capable of sexual reproduction. By using infusion techniques, a yogi can dissolve this subtle orb.

What pranayama should be used? The answer is whatever actually dissolves the gland.

After a while, Yogeshwarananda appeared. He came just as I infused enough energy into the trunk of the subtle body, so that the bottom one-third of it was cleared of old energy, dark and dense astral force. He said nothing either to me or Muktananda. I continued the infusion but I switched to working on the central spine which is behind the chest. There was some orangish energy there which needed to be dissipated with fresh subtle energy. After I did this, I got a mental signal from Muktananda to work on the stub kundalini which hangs about three inches under the brain stem. I infused that. It glowed with a golden hue.

normal kundalini stem
spine connected to brain

stub kundalini as subtle body brain stem
no connection to spinal passage

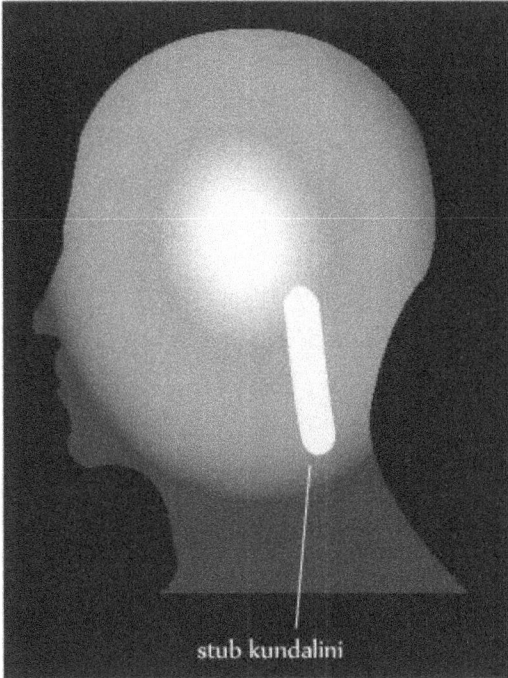

stub kundalini

However, Yogeshwarananda said that I should return to infusing the lower trunk. He remarked that I should infuse no excess in the subtle head. He said,

"Do this before leaving. You can complete that other practice after leaving."

He spoke about what should be done before death of the physical body and what can be done hereafter. Some practice should be completed while the physical body lives, since those techniques may not be possible while one lives as an astral body which has no physical counterpart.

Some practices can be done in both situations of having a physical body or not having one. But some can only be done while using a physical system.

Based on what he said I switched to the trunk of the physical body. I saw the face of Yogi Bhajan. He said, "Yogesh is correct. He who raises the lowest part of himself will succeed. He who sustains only the highest part of himself will fail."

Collar Bones

There is a method which Yogesh showed during this session. It is a way to breathe through the lower neck into the collar bones. As this is done when there is an exhale, energy is pushed through the neck. When there is an inhale, energy is pushed through the shoulder bones. This is done with rapid breathing. It allows fresh energy to enter some *hard to reach* places in the shoulders and arms.

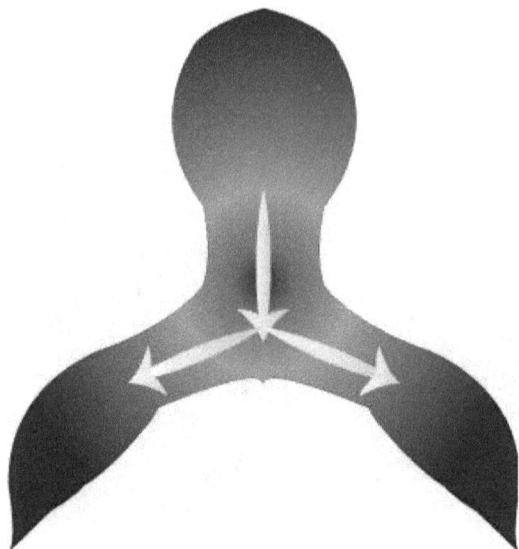

Sex Kanda Kriya / Muktananda

During breath infusion which I did for an hour, Muktananda was there on the astral side. He mumbled to himself about his inability to make enlightened souls in the developed countries of the United States and Europe. He was distressed about it.

During the session he showed a kanda bulb *up jump* kriya. There is more than one kanda bulb in the subtle body but the main one which is the concern of students who wish to assume yoga siddha bodies is the sex kanda.

It is situated between the anus and the root of the reproductive organ. It is like the shape of an egg. It is the center of the astral body. Some nadis spring from the kanda.

This particular kriya is possible if the student can perceive the kanda. Even if one knows the location of it, even then one can make it *up jump* if one cannot perceive it through pranaVision. That vision is infused astral energy which reached a highly charged state. When one looks through or into that energy, one may develop a perception.

At room temperature iron is a solid. It is dense. It has little if any perceptive qualities. If you heat it sufficiently, it will become red hot. It will glow. If you increase the temperate it will turn white hot. Then it will melt. It changes and has perceptive qualities. Sitting as a cold physical object it does not perceive anything. It is unresponsive. As soon as it turns white hot, it becomes reactive. When doing breath infusions something like this happens if one infuses sufficiently, where perception occurs through the infused energy at a certain stage of its intensity.

When one sees the bulb, it will be semitransparent and will have a white-yellow color. It will have an oval shape like an egg. In some experiences it appears to be like an onion bulb. It has a globe on the bottom with a few roots hanging. It has a thick stem on the top of it.

Muktananda caused the bulb to jump into a space in the throat. He told me to do the same thing. He did this to the sex kanda in my body. Then I did the same. There was no resistance from the bulb. It came up by a willpower action. As soon as it entered the space in the throat area, it disappeared as if it was swallowed and was instantly vaporized.

When I first did this, the bulb reappeared after a few seconds at the bottom of the trunk of the body. I did it again three more times. Then it did not reappear. During these actions I simultaneously continued the breath infusion, either doing a run of rapid breaths or stopping on an exhale and pulling the locks tightly. Sometimes I twisted to one side and then to the other, to cause kundalini to move through some nadi channels.

Muktananda made this remark:

"The throat space gap and the reproductive mechanisms are connected. They work together so that the reproductive mechanism sends instruction to the throat for what should be put into the body, what is to be swallowed. Eventually as one advances one will eliminate the kanda. If this is not done, one will take rebirth as a physical species.

"If the throat remains submissive to the sex kanda, one cannot at any stage become liberated because the psyche will be oriented to reproduction in creature existence. It is a decision for the yogi to make, regarding which world he/she wants to exist in. Existence will be there; you can be sure. It is a matter of which existence, where."

After the session, I sat to meditate. I spent forty-five minutes in a tight lotus. I do not recommend this unless the student's limbs can tolerate this posture as an easy pose. Otherwise one should sit comfortably. After those forty-five minutes I unwrapped the legs. I had to wait five minutes for blood flow to resume. Then I sat for another thirty minutes on a couch which was comfortable.

Yogeshwaranand left an instruction about my assumption of lotus every day. I must do this to comply with his directions but that does not mean that others should torture themselves with this. I started doing lotus since in 1970 when I used to lock myself in a metal locker in a barracks on Clark Air Base in the Philippines. It was painful then but I was determined to make my body do it. I mastered it before in many previous bodies. I was aware of my former practice. I wanted to re-establish it.

Since then I practiced different postures. Even though the body I am use is sixty years of age, I can do a reasonable full lotus but that is due to consistent practice for at least forty years. Restrictions for how to sit were put on me by Yogeshwarananda who is my primary teacher. To maintain the student relationship with him I do as advised.

During the meditation my main effort was to keep linked into the naad sound. Muktananda was present but mostly he mumbled to himself. Once he said to me,

"You must sit for longer periods, otherwise your time will run out and you would not gain the accomplishment. Get strict with yourself. Forget others. Let them do as they like. People, who are used to transmigrating as animals, have no sense of time. They think that they have forever for a serious spiritual practice. Know the urgency. With our help increase the meditation time."

Knees Knot Kriya

During practice with breath infusion, Yogeshwarananda appeared as soon as I infused the lower trunk. It took some time because of the nature of the air, and also because during the night, I had an astral encounter in the Philippines and another in the West Indies. The main drag on practice was the one in the Philippines. While I was there in 1970, I had a relationship with a young lady. Now suddenly I found myself as my astral body on the island.

The lady I knew there tracked me through a person I knew in the West Indies just about the same time around 1970. That person brought her to me astrally. My astral body just left Florida and went to the location in the Philippines.

The lady wanted to rehash the events of our relationship and discuss what happened to her since then. I listened. More or less she filled complaints about providence's treatment of her destiny.

She had this feeling that I was partially responsible for what happened after I left the island. It was one unfortunate thing after the other. After a time, gradually, I calmed her down by not saying anything and by agreeing to the complaints. Then I left that place. I got up about thirty minutes later than I should have to begin the practice. The breath infusion was slow at first. The subtle body being stupefied by the encounter with the woman, was slow to respond. In fact, during the first ten minutes it simply refused to take any of the breath energy but then after this something changed. It began to absorb the energy. Then I was released from the effects of her association.

During the infusion, sometimes, when the energy is compressed into the lower part of the body, one should when one stops on an inhale or exhale, apply the locks quickly and then stretch to the right or twist to the right, let the energy rise to that side or to the other side under compression, and then stretch to the other side and have the energy rise into the corresponding area under compression. This rises in the right and left channels which creep on either side of the sushumna central channel.

Usually I do not discuss *ida* and *pingala* but in some infusions the *sushumna* is not used. One uses either of the channels on either side. Sometimes one side is infused more than the other, as in the case where one stretches to one side and then kundalini energy or compressed astral force rises on that side or to the other side with intensity. Then one stretches to the other side and there is very little rise or no rise at all.

This happens because of the kind of energy which is in the atmosphere at the time of practice. The main thing is to look through the body, to be very attentive within the psyche during practice. If you have to, you may wrap a cloth around the eyes or use a ski cap and pull it down over the eyes.

A simple thing like not closing the eyes, not focusing internally, can cause an extra five, six or more years of practice, to reach an advanced stage. Once when Yogi Bhajan spoke about practice, he said this,

"The main cause of lack of progress is inattentiveness within the psyche. Keep the attention within the confines of the psyche, within the borders of the subtle body. Do not let the attention leak to anything during practice. Breathing and breathing and breathing for years on end, rapidly or as people usually do involuntary, will result in nothing if you are inattentive within the psyche. Track kundalini's slightest movement during practice.

When Yogeshwarananda appeared, I infused the lower trunk into a white heat state. The higher part of the trunk in the chest was in a grey energy state, which meant that it was not fully infused. It is not easy to infuse the entire trunk. One should not try to do it until one mastered infusing the sushumna central passage.

Yogeshwarananda directed me to stand in *tadasana*. This is a famous posture which was used by Arjuna when he was practiced *samadhi* states in

the Himalayas when he wanted to go to the angelic heavenly world to get
help from deities who reside there.

    I stood up in a partial tadasana. In this practice the entire sole or toes of
the feet stays on the ground. Then one lifts the arms with fingers
outstretched. The mental focus is in the thighs only.

    If the bottom of the trunk was infused, one can infuse the thighs. One
will find that there is a closed area in the joints at the knees, such that the
infused energy will not pass into the legs but will remain in the thighs.

    In the Vedic literatures, the Puranas, usually Vishnu is said to be the
patron deity of locomotion. Without locomotion one has to remain in one

place in a physical body like that of tree or a barnacle. With locomotion, one can change location. For locomotion the primary means are gripping and dragging like a snake, or using fins, wings and feet. Fins are a more essential development and after that wings or feet may develop.

If a yogi can bring the locomotion energy under control, he/she can side step many birth opportunities as a human being, animal or less. Desire is the big driving force. It causes a feeling that one needs certain fulfillments. Hence one takes a body here or there as given by providence. This process can be changed by controlling the locomotion energy of the subtle body.

When I sat to meditate, naad sound was in the back of the head, near the back top but only for three minutes, then it switched and was behind the lower neck about six inches away from the lower neck. I linked into it for the remaining part of the meditation.

Trunk Nadi Kriya

This is a procedure which was shown by Yogeshwarananda. This is for those students who pulled kundalini into the brain stem as a stub energy which glows.

Once kundalini is pulled up, the sushumna passage will remain in the trunk of the subtle body in the corresponding place of the physical spinal column. The yogi must repeatedly blast subtle energy through that unoccupied sushumna central passage. This results in a white heat buildup in the passage. When this white heat energy reaches certain saturation, the bottom part of the central passage will dissipate, vanish. There will be a glow in the bottom part.

After repeatedly blasting these areas, it will seem as if the lower sushumna passage disappears entirely but there will be some dark energy in the other parts of the lower trunk.

More practice will cause the top part of the central passage, from the navel chakra to the neck to vaporize. This is the stage at which this practice, which I will describe in the next paragraph, can be done.

With the sushumna passage vaporized and with it not reappearing as it did before, one does breath infusion, treating the entire trunk of the body as a *sushumna nadi*. This is a special practice. It will cause the student to meet with advanced yogis who mastered this.

Initially in this practice, one will find that most of the trunk has dark astral energy. This is when one looks into the trunk during breath infusion practice. There will be some light here and there, especially at the location of the base chakra where kundalini used to be positioned, but overall, the trunk will have a heavy energy within it.

The breath infusion will cause the lower part of the trunk to eventually fill with light, with a slight orange tint. This will change into a white heat light which glows at the bottom of the body. Over time, the entire trunk will have this white heat energy. The trunk itself, will seem to be the *sushumna nadi*.

Meditation should begin immediately after this practice. One should find the location of naad and listen to it to see if the frequency changed. One should also be sure to check if naad sound has two source locations, which are vortexes which one cannot enter.

As soon as one identifies the location of naad, one should link to it. According to the degree of linkages one will know if it is *dharana, dhyana* or *samadhi* linkage. If effort is used to link, it is *dharana* practice on naad. If the linkage seems to be automatic and spontaneous, it is *dhyana* linkage to naad. If one finds that as soon as there is contact the coreSelf stays in naad and makes no effort to locate itself anywhere else, that is *samadhi* linkage to this particular naad frequency.

If one finds that naad sound is all pervasive and that one cannot locate an origin point or a spot location where it is the loudest, one should understand that for some reason one's psychic perception is not keen enough to realize a node.

awakened kundalini
in sushumna nadi
spinal column

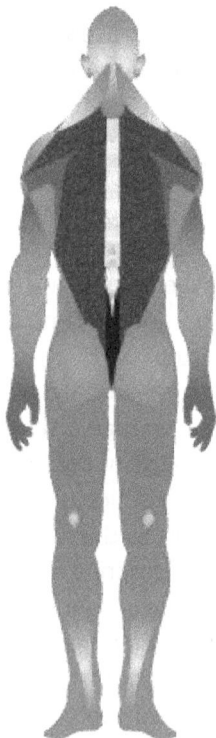

kundalini absent in spine
breath infusion brought
lower trunk to white glow condition

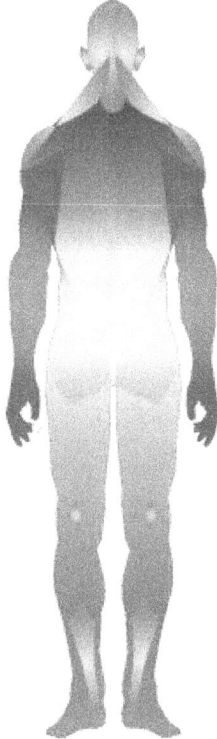

Yogi Finally Gains Some Authority

Today there was an interesting conversation with Yogi Bhajan on the psychic level of existence. For about at least eight years now I did some procedures during breath infusion, which were done with stress on blasting the sushumna passage.

This is a process in which the passage itself is brought to a white heat color. Then the walls of the cylindrical sushumna practically vaporizes. I used a procedure from Yogeshwarananda and some from Rishi Singh Gherwal which resulted in pulling kundalini into the head. This has to do with lifting kundalini so that it is a stub under the brain where the brain stem is located.

In that practice, due to kundalini being pulled into the brain, the yogi has a new chore for maintaining the trunk of the body without much help from kundalini, which is really the force which is assigned by nature for that service. At first when one achieves this kundalini lift, there will be small kundalinis firing here and there like lightning or like compressed bliss energy. These will occur by the accumulation of the infused energy which is pumped in vigorously during *breath of fire* practice.

The yogi does not cause these small kundalinis to happen. They occur because of the action of the infusion. During one session they occur in one place. On the next day or during the next session, they occur somewhere else seemingly in a random way like when lightning strikes.

The yogi does not visualize in these practices. If there is enough static electricity in the air, if there are charged clouds, there is no need to imagine lighting or visualize it. Lightning will occur if one waits and sees.

Due to completing these practices successfully, Yogi Bhajan was happy. He said:

"You can declare that you are authorized by me to teach kundalini yoga as a master teacher of the breath of fire *process."*

I asked him if I should an open ashram. Should I hang a sign? Should I post ads in yoga magazines? He got serious. He said,

"You are a student what do you know about opening ashrams? Who gave permission? I never said that. You are a boy. What is the matter? Do you want the responsibility which will break your back and send you to the monkey level?"

"Someone becomes a master. Then he is told by a master to teach. But others become masters and are not given the authority. It is for their good. Instruct one or two people who are submissive and wish to learn. Otherwise accelerate the practice. We want full success for you. Ashram start-up and teaching publicly is the most frequent cause of demotion. I do not wish that on those children whom I love dearly."

I joked when I asked the dear father, if I should open an ashram and advertise through yoga magazines, but he took the inquiry seriously.

The nice thing about having a close respectful relationship with teachers is that one cannot act whimsically. One cannot come up with plans to do anything. Unless they permit, one does not go off and begin anything for which one does not understand the liabilities and implications. One remains in the divine grace with its infallible protection which results in one not having to take whimsical troublesome rebirths in the mundane evolutionary cycle at the whim of providence.

Otherwise if one does not have a respectful and adhering relationship with a superior soul, one is left to one's devices with no idea of a deity and no coverage from doing things for which one will be sorry.

Yogi, Night Clubs and Sex

If one is serious about making spiritual progress, rising early to meditate is a must. If one finds that one cannot do this, it means that one's associations discourage one from this. One has to take support from yogis who rise early to gain success in this.

Despite the ideas about people being as good as Buddha and Christ, the truth is that most of us are not on par. In fact, our condition is that if we fail to take assistance from super people, the spiritual progress will be nil.

Anyone can imagine that he is as great as Buddha or Krishna. Anyone can take a sense of pride in thinking in that way but it remains to be seen if in fact we can live in a way which puts us into a divine condition.

Support is something we must have. The conversation cannot begin with idea of independence. The honest thing to do is to speak of selecting a different dependence, a different reliance.

To rise early one must take help from yogis who do so. It does not matter if these yogis live as physical bodies or have departed. In the ashram life one should rise early under the direction of the teacher, otherwise one should leave the place. I never lived in an ashram where it was tolerated that people could sleep in, during the morning. We had to rise at 3.30 am or even sooner, get cleaned up, get down to the meditation or temple hall, and do whatever was stipulated as the discipline. But how should someone be trained in this system if he is not in an ashram, if there is no teacher who compels him to rise early. Obviously, it is left to the person to command himself to comply.

Last night in the astral world a person in the UK questioned about the benefits of rising early to meditate. He said that he had to be with friends during the night and could not rise early.

In that case why do we discuss rising early if one has to be with friends? One has to make a decision about the priorities. If being with friends and visiting clubs are important, one will get the benefits of that. It is not that these affairs are devoid of advantages. Each type of association has advantages. Why tear apart the life with friends, the pleasure of sex and the need for night air on the body, when it gives an advantage?

But the question is: Is one willing to abandon that. Everything has its ups and downs. If one decides to rest early, one will not have the cool night air and the club atmosphere to enjoy. One will not meet sex partners. Sexual fulfillment will drop considerably. Everything has its price.

In the physical world, we know all too well what happens when we stick close to parents. They make suggestions and dictate our lives. But it is the same with friends and mates? There are stipulations with yoga teachers as well.

In my experience shifting from relatives and friends to yoga gurus, I had the same problem of expectations and demands. But in the story of my life, I find that I am constantly under the discipline of yogi gurus with their expectations and demands. Why do I bother? Why should I not neglect the gurus?

The reason is that everything has its price.

With the yoga gurus, I am like a son, and not just a son but a son who is a minor. When you are a minor, you do not have adult needs. You do not have sexual desires. You have gender but not the sexual expression of it. With the yoga guru, something like that develops. Once you are a child in the care of a parent, the whole scheme of adult life does not haunt you. You do not feel the need to pursue sex.

You do not feel the need to drink liquor. In fact, it burns the mouth. You cannot smoke marijuana. You do not masturbate. Your body is not mature. If a woman is there, she is like a sister or mother. If a man is there he is like a brother or a father. The idea of sexual participation is absent.

Once when I did yoga practice in the astral world with some other students, Yogi Bhajan appeared. He said, "What are you boys doing? Do that posture like this. Breathe in this way."

Who did he speak to? We were men who were sexually experienced. He addressed us as boys. What is that? What should we say to him? "I am not a boy. I am a man. I am sexually experienced. In fact, I am God too. Have some respect teacher!"

Once when I was with Yogeshwarananda, he said this, "Where is the lady, my daughter? You two should stay together as brother and sister. Do not separate. Related children should stay together and behave in a way which the parents would appreciate."

He spoke of Marcia Beloved. He did not see us as capable adults who could enjoy sex. Juvenile children have no needs for sexual indulgence. It does not cross their minds.

If I do not rise early what will happen to my relationship with these teachers? Lucky for me I have some psychic perception but some people feel that it is all in my mind and that there is no astral world, no astral persons, no psychology which will survive as me or you after death of the physical body.

I have those relationships with astral gurus. For me I must rise early and practice. As a child, you know how it is when the parents say you must rise at 6am. You have no choice. You do not think that you can sleep beyond the limit. You do not feel that you will be out and about in the clubs making moves to get sex during the night. You do not think that you have to smoke or drink beer.

Even though I use a body which is sixty years of age, still in the presence of my gurus I am an infant. I just cannot imagine what it will be like if I were to treat my yoga gurus in such a way as to not live up to their expectations. They think,

"The little one wants to be with women, with mature girls, to have sex with them. He is crazy. Something malfunctioned in his brain."

"He wants to smoke marijuana, drink liquor and ruin his psyche."

"He wants to be in night clubs, dancing, flirting and having sex. Whose son, is he?"

Breath Infusion Proficiency

After practicing breath infusion for some time, At least for about two years on a daily basis, at least once per day, preferably twice per day, one develops a sense for how much air the physical system can absorb and how much the subtle body can process.

When one first begins the practice, for the first six months, one plays. One does not understand the circumstances.

This is because the lung cells have not changed their attitude. They feel that it is up to them to absorb air on the basis of what the cells in the body request. These requests of the cells are monitored and supervised by the nerves which are in turn supervised by the brain.

What is the need for absorbing so much air? In one session of practice, this yogi absorbs the quantity of air which an ordinary human being would take in during an entire month of normal breathing. Why do this? Nature designed a fine system of breath intake and expulsion. What is the need to adjust it?

The body, specifically the brain, knows when the body needs more air. Proof of this comes up when the body has to run. Then it will increase the heart and lung intake rate. The body knows when it needs more air. Thus, why does yogi spend so much time and endeavor strenuously to take in more air? Why hyperventilate, especial since some medical professionals say that it causes dizziness and headaches?

Initially when one does breathe infusion, the lungs simply refuse to take the extra air. What happens is that the lungs allow air to enter and leave the lung, but it refuses to absorb any of it.

But if one continues the practice, this attitude of the cells changes. They take the air which you breathe in during the rapid breathing. The lungs absorb this air.

There are two phases of this. The first is the change which occurs when after about six months of practice the lungs decide that they will absorb the air. But then absorbing air and packing it into the blood cells, corpuscles, is not everything. How much can be absorbed at any given time? What do you do when you absorb this extra air and it is absorbed by corpuscles? Then the other factor comes into play, the next phase, which is distribution of the absorbed air.

How is it distributed? If several boxes are brought into a building, where will they be stacked? In which rooms will they be put?

Thus, when the student yogi does the rapid breathing in a certain posture, if he or she is attentive within the psyche, the build-up of stored air will be felt. He will know when to stop the rapid breathing, apply locks and then help the system to diffuse and distribute that stored energy.

The trick initially is to force the energy down. See diagrams below. That is how it begins. Stuff in air. When you feel that it is no longer being absorbed because the lungs feel that they cannot store more, stop the rapid breathing. Apply the locks. Focus within the subtle body. Push the energy down mentally just as you contract the muscles and tendons with the locks. This will show you how the energy may be distributed.

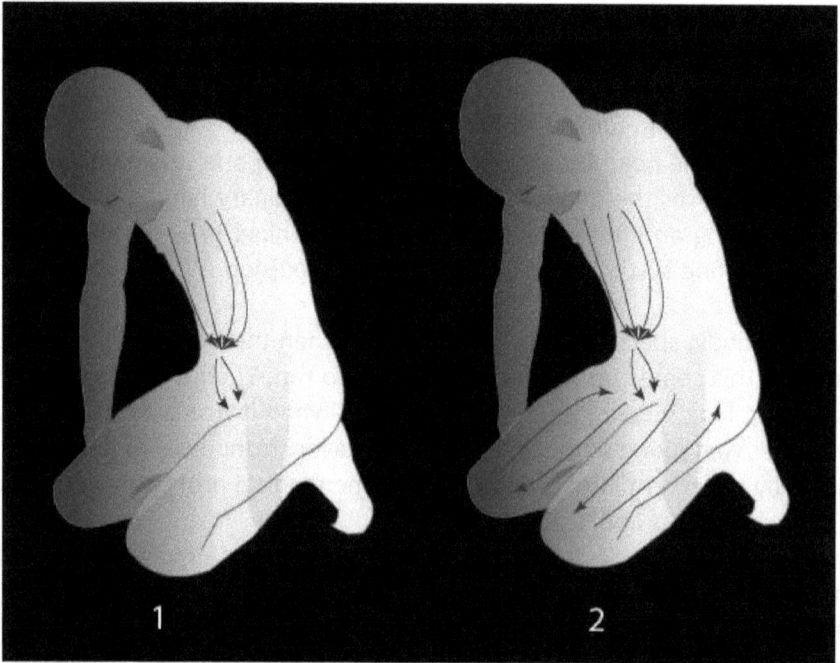

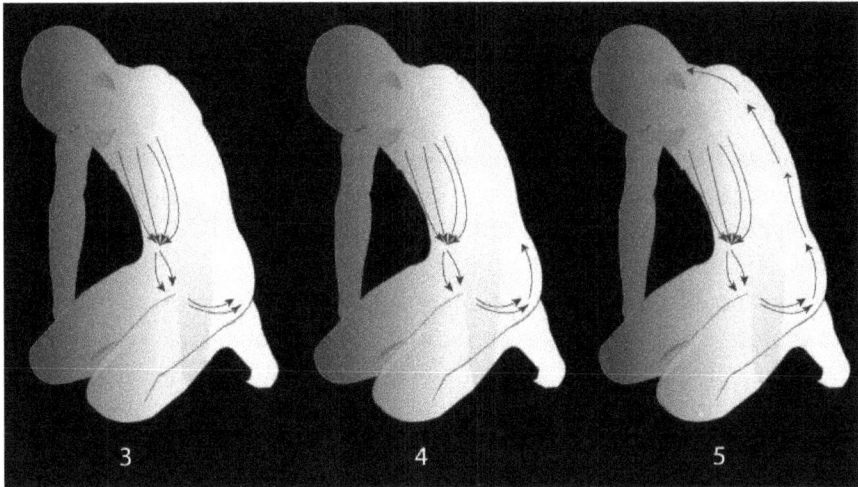

Instead of gasping for air because your system is starved of air when you stop and apply the locks, you will forget that if the system absorbed air and stored it but has not distributed it. Your attention will be on the distribution and not on the lack of it. As soon as you sense that the air was diffused into other parts of the body or that it was distributed, you should start the rapid breathing again.

This is done repeatedly until one is satisfied that all parts received sufficient air.

Initially a student finds that he cannot hold the breath out or in for long after rapid breathing. This is because the lungs were filled with air but did not absorb it. But if one practices, one will find that the priority after stopping the rapid breathing and applying the locks is the distribution of the stored air.

If the system stored much excess air, it will not be concerned with getting more air but with distributing the stored amount. It will not be anxious to breathe out but will be focused on air distribution.

As one advances in this practice, one will discover areas of the physical and subtle bodies which are fresh-air starved. These are blocked areas.

Rays of Light in the Psyche

This morning during exercises, near the end of a thirty-five-minute session, I experienced all-pervasive rays of white light in the entire psyche. It was like a floodlight in the head space, with the light radiating from the center outward. The rays were different shades and sheens of white light.

Just prior to this, after a series of breathing and application of locks, kundalini spread evenly throughout the body and head. I pressed the eyes while breathing rapidly. This is when I experienced the light. It lasted a couple of seconds, and was so bright that I wanted to move away from it.

Dangers of Teaching Meditation

It is said that fools rush in where wise men fear to tread. Taking that statement apart bit by bit, it means that one ventures into a domain in which one will be hurt but one does not know it because the domain is attractive initially. It seems that one will gain by going there.

This is based on the evolutionary drive for exploitation which we get from nature for exploitative opportunities. Everyone looks for the next advantage. Somehow, we convince ourselves that we are magnanimous people who are selfless. But our actions tell a different story. Teaching yoga and meditation is a dangerous adventure but many are attracted to it and want to make a livelihood using yoga and meditation.

I never saw a single instruction in any of the standard yoga books which gives anyone the right to use yoga commercially. Check the *Shiva Samhita*, *Hatha Yoga Pradipika*, *Yoga Sutras* and the *Bhagavad Gita*.

Even though I did these practices for over forty years, still I am affected by the association of the persons whom I teach. This is a fault in teaching. All teachers are affected by the energy of students. Most of this energy is negative because many students are reluctant to assume the disciplines required. The teacher struggles with students who argue and want to redefine yoga.

Teaching is dangerous because the teacher must deal with the feedback from the students and the negativity which comes from their resultant consequential energies which come due to their present and previous social interactions.

If a student has negative energies coming to him/her by virtue of actions before meeting the teacher, some of those energies will reach the teacher and affect him/her accordingly. There is no way around it except to limit the association of students and by demanding that they assume the disciplines required.

But if one commercializes yoga and meditation, additional negative consequences come into play.

Personally, I am against the commercialization of yoga. The original system, and it is plastered in the Sanskrit books, is called *dakshina*, which is a Sanskrit word meaning a donation or fee offered to a teacher as remuneration for instructions. This was based on a teacher-student relationship like that of a father-son. It was not an institutionalized fee like paying for a course at a university.

I taught yoga and meditation since around 1973. I never charged a fee to anyone. I never taught anyone on the basis of money. The yoga and meditation which I teach, disappears in my mind if there is mention of money as a principle of exchange for the teaching. The energy of yoga and meditation, the energy which I have, immediately leaves my psyche as soon as there is an idea of commercialization.

Yoga and meditation techniques live with me like living with a conditional wife. Such a wife threatens to leave the husband if he violates certain agreements. Since the husband is dependent on this wife, he has to toe the line or lose the services and agreeable company of the woman.

Since I am dependent on yoga and meditation in that conjugal way, I am stuck and do not dare do anything to cause true yoga and genuine deep meditation to abandon me.

There is a literal side to this. In the Nath sampradaya of Gorakshnath, there is a legend about one of our yoga gurus, whom we are eternally indebted to for giving us the kundalini conquest techniques. To be clear, this is not a myth.

In the beginning when Lord Shiva was the only person doing yoga and the only one of the celestial people who understood what it was and what it would do. He practiced yoga by himself but his wife was present, the celestial goddess who was later called *Durga* or *Parvati*.

She practiced but she was not serious about it. Still, she was the first student. *Gorakshnath* was the disciple of *Matsyendranath* who learned yoga directly from Lord Shiva when *Parvati* was taught. At the time *Matsyendranath* was not even in a human body. He evolved from a fish form but since Lord Shiva and Parvati was by a lake, *Matsyendranath* overheard what Shiva told *Parvati* about yoga.

Later this same instruction was used by Matsyendranath in a human body to master the yoga kriyas. The fact is that without getting help from the goddess one cannot master this yoga. Yoga is like marrying a sophisticated spoilt young woman who is used to having her needs met. If one marries such a woman one will have to do whatever is required to keep her happy, otherwise in a disagreeable mood she will go away.

One cannot commercialize the real yoga and meditation, or it will leave immediately. Muktananda did to some extent commercial yoga because he had wealthy students who encouraged that. Mahesh Yogi also fell into that system of commercialization with his TM trademark. These are mistakes. As soon as a guru does this, yoga go far away and another energy comes which looks like the process and serves a new type of yoga which leads nowhere in the spiritual direction.

In addition, fortunately for me I never paid a penny for yoga instructions. I never attended a class where I paid a fee. Mostly I learned yoga in the astral world from masters using subtle bodies. I did learn from Yogi Bhajan when he was physically present but he never discussed money. I learnt from Arthur Beverford but I was like a son-student to him only. There was never the mention of fees.

I took instructions from a few advanced teachers who commercialized yoga but I never paid either one because I took instructions from those persons in the astral world. On the physical side I could not approach these teachers because they had organizations around them which make it difficult to get close unless one paid large sums of money.

There was a time when Muktananda used to be in such a position. The same thing happened with Yogananda and some others. In the Hare Krishna Movement, some of this occurred as well where sometimes to get initiations one has to a render a large sum of money. Somehow by the grace of providence, I did not have to fit those tabs. Hare Krishnas do not teach *ashtanga* yoga. They do not teach meditation as it is defined by Patanjali or by Krishna in the Bhagavad Gita. They say that such yoga and meditation is not relevant in this era.

A student may offer a donation or assistance in expenses publishing books and doing other things for the sake of getting yoga and meditation information to others. For such donation, I accept the offers because these motives do not offend the practice which I do.

Call it what you like but the meditation and yoga which I do would vanish if a person uses it commercially. That person may go on teaching and may even use terms from my literature and say that I taught that but still the real substance of what I taught will leave that person.

Students should be careful to manage their negative features so that the energy does not feed back to the teacher. After all, if you are a good patient you will not want the doctor to contract your disease. Why spread the disease to the teacher? Better to take the disciplines required and keep oneself confined until one is purified.

Sex at Seventy

Last night in the astral world I was in a conversation concerning a question one person asked:

How does one know when to stop sexual intercourse? Is there a limiting age? Suppose the partner wants to continue, what should one do? Suppose one is over seventy? Suppose one is ninty? Should one get medical treatment to deal with being sexually dysfunctional?

If we discuss yoga by the system of Patanjali, sexual behavior pass about fifty years of age is out of the question. Patanjali listed Vedic style restricted association as required for yogis. For other systems, there are rules of sexual conduct.

For us it is a matter of compared value. If I continue sexual intercourse beyond fifty years of age, until my body dies, with or without the aid of sexual drugs then it is acceptable if doing that does not directly or indirect retard the spiritual practice? If it decelerates the practice, even then I may not have the power to stop the indulgence.

If one practices kundalini yoga and if the objective is to keep kundalini in a charged upward state, sexual intercourse will be counterproductive since it will release the energy of kundalini through the sexual apparatus. This will result in a drop in intensity of kundalini's upward thrust into the head.

Individuality in Yoga

During practice this morning Yogeshwarananda made a remark about guru influence. He explained that the best manifestation of a yoga guru's influence in the life of a student is the consistent practice of the disciplines. He said.

Convince someone to take the preliminary steps of yoga. That is success in teaching yoga. Failure to convince the student is failure to penetrate the lifestyle of the person.

Someone may praise a yoga guru but not assume the disciplines. That is a failed student. Because we are selves, the individual must do the practice personally. One must achieve it individually. No amount of collective unity can give us the deep advancement. It is such that individual effort, personal assessment of the psychological condition, personal mystic exertion to alter the inner nature, is required. To help a student means to help the student to get the individual psyche in order.

Creation of Yoga Siddha Body

Babaji was present during the afternoon session. He dictated this:

The development of a yoga siddha body is the change which occurs in the subtle body when the negative energies are extracted and are replaced with super-charged energy. One way to understand this is to consider the condition of the fluids in the physical form. Say that a person eats much spoilt food. That may be digested and may provide sustenance for the physical system but with the blood and fluids being created from that diet, as a special type of blood. Call it polluted blood.

Another person who eats fresh fruits and vegetables only, will have a different type of blood.

In the subtle body there is energy. If that energy is stale and heavy, if it is polluted, that body will reside in a certain plane of existence which is suited to an astral form of that constitution. Similarly, if the subtle body has a light, fresh energy, it will manifest on a higher plane which is suitable to that subtlety.

It is not a matter of religion. If one is religious and if the subtle body is heavy and dense, one will go to a corresponding astral place after death.

Religion neither denies nor guarantees anything unless it results in purity of energy in the subtle body. Suppose a man is an atheist. He does not believe in a Supreme Person, in God. Then, even if he has that belief, if his subtle body is light and surcharged properly, he will go to a higher realm after death, even into a heaven where there is God or a sub-deity.

If the subtle body lacks the proper energy content, the person is restricted to places which are compatible to that condition. This is why the effort at yoga in terms of the eightfold system given by Patanjali makes sense. Let us stick to Patanjali and his eight-part system and not be involved in novel definitions of yoga. Krishna endorsed the system of Patanjali way before Patanjali wrote that down. If Krishna approved of it there is no need for any lesser person to redefine it.

During the exercise I did a specific thigh stretch. Bringing the thighs under control is a vital part of the urdhvareta sexual energy uplift practice. The thighs are the main allies for energy of the reproductive organs. Thus, if one does not conquer the thighs it is unlikely that one will ever master the urdhvareta sexual energy uplift practice.

Babaji made remarks about the thigh stretch / carbon dioxide extraction exercises. He said this.

The real value in that practice is that it is the only way to get the pollution in the legs and feet extracted. There is polluted energy in the legs and feet. The heart and lung are unable to efficiently remove polluted energy from these lower extremities but if the negative energy in the thighs are extracted, say as low down as the knees, that causes an up pull in the legs and feet where the polluted energy there rises into the thighs and the yogi can extract it from the thighs.

These practices take time but if one really cares, one will see that it is done efficiently.

Who wants a yoga siddha body? Whosoever desires that may do these practices.

Babaji / Yoga Siddha Body Features

During the afternoon session I had a visitor, Tobe Terrell. He uses a body that is over seventy years of age, but he pushes himself with the aggressive *breath of fire* practice. It is said that a human body is so valuable that it can give the spirit using it, the chance for liberation. One must muster the courage to practice the right techniques.

It does not matter if the body is a black, white, green, tall, short, or even diseased, provided it is a human form that has an erect spine. For pranayama, a good set of lungs are required. There should be a diaphragm that will do some work instead of trudging lazily through life.

Tobe mastered the practice quickly. He has the will and mindset for it. This afternoon I went out earlier because he was involved in some activity and said he would be out in about five or ten minutes. During that time, I did some postures, some of the more difficult ones which are not suited to a beginner, especially one who uses an old body.

When Tobe arrived, I did the session with him in consideration. This means that I became attuned to his body and needs. I use postures that apply to his psyche. That is different to practicing on my own where I do postures which are suited to my stage of practice.

Working with others, teaching others, is something like when a large oil tanker loses engine power and has to be pulled to its destination by a powerful tug boat. The tug is small in comparison to the tanker but it has a powerful and efficient engine which allows it to pull the heavy vessel.

By itself, the tug can go very fast but when it is hitched to the tanker, it moves much slower. Teaching kundalini yoga takes mystic perception because kundalini is not a physical thing which you can see with physical eyes. You have to be very advanced in mystic practice to teach it. It is not like teaching asanas where the teacher checks for physical posture. The key here is psychic energy and its movement. The teacher must be aware of the psychic parameters of the student's body. During the practice, the teacher monitors the infused force and the kundalini.

When we exercised, Babaji arrived in his sunlight body. This is a body made of light, so that it is difficult to see it because he is in a realm of clear light. This is like when there is a jelly fish in the ocean and that creature has a body which is transparent. It is hard to see it in the first place. If one sees it, it is hard to determine where it begins and where it ends. It is not merged with the ocean but its body's transparency and coloring which is exactly that of the ocean makes it difficult to see it.

When Babaji manifested it was like he came from nowhere, like somebody stepping into one dimension from being in another dimension. He said:

"A yoga siddha body is created when the yogi has the trunk of the subtle body completely cleared of low astral energy, when just subtle energy of the highest quality, is in the form. It is not a matter of belief. It occurs by yoga practice, except in the case of those who transferred from the other side, the divine beings."

When he said this, we did a posture. Then we stopped breathing and held the last breath in. At that time Tobe blew out the air since his body needed air. When I heard him exhale, I said inhale soon after, then I said exhale, then inhale then exhale then inhale and then lastly inhale and hold.

All the while I need no air, because both my subtle and physical bodies absorb volumes of air during the breathing as compared to Tobe who have not mastered the practice.

Doing rapid breathing is no guarantee that the physical and subtle lungs absorb in the air. The air may be going into the lungs and the lungs may refuse to absorb it. In which case the body will not be infused with all the air which is inhaled. On another note, even if the body takes in the air, if many cells are polluted, it will take some time for that infused air to flush the negative gases. In some cases, cells in the body, even in the lung are attached to the negative gases. These will rebel and refuse to absorb the air. A student must struggle with this until he/she gets the body reformed from its addiction to carbon dioxide.

Noting Tobe's breath, Babaji said this:

"What is the difference? Why does he need air so quickly after a rapid breathing session? Is his psyche not taking the energy efficiently? Just by gauging that efficiency, one can tell if a yogi will get a yoga siddha body after leaving physical existence. It is not a belief. It can be rated by the breath absorption capacity. Pranayama is essential to the practice."

Mental - Emotional Actions in Breath Infusion Practice

This morning, during breath infusion, Muktananda came about five minutes after the session began. He was present then on the astral side. He had a question for me.

"Why do students crave sensational experiences during spiritual practice? There is so much which happens otherwise and which should be noticed. People are focused on physical consciousness. If something is subtle, they miss it entirely."

It seems to me that he answered the question I replied:

"Kundalini is the motivating force for their sensual or otherwise decisions. It requires sensation since it feeds on that. So long as a student does not master kundalini, the need for physical sensation will continue. They will continue to ignore what is subtle, regarding that as being non-existent."

I did infusion practice in different postures. He supervised some; advising this and advising that, especially in regards to the subtle actions being taken in the psyche. It is one thing to have somebody tell you how to do a posture. That is a physical thing which can be demonstrated. What about subtle actions, mental and emotional actions within the psyche? Are the mental actions formless indescribable motions? Are the emotional actions specific?

Higher yoga has more to do with emotional and mental actions. Sometimes one must be willing to trust a yogi who enters the psyche. First of all, does one feel that the psyche, or mind is a chamber? Is it or is it not? Are you merged in the absolute so you do not have a border or diminishing limit, not even a mental or emotional one?

After I got to the point in the exercises where the trunk of the body was cleared of apana energy, carbon dioxide and other negative gases and subtle airs, Yogeshwarananda appeared. I made a mental note of the event since that is a marker for his existential residence. A yogi appears when one hits the level of consciousness, he resides in. Because Yogesh is on a higher level, he is usually reached after about twenty or thirty minutes of practice for the least when the subtle body loses the heavy subtle energy and it transits to a higher plane. Muktananda works from a lower level than Yogesh.

Yogeshwaranand ignored the presence of Muktananda. Then Yogesh said this,

"You are getting there. Be persistent. He is not a bad guru. He can help. I read his book in the astral world. He was sincere when he did the austerities. Other acts of his are despicable but who cares? In a world like this, moral failure is the rule. He is quite proficient."

Then he said, "Keep going. Push hard."

That was when I shifted focus on breath infusion from the trunk of the body to the head. It was a cool morning in Gainesville Florida at Tobe Terrell's Zen Hostel. Seems like the place was in Japan or China, back in say the 1400's with several inmates of a Taoism discipline. But that was not the case. It is America 2011. I pushed on until the head was infused with fresh astral energy, all dark pockets of it were removed.

Learning Kundalini Yoga without a teacher

Kundalini yoga cannot be learnt in total simply by watching a video. It concerns what happens in the subtle body not the physical one. From the physical postures, one cannot see what happens in the subtle one. It has little to do with the physical body. It is not a physical process essentially. It uses the physical body because that body is in a position to influence the subtle one.

You can learn it from books or from videos if you subsidize that by getting instructions from a physical or an astral teacher. There must be a teacher. Look at my situation, I did this practice since at least 1972. I learnt from a few physical teachers but most of the instruction was in the astral world from teachers who I never met physically. If someone who is as proficient as I am requires a teacher even now, it follows that others who are less proficient would require help.

If a student does not have psychic perception, he needs a physical teacher. If his psychic perception is good, he needs astral instruction. People who are aware of the physical body only cannot understand this process.

Kundalini yoga is a real process if one works on the subtle body and if one correctly infuses it, otherwise it is imaginative gratification.

To learn this requires some personal association. I learnt this from an individual person not from the void, not from the oneness. Even today, I take lessons from people on the astral planes.

This practice is for those who dare to tread the path of *nivritti marga*. It is not an easy path, because it means that someone who is under the full control of nature made a decision to fight nature, a force which was his benefactor and slave-master from time long past.

Pravritti means someone who is interested in the opportunities for survival offered by nature. So long as that interest is there one cannot be successful in the kundalini practice. This is because kundalini is a most faithful servant of nature. It will not give up that allegiance. It will fight the individual self in defense of nature.

Patanjali made it clear that the no-thought zone is essential. Unfortunately, the matter does not end there. One can spend the next million years in that zone and not advance any further, not go to a spiritual dimension. That happened.

There is a process called *jada samadhi,* it means that one can go into a samadhi which is in the mode of ignorance. Many people do this and feel that they attained perfection.

It is not the *samadhi*, it is the level on which it occurs.

Sex-Energy Pull-Up

Breath infusion this morning was great. There were isolated kundalinis rising and spreading here and there, mostly in the trunk of the subtle body.

These were mini-kundalinis rising and spreading. They were like compact ice crystals, rammed together in a tight squeeze, emanating tight bliss energy. At one point Muktananda appeared. He did not enter my psyche. He stood outside in his subtle body. As I looked down in the psyche seeing the infused breath energy which was rammed below the navel, he also looked. I could feel his looking energy passing through my subtle form.

He then instructed that the energy, once it collected in the pubic area, should be pulled up and out of the body through the top of the head. This however is not a quick shot or a procedure for visualizing that this will happen or visualizing with the confidence that one's willpower will make this happen.

First one rams the energy down by breath infusion such that any energy that comes in is pushed down and is not allowed to rise through the front of the body. When that rammed energy is compacted, it will reach a stage where the navel area can take no more of it. If one keep infusing on and on after that stage the energy does one of three things:

- explode at the navel of the subtle body.
- goes downward to the pubic area.
- goes upward and escape from the subtle body through the same passage through which it was inserted into the subtle body.

The desired result is the one where it either explodes and the energy of the explosion is pushed down to the groin-pubic area, or it goes to the pubic area in a compacted form before exploding.

Once the energy gets to the groin, more breath infusion should be practiced. One should keep this going until the energy explodes there. Sometimes the energy will jump to the kundalini base chakra and ignite that, causing kundalini to move in some direction to some other area of the psyche.

In Muktananda's practice the energy is held at the pubic area until it cannot be held there any longer. Then it explodes. As it does so it is pulled through the center of the body into the brain.

This is one method for *urdhva reta* practice, being the practice of causing sexual energy to course upward through the subtle body rather than to be expressed downward in sexual climax. Muktananda made this remark:

"Sex energy can be used directly without having to route it to the kundalini. It can be pulled into the head directly. In fact, from the time the hormonal energy is developed or produced in any part of the body, it can be absorbed. It does not have to go through the reproduction glands."

As soon as he made this remark, I felt the presence of Yogeshwarananda but while with Muktananda his subtle body was the full size,

Yogeshwarananda's form was only perceived as the top half of his body, as if from below the chest his body was missing.

This meant that he manifested himself partially into the dimension Muktananda was in. He looked at Muktananda with a look of disgust and said:

"Trickster. That is what you are! What sort of yogi it is who tells people he can give them spiritual perception by touching them? What nonsense? Why were you posing as a world-class guru?"

At this point Swami Muktananda got a little disturbed. Yogeshwarananda pointed to me and said, "I like him because he leaves markers for others. He does not make disciples. He learns, like being a student forever."

Before Muktananda could defend himself, Yogeshwarananda left. Then Muktananda said to me, "Whatever it is, it has critics. What can I say? People are critical."

Reproducing Children Without Males

In the *sex you!* book I explained that to get a human body one has to initiate the form in the father's body and then be transferred into the mother's form. Someone challenged this idea. It is a worthy challenge but in mystic perception, one is not concerned with physical evidence, or with the value of physical proofs.

However, there is another way to look at what I said and instead of hearing that the human body must begin in the father's form, one can consider that the lifeForce of the child begins in the father's form. The lifeForce of the entity who is to take birth takes possession of male sperm. The female contribution, the unfertilized human egg which is said to be 50%, does not have that lifeForce of the person who is to be a baby.

For birth of a child at least three lifeForces are involved: the entity who gets the body, the father and the mother.

In the case of some other species of life, the mother's body may facilitate a lifeForce in which case no father is necessary.

Sometimes it is hard to imagine how this creation begun but right before our eyes, there are instances of pathogenesis where a female species has a virgin birth because that female body has facilities to channel the lifeForce of its offspring.

Purpose of Life-force

Procreation is not the life-force's primary concern but it is the subsidiary interest by necessity because of the fact that in this type of creation, everything is temporarily manifested. Forms here do not exist on their own.

They are propped by conditions. If conditions are unfavorable, a particular thing deteriorates or breaks down. Its form is de-constructed.

Kundalini is here to have a good time, or to put in Patanjali's words to gain experience. However, since it finds that the means of acquiring experience is temporary, it becomes interested in survival. By instinct it knows that it cannot continue existing in a particular form forever. It engages in reproduction to procure for itself future forms, so that when the present form dies, it can jump into one of its descendants and develop an embryo which will grow into a new body.

It does this repeatedly.

Its real interest is having fun, or experiencing but it is intelligent enough to know that there will be a shift in the future such that it will lose the body, which is its chief means of experiencing this place. That causes it to be anxious about survival.

This paranoia makes it appear that survival is its main interest but actually enjoyment or procurement of experience is the purpose.

Its real interest is excitement, but it is intelligent enough to know that there will be a shift in the future such that it will lose the body, which is its chief means of experiencing this place. That causes it to be desperate for survival.

Part 5

Kundalini Rising

Energy up the spine that is like cool air, with lights, is kundalini. Rising of kundalini can cause headaches but usually these will occur immediately after. One can have black outs or gold outs. Black out means that one has a blank and when one is again objectively aware one has no recall.

Gold out means that the bliss energy produced when kundalini rises into the head is felt as frosty spiritual energy as a golden light shimmering in all directions. When this happens, one will return to normal awareness with a distinct and clear memory of what happened. One will find the body in whatever position it was in when it occurred, provided the body was lying down. If the body was standing or sitting it would have fallen or leaned downward. One will find oneself awake in the body in that condition.

Activated Kundalini

This varies from person to person. There is a no hard and fast rule for activated kundalini. For instance, someone who has no interest in spiritual cultivation may experience kundalini rising. Another person who has the interest may experience it also. But know one thing for sure. The same kundalini rises when one gets goose bumps due to a disaster, emergency or shock event. The same kundalini is experienced repeatedly as sexual climax, except that it fires through the genitals mostly. But even in sex climax experience, it fires through the spine and into the brain, into the lips, into the fingers and toes, into the breasts etc.

For a yogi rising of kundalini is important because that allows higher perception and also curbing of kundalini from its primordial animal instincts. Yogis who are versed in the locks do not have headaches, because the locks restrict and guide the passage of the aroused kundalini.

There is anus lock, perineum-urinary muscle lock, stomach lock, neck lock, and mind lock at the third eye. These are the basic ones but they are others. Usually these are applied during breath infusion, especially after fresh air is infused in certain postures. When a yogi sits to meditate, he may or may not use locks.

Sex during Elderly Years

Last night in the astral world, a friend asked about the time when a person may stop sexual intercourse in an old body.

At the time I could not answer the inquiry. I laughed. What a question? I remember when I lived in Port Charlotte, Florida some years ago around 2002. There was a report in a local newspaper that in Sarasota, Florida, there were swinging clubs for persons who were between sixty-five and death. Sixty-five is the average age for retirement in the United States. This club was for retirees. It was an arrangement for meeting to have sexual intercourse in an elderly body.

When should someone lose interest in this behavior?

It depends on the culture and needs. For instance, where my body grew up in South American, the concept of having sex after sixty-five was not in vogue. Nobody thought like that. No one expected that as a privilege. Culturally it was taboo but people also did not expect to use an old body in that way. But there was an instance in my own family where I realized that some elderly people considered the possibility.

A great aunt brought it to my attention that her husband my great uncle, could not perform sexually after he was fifty-five. She was distressed about it. She resented him. He had sexual dysfunction. When the elderly lady told me that I was very surprised but I pretended that the statement did not jolt me.

In the skill of the kundalini yoga I practice, sexual indulgence is an unwanted feature except when it is done to beget children which will cause a karmic obligation to be absolved. Besides using sex for generating progeny, classic yoga, Patanjali yoga, has no use for sexual indulgence.

But there are sects for tantric yoga and kundalini yoga which give process for increasing sexual pleasure, prolonging it and enjoying it. There are also subtle dimensions in the astral world where people engage in sexual intercourse for days, weeks or months even, continuous. It all depends on what interest and culture one develops as one transmigrates.

As far as doing it for the natural pleasure which it provides, in kundalini yoga we use the energy to get the pleasure in the head of the subtle body, by moving it up the spine. We consider the head pleasure to be a higher pleasure and so we are eager to use it there. If the hormone and lifeForce energies are mixed and then used for sex expression, they cannot be used for pleasure in the head. This is why yogis are concerned to conserve it from sexual usage.

Both sex pleasure and the pleasure of risen kundalini in the head are pleasure. Look at these terms and note that *ananda* is the end of each word:

prajananda = *prajaa* (begetting) + *ananda* (bliss pleasure)

brahmananda + *brahma* (spirit) + *ananda* (bliss pleasure)

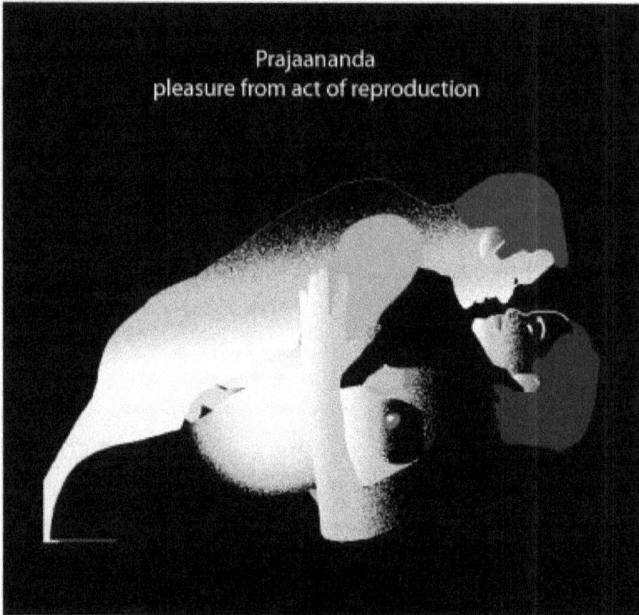

Prajaananda
pleasure from act of reproduction

A yogi is interested in *brahmananda* or spiritual pleasure. To increase that the yogi avoids sex pleasure expression.

The question of when to stop at what age of the body, would hinge on a person's needs and desires.

I explained in my books that it is the same kundalini which expresses itself though sex pleasure which is used to trigger spiritual pleasure. It may be hard to understand that sex pleasure is conducted by the kundalini, but I insist on that.

A sure way to shut down one's third eye if it is functional and open, is to get involved in sexual pleasure. It is a matter of making up one's mind about one's objective and also one should note the effects of one's activities and make decisions accordingly. Of course, sex pleasure is a basic instinct and even if one desires not to be involved with it, one's decision may prove to be ineffective because of the impulsive force of nature, which does on occasion force one to go against one's will.

Yogi enters memory of Student

During breath infusion this morning, suddenly there was a flash in the left thigh bone, on the top part of it. After this both thigh bones were infused and assumed the color of white-hot metal. I did some stretches which caused the thigh bone to be infused.

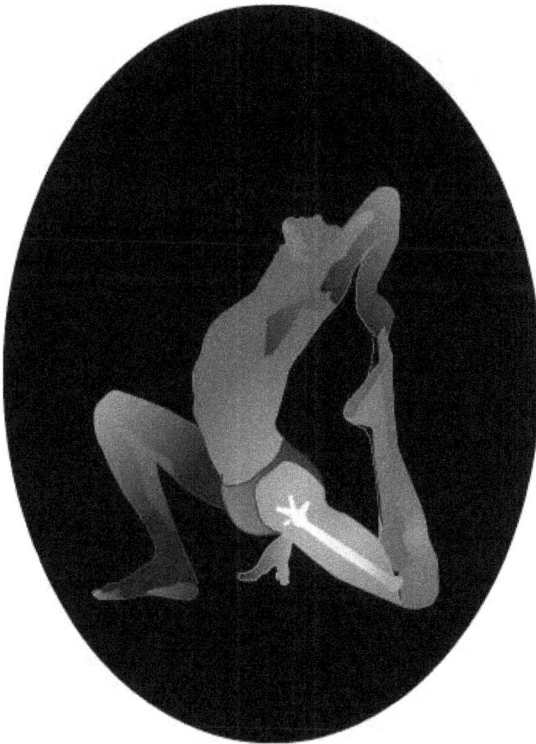

These lower parts of the body are important in the effort to uplift the kundalini and its outposts which are in remote parts of the body. For the development of a yoga siddha form after leaving this body, one must have the entire subtle body saturated with a high grade of subtle energy. If just the head, or if just certain chakras have that energy, while the rest of the system is with heavy astral force, one will fail to assume a yoga siddha form.

This is similar to the idea of being a mermaid. One is part human part aquatic such that one cannot be either and essentially the fish part predominates. This half state is that of a crocodile, where it lives on land part of the time and lives in water part of the time. It cannot stay on land and it must come out of the water some of the time.

Another example is that of peacock. It is a very beautiful creature to see but its habits are that of a vicious bird. Despite the beauty, mentally it thinks of killing and eating insects and worms. Thus, if the subtle body is only partially filled with light, the person will go to lower dimensions which are suited to the heavy energy in that body. In the end the lowest level of the psyche will take the rest of it to a lower category.

As I did the practice, Yogeshwarananda entered the subtle head. I thought that I would never see him again since he did go into the causal ocean of energy from which yogis usually do not return to this side of existence.

This appearance of his in my head was such that I determined that he abandoned to some extent his endeavor to stay in the causal energy. I did not question him for a reason.

However, he was in my psyche checking a memory chamber which is below the neck. It was funny because he pulled out something and threw it out of my subtle body, then he pulled more and more like a person pulling things from a duffle bag and throwing them at a distance.

He kept saying, "O what is this? What is this? Why did you do this? Where did this happen? What sort of yogi are you?"

Since I did breath infusion while this happened, I did not dare to laugh since that would shatter my focus and ruin the session. He pulled up a scene from a movie which I saw years ago. He looked at it in disgust. This is because yogis are not supposed to do anything which creates more impressions in the mind. Patanjali prohibited yogis from doing anything which increases the chittavrittis or impressions in the mind which obstruct the practice of higher meditation.

Just after he pulled that impression from the movie, he pulled out a few small impressions of insignificant things and then he pulled something and said, "This is it! How did this happen. This is what I search for."

That was an impression about my seeing the Krishna boy form in the divine world. This happened years ago (1993). It was one memory impressions of it that Yogeshwarananda found. That was not the original impression but it was a copy of the original. He turned to me and said, "I have to work on this, the spiritual body. How did you achieve this? The deity picks and chooses. If you are not chosen, he does not appear to you in which case you will never know of that place."

This conversation continued as I did breath infusion. Yogeshwarananda said that I need to increase the breath infusion practice to at least one hour. When he said that I did the practice for forty-five minutes. He said that was the warm up and that there should be another hour with focus on the head. Then one should stop that and sit to meditate, doing samyama as advised by Patanjali.

Basically, that means about two hours of postures and breath infusion and then sitting to meditate for at least one hour. Usually I do forty minutes or more of postures and breath infusion and then forty minutes or more of meditation practice. But in his view that is not enough.

Yogeshwarananda showed some breath infusion practice which is done to the head of the subtle body, in different parts of the head, here and there.

Yogi Touching Students

I got an inquiry about touching students when showing yoga exercises.

First of all, my training is that yoga should only be taught if one is commissioned by a teacher. The main reason for this is accountability. If one teaches but one is not commissioned by an advanced person, who is one accountable to, what social standards should one observe in that case?

When there is a teacher, it is easy to determine what is approved behavior. Patanjali listed a set of yamas and niyamas which define dos and don'ts. If there is no teacher from whom one can get a code of conduct, one has to create one and use it.

When teaching postures, it becomes necessary to hold someone's body but that carries with it the danger of sexual energy exchange. Then there is the question of what to do with the sexual energy which entered one's psyche from a student?

If possible, male teachers should have female assistants who demonstrate to female students and who touch female students. If a male teacher touches a female student there is a risk that sexual energy will pass in either direction. The result will be that either the teacher or student or both will be affected.

The teacher of the teacher may not approve of certain associations with some students. Once I ran an ashram during the years of 1973-1974. I taught both kundalini yoga which I learnt from Yogi Bhajan and also the postures and third eye meditation, I learnt from Arthur Beverford. Once I called Beverford.

I was in Springfield, Missouri. He was in Ventura, California. When I explained to him how I managed the ashram, he did not like certain things. Like for instance he did not like that I awakened students at 4am for posture practice and meditation. He thought it was too early. He had other objections.

If one teaches a certain method on behalf of a teacher, one should be clear with oneself how much of that teacher's methods one may use.

Karma is not an illusion, at least not on this physical level and also not in the astral world. It is a real. It affects people. It frustrates plans. Patanjali, near the end of his sutras talk about *dharmamegha*, which is the cloud *(megha)* of righteousness rules *(dharma)*. It means that as a spiritual teacher, one would be a fool not to know what the risks are when influencing people.

I am lucky because I only have to teach one or two people. I am not required by any of my teachers to teach many. And in fact, for myself, I am disinclined to being a teacher or leader. Why?

Because essentially, I do not like to do hard work. Teaching yoga in a sincere way is hard work. For me I must have coverage from a yoga guru or deity, especially from Shiva and Krishna.

If I hold a yoga class and begin teaching what Yogeshwaranand showed, I should remember that I am teaching on his behalf. If I explain the *Bhagavad Gita,* I explain that Krishna thinks He is God and gave rules and conditions for his devotes.

If I am teaching on behalf of Beverford, I explain that he believed in a primal creative cause. He did not believe that one person, an individual identity was the Cause of all causes.

If someone teaches on my behalf, I gave rules and explain where I will commit myself and where I assist if an upset occurs and the person gets into a karmic fix.

I hide myself so that no one knows that I teach yoga. Just an hour ago I heard a man telling a lady that there was a guy nearby who is an expert on yoga. When I heard that the hairs raised on my skin. I thought, "This guy is my enemy."

Any association means exchange of energy. It does not always go in one's favor. What happens may go beyond what one can control.

Personally, I do not believe that yoga should be taught to everybody. I feel that unless one is supported by higher yogis, one's yoga teaching will result in one's undoing. For me it is easy to be a student yogi without ever being a teacher.

The other day I spoke to Tobe Terrell and he said something profound which is: *Is the desire to teach stronger than the desire to learn?* That subject was discussed in my book *Spiritual Master.*

Lucky for me I feel that there is a Supreme Person, a specific person that no one will merge into and share power. My idea is that this person is responsible for what happens in the world. To my view instead of that person sleeping in Paradise, and me worrying myself to death on earth about the problems of human beings, I will go to sleep in paradise and the Supreme Person should be the one who worries about everything. Why should I care if He does not give a hoot?

It is a callous obviously but that is my view.

Stingy Kundalini

During breath infusion, I had some luck making small kundalinis. For the past week, breath infusion was not as desired because the atmosphere was not properly surcharged with sun energy. Still, I maintained the practice. On some days sun surcharged subtle air is hard to come by because of natural or man-made chemicals in the air and differing weather patterns. A yogi must live in peace with these variations. He should maintain the practice no matter what.

With sixty years and counting, with ultimate collapse of the body staring me in the face, it is in my interest to reinforce the practice. During the breath infusion, there were two small kundalinis which were in the face. These shot downward into the cheeks on both sides. This felt like cool foam shooting through the cheeks. It was a bright white color.

Five minutes after that occurred, there was a kundalini force in the frontal chest area, this shot through the neck on the right and left sides near the front of the neck. Neck clearance is important since the neck constricts and limits the exchange of energy between the trunk of the subtle body and the head of it.

If the neck is blasted properly in practice, the energy from the trunk will flow into the brain and visa versa. One of kundalini's bad habits is to keep the neck blocked. It allows food and breath energy to pass through the neck downwards. From this energy it manufactures hormones. It then uses these hormones for sex expression.

Kundalini is stingy about passing any of that energy into the head, except that it sends some of that energy as sexual charges into the senses. This gives the senses some intelligence about what to do to procure sexual pleasure.

A yogi has it as a task to disrupt this process of kundalini. By blasting through the neck, kundalini is no longer allowed to store this hormone energy just for sex. It can be used to increase clairvoyance and other psychic perceptions, which help the yogi to better manage social involvements and to discover methods of spiritual realization.

When I worked on the lower part of the body, there was a time when the thighs became surcharged with energy. This energy usually stays in the thighs and is used by kundalini to motivate the sexual urge and to drive the aggressive energy used during sexual intercourse. I pulled that energy out of the thighs into the trunk of the body. Then I pulled it into the brain. This is part of what is called the *urdhvareta* practice, where a yogi lifts the sexual charge of energy into the brain.

Sun-Charged Air

Yogis are reliant on sun charged air for progress. This is because the consciousness or awareness which we work with on this plane is dependent on the sun. The sun planet though a physical orb is also an astral reality. The astral bodies rely on it just as the physical bodies need it.

In India there is the *gayatri* (gai-tree or gai-a-tree) mantra. This mantra was misapplied because various sects in India claim it as their own and change its application according to the purpose of the Sect. In addition, many people from other cultures confiscate this mantra and publish it with meanings which make sense within the context of their philosophy and motive.

However, in the religious history of India, this mantra has to do with brahmins praying to and making contact with the sun-god three times per day, at sunrise, at noon and at sun set. It is a mantra for greeting the sun-god and taking assistance from him as well as remembering that we depend on him. Brahmins wrap a sacred thread around the right thumb daily thrice per day while saying this mantra and meditating to make astral contact with the sun-god. This is called *upavita*.

The words of *savitur, dhimahi, dhiyo (dhiyah)* mean the shining light of the sun god. *Savitur* is an altered word form of *Savita* who is the sun god *Aditya* or *Surya*, the son of *Aditi*.

As great a person as Krishna stated that the yogis use either sun or moon energy at the time of death to either go and not return to earthly rebirth or to return to the earth after staying in an adjacent astral world. This is explained in the *Bhagavad Gita*. If the astral body is not properly surcharged with sun energy, a yogi is stuck. It will not matter what his philosophy is.

We are not independent. We are not going to be absolute anytime soon. This is why yogis are advised to do breath infusion to energize the subtle body with the right type of energy which elevates and shifts it to higher planes.

Physically the sun is a physical object. In fact, it is a subtle physical object. It is also personal, just like on this planet we have persons. Of course, we cannot physically perceive anyone on the sun but that does not mean that there are no persons there.

Ancient yogis made formal contact and offered appreciation to the sun god *Savita (Surya, Aditya)*. Without sun energy both on the physical and subtle level, we would sink down to a very low existence, especially on the astral side.

How Kundalini Leaves the Body at Death

During breath infusion this morning Swami Rama came. He discussed how a yogi should handle the psyche when the physical body is on the verse of dying. He stated this.

Many meditators have no idea of what to do when death comes. Their idea is that it will be all good since they will merge into the Absolute or go to an astral paradise, but that is not the way of the yogis. For yogis we learn what kundalini will do before the time of death. Then we can either go along with kundalini's method or try to resist it or even try to force it to do something else.

Some persons think that God will make it good for them at the time of death and that He will compensate their deficiencies but this idea is only as good as what God did in terms of preventing the physical body from disease.

If we accept that there is a God, if that God will help one in the subtle body at the time of death, what is the explanation as to why that God does nothing to adjust the diseased condition of the physical form as it approaches death? Has that God said that he will fix the subtle body's condition at death even though he rendered no care for the physical body in that way?

Kundalini is the single element which controls what will happen at death, regarding where the individual soul will transit. The condition of kundalini and its condition alone determines that.

When the body gets to an elderly stage and when its functions deteriorate, kundalini uses one standard method which is to close down one part of the body after the other, beginning with the extremities and vital organs. Even parts of the brain malfunction. It is like when a person is on the verge of sleeping at night. He turns off the lights one by one and leaves a small lamp lit in the bedroom. Kundalini does this by ceasing various functions and organs one by one.

A yogi should take note of this and should not, like modern people, take medication which affords one the luxury of not knowing what kundalini does.

The student yogis like all other human beings are usually forced to go along with kundalini when death is near. This means focusing on the one or two major health defects in the system at that time. This health defect serves as gateways to the afterlife for kundalini. But an advanced yogi should not use such easy gateways because they lead to lower astral planes and to haphazard incidental rebirths in which the person has no idea what will happen and how history will unfold in the next life.

At first, kundalini begins to reduce its energy outlay at the base chakra. It retreats from all exit points or sensual orifices. This is experienced as blindness in the eyes, lack of hearing in the ears, insensitivity or numbness in the skin, lack of taste in the tongue, lack of odor in the nostrils.

This is like when a king who governs a large territory begins to lose control and is attacked by challenging rulers from other places. At that time the king builds a central fort in his territory. The idea is that he can be barricaded from his rivals and live in peace behind the walls of a stockade.

Unfortunately, his rivals, who went away when he first did that, return with siege engines and battering-rams. They pound his city walls.

Hearing the constant threat of the rivals and being aware that his end may be near; this king planned to escape from the city, which was designed to protect him but which became a trap for him. At last when the energy breaches the city wall, the king himself in disguise tries to escape through the same breach which his enemies made in the city wall.

Kundalini is just like this in that it tries to leave at death through the main disease which kills the body. Say for instance, that it is tuberculosis, then kundalini will leave through the lungs. If it is a venereal disease, then it will leave through the genitals, if it is constipation or diarrhea, it will leave through the anus. If it is Alzheimer, it will leave through the malfunctioned brain cells which caused that. If it is heart failure it will leave through the faulty heart valve.

A yogi must however try to get kundalini to take a different course at the time of death so that it does not travel along the lines of the terminal disease which the body will have.

Swamis and Sex Desire

A swami who passed about a week ago, came this morning just when I was to rise to do exercises. He said that since he is departed and is free to use other methods, he wants to consider yoga practice. This is a swami who was an officiating spiritual master in the Hare Krishna Movement. Due to prohibitions concerning yoga in their society, he could not practice while he used a physical body.

Due to having homosexual tendencies, he was trapped in pedophile activities with some boys who were in the boarding school in the religious society. He said to me,

"Yoga was not allowed by our teacher. I feel that perhaps it would have helped us to curb sex desire. We could have done it for say half-an-hour or even one hour, early in the morning and then we could have cleaned up and then attended to worship procedures and chanting schedule. There was time enough for it."

"Many of us had to deal with sex desire. We had no way to cancel it. Yoga especially the asanas and the pranayama practice may be effective."

When I began the postures and breath infusion, he followed what I did. After about ten minutes another Swami who was his main assistant and god-brother came there. This person used to be the main teacher at a boarding school where I taught when I was in the society. He also had homosexual tendencies and was accused of having sexual relationships with boys. Seeing the Swami doing the exercises, he began to do the exercises as well. He showed some congeniality towards me even though he was hostile when I lived in the ashram and worked in the school under his supervision.

Once when I lived in their ashram, this other Swami approached me to inform me that I could take nights off, to be with my wife. He was concerned that I was deprived of sexual intercourse. Since they discovered that I was not as needy for sex as they thought I should be, they began to wonder about that. Eventually they felt that yoga practice was the cause, even though in their ashram yoga was banned and I never did it while I was there for that very reason.

It is interesting how human beings get a religious belief and become fanatical about it, to the extent that they cannot properly evaluate it for what it really is. They cannot adjust themselves until they leave the physical body. They become afraid of condemnation in the religious society. They feel they must protect the status among their religious peers.

Swami Rama / Reserving the Sexual Energies

The afternoon session of breath infusion went well. During the practice I felt the presence of Swami Rama on my right. He spoke as I practiced. His discussion concerned these Patanjali verses:

अविद्यास्मितारागद्वेषाभिनिवेशाः क्लेशाः ॥३॥

avidyā asmitā rāga dveṣa abhiniveśaḥ kleśāḥ

avidyā – spiritual ignorance; asmitā – misplaced identity; rāga – a tendency of emotional attachment; dveṣa – impulsive emotional disaffection; abhiniveśaḥ – strong focus on mundane existence which is due to an instinctive fear of death; kleśāḥ – the mento-emotional afflictions.

The mental and emotional afflictions are spiritual ignorance, misplaced identity, emotional attachment, impulsive emotional disaffection and a strong focus on mundane existence, which is due to an instinctive fear of death. Yoga Sutras 2.3)

स्वरसवाही विदुषोऽपि तथारूढोऽभिनिवेशः ॥९॥

svarasavāhī viduṣaḥ 'pi tatha rūḍho 'bhiniveśaḥ

svarasavāhī = sva – own + rasa – essence + vāhī – flow, current, instinct for self-preservation (svarasavāhī – its own flow of energy of self-preservation); viduṣaḥ – the wise man; 'pi = api – also; tatha – just as, so it is; rūḍho = rūḍhah – developed produced; 'bhiniveśaḥ = abhiniveśaḥ – strong focus on mundane existence due to instinctive fear of death.

As it is, the strong focus on mundane existence, which is due to the instinctive fear of death, which is sustained by its own potencies, and which operates for self-preservation, is developed even in the wise man. (Yoga Sutras 2.9)

ते प्रतिप्रसवहेयाः सूक्ष्माः ॥१०॥

te pratiprasavaheyāḥ sūkṣmāḥ

te – these, they; prati – opposing, reverting back; prasava – expressing, going outwards; heyāḥ – what is fit to be left or abandoned; sūkṣmāḥ – subtle energies.

These subtle motivations are to be abandoned by reverting their expression backwards. (Yoga Sutras 2.9)

He explained this.

Each person who takes a physical body has to at some point in the initial formation of that form; submit to the curling action of kundalini. In this curling action, kundalini concentrates certain energies which are required as a starting point for the new body.

Even a great yogin, a siddha, who takes a new physical body, is subjected to this. Few persons however can break the choke-hold of kundalini and its temperament which is to create a concentration of energy for sexual preoccupation.

Before puberty there is no carnal knowledge in the body. In fact, if you take a juvenile who has not reached puberty and expose that person to sexual intercourse, there would be no experience of a climax, because at that stage the body does not support sexual pleasure.

However, for an adult once there is exposure, it becomes the most forceful impulsion. Because of this forcefulness a student yogi does the practice in a half-hearted way, whereby he/she cannot concentrate fully on the internal plane.

Kundalini is on the alert to procure sexual pleasure. That becomes its main focus after puberty. Thus, when the student begins, he/she is stymied by the need for sexual pleasure. Kundalini for its own part, stores the hormones with the intention of using that energy during the expression of sexual affection.

Why should the student yogi go all out, when he/she can do enough yoga to make-by? Why infuse the sexual energy and then by a thorough infusion scatter it evenly the body? You may not get intense pleasure if the energy is scattered, so why do yoga to that proficiency if it will deprive you of the pleasure intensity yielded by reserving the sexual energy for the genitals and their related sensual facilities?

Army Marches through a Yogi Body

Last night I was asked to give a short lecture and supervise a class on the *Ramayana* of Valmiki, which is a standard religious book from India. After the function, I was offered a meal, which due to the tradition of these events, I could not refuse. It was 8pm when I finished the meal. I knew it was a punitive act but still, due to social requirements, I took it.

The result was that during the night there was a small army moving through my system, at a time when there is usually total silence and rest for most of the cells of the physical body. The meal was one-third the size of a full meal. A full meal would have been like ten battalions with heavy tanks bombarding a large city, pulverizing it to dust. Instead this was like a small squadron with a few snipers and two or three gunships with light artillery.

During the night I awoke twice when there was some firing of the artillery. I thought to myself, "I wish this infantry would fall and die or go to sleep for the night.

The real question is:

How do people do this night after night with heavy meals? That is like when you are in the city which is shelled by an enemy. You get so accustomed to the loud explosions that you sleep anyway even though when you awaken the next morning the building you slept in, vaporized due to the explosions?

I was late to do the breath infusion, doing it near 6am rather than 4am. This is one of the disadvantages of night eating, that one becomes inclined to rising later usually after 6am. I struggled to push down some heavy energy through the chest, down into the navel area and then out through the bottom of the trunk of the subtle body. I worked on this for about twenty minutes until I felt that the energy moved out of the system.

After that I worked on infusing the head of the subtle body. I worked on blasting the thought, image, idea area of the subtle head. I had some success with that.

Sex Pleasure / Yogi Bhajan

Breath infusion practice this morning was successful. Somehow, I created a kundalini force which saturated the entire trunk of the subtle body, even the arms. A pearl-like energy shook through the trunk and went into the arms with a bliss aspect and with distribution of small pearly energy molecules.

After this happened, I shifted and focused on infusing the head of the subtle body, beginning with the area where thoughts are generated, and then moving to the back top of the head.

Yogi Bhajan's head appeared for a short time near the end of the session. He said this.

In the West most students were stymied by sex desire. They underestimated what the Indians who do kundalini yogi experienced. It is not that all Indians are advanced. Some are just as restricted in the practice, as those who took bodies in the West.

"It is a fact that when you take a body from the Western culture, you are automatically restricted because of the nature of the environment and because of the stress on sexual freedom. The focus of the culture in the

West is for personal sexual gratification. The society is designed to facilitate that. But sex pleasure has little use in yoga.

"Kundalini is keeping the individual spiritual beings restricted in one way or the other but its hold on them through sexual facility is tight. Imagine that you are in a maximum-security prison and then they put you in solitary confinement. When one is attracted to sex, when one is sex-centered, and when one sees that sex pleasure is the ultimate basic enjoyment nature has to offer, one is under the maximum confinement. This continues even when one is introduced to kundalini yoga.

"When I was alive, I stressed responsibility as a replacement for sex. No one knew what I spoke. They looked at me as if I did not know what I discussed because in the case of sex, the enjoyment is real and immediate. In the case of responsibility, the enjoyment is postponed for the future. It is not saturated. Everyone looked at me as if I was ignorant of the value of sexual pleasure.

"I very well know what it is but in the long run, responsibility will give a greater profit in the cultural world if that is what one is after.

"After high school, youths acquire apartments. This concerns the privacy needed for sex. As soon as puberty sets in one is confronted with this need for privacy which becomes an obsession. However, along with the need for sex, the aspect of responsibility faces the individual. Sex offers a reward upfront in the form of indulgent pleasure, while responsibility holds back the reward, and demands service without yielding pleasure at the onset."

Yogi Bhajan spoke of those who confronted him as disciples when he came to the United States. Many youths from the counter-culture were attracted to him. They desired enlightenment along the lines they discovered while using hallucinogenic drugs like LSD, but behind the scenes there was an aggressive need for sex which over-shadowed the desire for enlightenment.

The sense of responsibility had no voice in the matter, because the sex pleasure need was prominent. It did not allow any other part of the psyche to speak. As far as the experience they derived from hallucinogenic drugs, that too involved sex pleasure and that was neglectful of responsibility.

Evidence of this is there in a leader of counter culture, Timothy Leary, who urged college students to turn on, tune in and drop out if necessary. Pleasure was the highlight.

Responsibility for progeny is inclusive in the range of aspects for which we are accountable to providence. Ultimately in terms of reincarnation the responsibility for progeny is the biggest bill which one will be held accountable for. This is because to get the next body, one needs to induce someone to take responsibility for one's infant form.

Suppose my parent(s) beget my baby form and then they leave it to fend for itself while they procure more and more sexual pleasure. That pleasure to me will be the cause of my death. For them it would be pleasure and fulfillment of personal needs. For me it is neglect.

Responsibility includes responsibility for the progeny produced when using the sex force. If I try to get a body but my would-be father or mother, uses a contraceptive they effectively skirt the responsibility for my upbringing. They get what they need the most which is sexual pleasure, I would get what I do not desire which is frustration for being deprived of an embryo.

Yogi Learns from Two Businessmen

The night was quiet and mostly uneventful which is really great for a yogi. It is a good result of practice if one finds that during the night one does not have much social involvement with people whose primary interest is everything but yoga.

I did breath infusion just after 4am. At first no one was present astrally but then Muktananda appeared as an astral body. I focused down in the trunk of the body I infused energy into the thighs. He made this remark.

"Those who are unable to keep the attention in the psyche during asana postures and breath infusion will not reach the heights of Patanjali yoga. Subsequently they go about speaking of things of which they have no knowledge. Baba used to whack us if at any time during practice, our attention strayed outside of the psyche. In the subtle body, you would get this stinging whack on your back. Then you realized that your attention strayed. It is nice that you keep your attention inside even though there is no one here to inflict pain on you for violating that."

By Baba he meant Siddha Swami Nityananda.

During breath infusion, the air was cold but I persisted. Presently my circumstance does not allow me to practice the breath infusion outdoors. Sometimes circumstances are not ideal but a yogi should not allow that to deter practice nor distract one from the real issue which is to take any opportunity and make do with it.

For breath infusion one should never use polluted indoor air. There must be ventilation so that fresh air reaches the nostrils.

If one lives in the Northern Hemisphere, one should when the weather is cold, do the breath infusion indoors with windows opened partially so as to warm the fresh air but if that is not practical, one should practice anyway. I dress warm and go outdoors. People make many sacrifices and go through many loops of hardship and austerity for physical aims. Hence, there is no reason why a yogi cannot take their example and apply their persistence and sacrifice to spiritual practice. There is much to learn from dedicated persistent materialistic people.

Yesterday I was with a few businessmen. They went to a wholesaler to purchase items for retail sale. It was interesting how they badgered and whittled-down the wholesaler on prices. They were persistent and stripped the man to the bare bones to get the cheapest prices so that on the retail side they would make the highest profits. There was no shame on their part in this. It was all about profit. As far as they were concerned the wholesaler should make no gains from the purchase. He should give it to them at the price at which he bought it or less even. They were vicious like efficient predators, like eagles and lions, which strip everything to the bone and crack the bone and take the marrow within it if that is necessary.

There is something to learn from these people about how efficient to be in spiritual practice. These people are noted by a yogi, regarding their lack of conscience and total efficiency. After they completed the transaction, I interviewed the two men about it, asking them if there was some satisfaction in getting the best prices from the wholesaler.

They explained to me that of course there was and that if they did not do that, the whole thing would be spoilt for them. "We must get that price down to the bare bones," they said, "then we are satisfied. The pleasure is in getting the best prices so that we can make the highest possible profit."

I was struck with wonder because I was never able to see life in that way. These fellas had some circuits which were missing in my psyche. Still, it was an important lesson in how to deal with life and get from it what you must to fulfill your nature. If these materialistic persons can do this, why should yogis sit back and get nothing out of spiritual practice.

Male Yogi doing Female Practice

I got up at 4am. I was with some people who stayed in an ashram in Scandinavia. This was an ashram of Swami Muktananda who is now deceased and who many people doubt was a worthy guru. At the ashram, a lady arrived who used a Scandinavian body. There were other ladies there who were of Scandinavian descent. This was on the astral side. Muktananda must have ashrams in the Scandinavian countries, like Sweden, Finland and Norway.

At the ashram in the astral I did not see the Swami. I spoke to three of the Scandinavian women. One just arrived at the ashram. I gave her instructions on how to stay there and in which room she would be domiciled.

Soon after that I rose to do exercises, Muktananda showed up with the same lady who I instructed at the ashram. It was then that I realized that it was his ashram. Now I was on the physical side with astral perception. The swami and the lady were on the astral side only.

As I did postures, he showed her what happened in my subtle body, where the infused energy was and what it did to the subtle body. She was struck with wonder expressing that she had no idea that yoga was anything but a physical practice.

He had me show her a yoni clearance exercise which is done by yoginis (female yogis). Yoni is a Sanskrit word for female genital organ. In this exercise, the person focuses on the genital organ on the subtle side of existence (in the subtle body) and works with breath infusion to remove the lusty attitude of the organ. This involves moving the energy which is usually sheltered in the organ and changing that energy into a higher infused force.

The genital organ is naturally the chief servant of the mode of passion but it can be reformed. It can be made to serve the mode of clarity. However, that change occurs only under the pressure of yoga techniques.

Even though my body is male, I can sometimes assume postures which are for females. At the onset, the embryo has the potential for either male, female or neuter gender.

For that matter these bodies have more female potential than they have male. Assumption of postures which are particular to the female form is easy. The lady was wonder struck when she saw what the breath infusion did in the subtle body. Even though she did yoga in her physical form for many years and had perfected many postures, she never imagined anything like that.

Now she knows that yoga is not a practice for physical health and beauty. A question may arise as to whether this person would remember that astral encounter when she returns to the physical side after that astral projection. The answer:

She may or may not.

She is the Swami's disciple. That is his worry.

After I did the infusion having to do with the trunk of the body, I switched to finalize the practice with infusion of the intellect. The swami wanted the lady to take note of that. Since the orb is so subtle even to subtle perception in the subtle body, the lady could not see what the infusion did as she did with the infusion in the trunk of the body.

The swami explained what I did to the orb. Because the lady had some doubts about his practice as compared to mine, he said this, "Yes, no one sees me doing these practices. I mastered these in my youth; I do not need to practice these now. Do not worry about my practice. Focus on what you need to do at this stage. You cannot always do what a guru does. You are at another stage. I brought you to him because he is at a stage of practice which you can learn something from. Each yogi is at a different stage of progression. One learns best from the one who uses the method which would cause you to progress the most."

After that the swami went away. The lady left with a look of wonder.

Subtle Body Focus

During the afternoon session I worked on the energy flush-way which is at the bottom of the trunk of the subtle body. This is the equivalent of the anal pouch which is the rectum. In the subtle body however, there is no long winding alimentary track or upper intestines. The subtle body is not concerned with digesting solid matter but with using energy which is made from light (like in sunlight). The Sanskrit term for this energy is *prana* (praa-nuh).

This flush-way should be of a light color. It should not be dark in the subtle body. By breath infusion one can clear this flush way so that it promptly expels energy which was used by the subtle body and which should be expelled from it. Again, this type of expulsion is not like evacuating solid matter or feces from the physical body.

I also worked on two corresponding areas in the upper back. These are like two plates of energy. Usually this energy is dark but a yogi can infuse it with breath. If the infusion is sufficient, this area will change from a dark cloud of heavy subtle energy to a whitish very light energy.

In this way, a yogi can do his work in attaining a yoga siddha form. There is no point in getting too crazy about maintain the physical body because no matter what one does, one will still lose it within at least one hundred years of its life. The subtle body lasts for the duration of the galaxy. It is worth the effort to keep it in tip-top shape.

If one's subtle body is not automatically kept in a high vibration all by itself without endeavor, it becomes necessary to strive with breath infusion to push the subtle body up to higher planes.

One stumbling block is the lack of experience of higher subtle dimensions. Many spiritual seekers do not get experiences of these zones. They feel that these are a myth or something imagined by mystics. Thus, it is reasonable for such seekers not to endeavor for this.

A yogi will notice that with an increase in breath infusion, the physical body appears to be healthier. For instance, when breath infusion is done with focus on the rectum, a yogi may notice that there is more prompt evacuation. Seeing this, a yogi who is not properly grounded in transcendence may get the idea that yoga is for improving the health of the physical body. This will result in more focus on the physical form resulting in a yogi who has a misunderstanding about yoga.

Even though one may notice that there are physical health benefits to yoga, one should not be distracted by this but should keep the focus on the enduring subtle body and not be concerned with the short-lived physical system, which will soon have a terminal illness no matter how healthy it may be.

Yogi Put Up a White Flag

For the afternoon session I had a visitor, Muktananda. As it turns out, the sudden urge to do an afternoon session come from him. He deposited energy in my psyche which nullified some other energy which blocked that afternoon practice. This may be considered a case of having to take help from a yoga guru to make progress.

If one is unable to transcend negative influences, one may take energy from a teacher who is resistant to such forces. That may be enough to cause one to overcome the retardative force.

Muktananda gave this notation.

"Eventually one comes to realize that one fights a losing battle against kundalini which is present in one's body as the lifeForce. In a losing battle even if one is courageous, one will only go on fighting if one does not understand the odds. Once the fighter sees that the odds are against him and that there is nothing he can do to tip it in his direction, he becomes discouraged from fighting and puts up a white flag.

In yoga there is no such thing as committing suicide to avoid capture by the enemy because the yogi is confronted with the fact that he will survive the body. Killing the body is no way out because even then physical nature will be present on the subtle side of existence and then again, the yogi will have to face the enemy. Hence the only thing left to do is to put up a white flag.

The yogi calls a bluff with the white flag because a hero cannot surrender to the enemy. The yogi surrenders but in the back of his mind, he thinks of another way. He is captured by the enemy after putting up that white flag but still he thinks of a way out.

What is that way out?

It is the realization that to escape capture one must go into another dimension where physical nature has no influence. That other place is called the chit akash.

The psyche of the yogi should be altered in such a way that it is no longer responsive to the sensation which it once craved in physical existence. A thorough overhaul is required. Who should do it for the yogi? Should it be God? Should it be a yoga guru?

Infusing Sun Light Energy into Subtle Body

Swami Muktananda directed me in a posture for removing dark subtle energy from the back thigh-buttocks area. This is done while the back part of body faces the sun. The yogi pulls in sunlight energy from the sun's rays into the subtle body. This is done by doing breath infusion with attention on that specific area.

See the diagram with the sun energy penetrating the specified area.

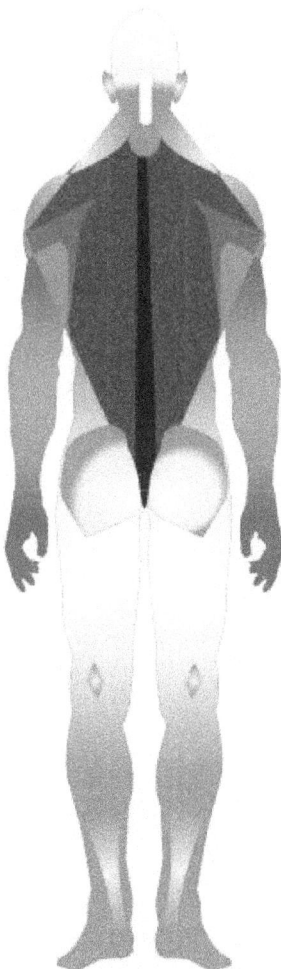

Yogi runs from pleasure/reproduction

The main infusion area this morning was the thighs, which got white hot in the subtle body. The subjugation of the thighs is part of sexual energy conversion practice. Sexual energy is necessary for reproduction but sex energy has an addictive pleasure aspect.

Pleasure becomes a vice when the entity decides that it should be procured and should be detached from responsibility for progeny. When nature first introduces sexual pleasure, it does so with the intention of luring the entity to reproduce but the entity soon finds a way to outsmart nature by frustrating the reproductive feature and taking the pleasure. This however makes for a vice which causes the entity to owe nature for the energy enjoyed. Nature then reacts by setting up complex nearly-unsolvable destinies in the person's future so that when that person comes out again in the creation in a physical environment, he/she is stymied or is in a stunted life form in which nothing can be done to circumvent nature's reproduction-pleasure system.

Realizing that nature's pleasure system can only be separated from its reproductive functions with dire consequences, the yogi decides to go for celibate practice. It is not a religion. It is sheer mathematics, because when one figures it out, one loses in the effort to cull the pleasure from the reproduction business. Nature is the one which does the tally. The entity is not the accounting agent in this case. Nature tallies in its interest.

King Self and Goof-Off Servant Kundalini

During exercises this morning, Swami Rama appeared for a few minutes. He wanted me to focus on the sacral bone. This is the bone structure which is in the buttocks.

This place is usually kept under lock and key by the kundalini lifeForce but when the yogi gets kundalini pulled into the head out of the spine, it is left to the yogi to infuse the system with fresh air energy.

The real value in lifting kundalini is that the yogi sees that what he/she took for granted was amiss. The normal configuration in the psyche is for the self to be a loafer, a lazy bum, a person who is a crippled king who can do nothing for himself but who is dependent on servants

If that king dismisses the servants what will be his lot? He is helpless and cannot serve himself? When the yogi lifts kundalini, it is left to the yogi to infuse energy into the psyche. The yogi realizes that the kundalini lifeForce was a bungling incompetent all along. While the self, as king was laid back doing nothing but enjoying the benefits of its servants like the kundalini lifeForce, the intellect, the sense of identity, the senses and memory, some functions were neglected by kundalini.

Instead of aggressively servicing the entire body, the kundalini neglected certain parts of the system. This is discovered only after the self must do this for itself and it finds many dark energy-deficient areas in the psyche.

Swami Rama told me to work on the sacral bone. Then he faded astrally. I spent the whole session focusing it. It was so dark and so de-energized that I realized that kundalini neglected it.

Kundalini's main interest in an adult body is sex and social power. It puts its energies into manufacturing sex hormones and in doing whatever is necessary to maintain and promote the status quo. It is not interested in anything else. It neglects any and all parts of the psyche which are not directly related to sex and status. Many of us live our entire lives with kundalini dominating for sex and status pursuits.

Swami Rama convinced me that if one works on any energy deficient area of the psyche which is below the neck of the subtle form, that increase in infusion of energy into that area would result in an advanced condition of mind when one sits to meditate.

When I first sat, naad blared loudly outside at the location where the right physical ear is located. I noted it but then I got a message imprint which Swami Rama left in my psyche. It read:

Naad should be seen as nutrition for the self, as replacement for sensation. Let the self consume naad. Become saturated with it.

Agnisara Tubes in Subtle Body

The *agnisara* process is still effective with psychic penetration during the meditation session after practice.

However, it shifted in two ways. At first the shift was to the back a little. Then it rose to the chest area, on the inside of the chest near the spine. This shift caused a mini-kundalini to form. When that got white hot with intensity, it flashed. Kundalini joined with it and came under the neck into the shoulders. I applied the neck lock and suppressed it from entering the head which is what Swami Rama advised during this particular phase of *agnisara* practice.

The idea is to pull kundalini into the head and cause it not to be in the trunk below the neck. Then the yogi should generate mini-kundalinis by using the breath energy charge confined in various nadis throughout the trunk. It begins with finding the subtle excretion track which is from the navel down through the body.

One experiences it as a tube about one and one-half inches wide but it gets bigger at times and may change into an oval shape. The yogi should target that repeatedly until it disappears. That happens after repeated intense infusion with breath, with full focus on the tube so that even if a thought arises, the thought or image is immediately dropped into the tube and is pulverized out of existence by the infused energy.

After that primary tube is annihilated, another tube appears which goes from the navel front area of the body to the anus, to a little before the anus. This tube is more slanted than the first tube since at the bottom, it leans back more. The yogi should work on this and then blast this one away with the infusion.

Initially the tube becomes evident to the yogi. The infused energy flows through it but as the yogi intensifies everything, the dusty cloudy energy in the tube turns white hot like when metal is near the molten stage under intense heat. If the yogi continues the infusion, the intensity causes the tube to disappear.

The yogi will find that another tube a sliver tube, a very narrow one, appears. The attention shifts to that wherever it may be in some part of the body or even in the thighs, legs or feet.

The problem facing a yogi who does these methods is discouragement. This comes in the form of the inability to persist with the practice day after day, and also in the form of a discouragement energy which causes the yogi to do insufficient breath infusion to energize the tube. If the yogi fails to take help from more advanced yogis, he will not resist the discouragement energy.

A student yogi, all by himself/herself cannot complete these kriyas because the all-surrounding discouragement energy is more powerful than the will or desire of the yogi. Assistance must be taken from yoga gurus.

The *agnisara* tubes below are central in the subtle body.

tube below is from navel
to perineum area (pubic floor)

tube below is from navel to near anus
but not touching anus
this is between anus and perineum area

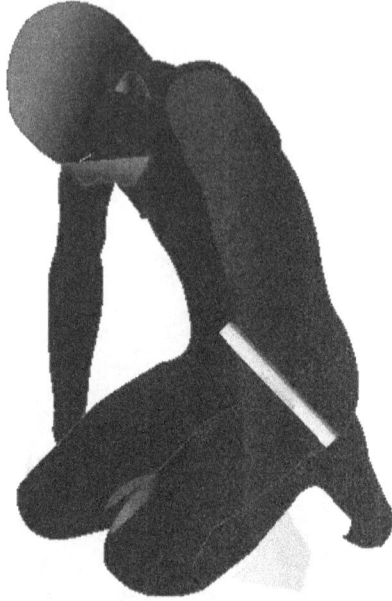

tube is near spine on the inside of the body
centered in the subtle body
it feels like a sliver of molten metal in white heat

Mini Kundalini

The mini kundalini mentioned is not the standard kundalini which governs the construction of the physical body and which usually governs the final departure from it at death of the form. This mini-kundalini is one that is created by the infused breath energy when doing the *agnisara* practice.

This practice is not the standard *agnisara* practice which is done with the regular kundalini. This is a practice which is done after the yogi forced kundalini out of the spine into the head. There were some previous descriptions where I described how a yogi caused kundalini to abandon the base chakra, then it hangs in the spine and then from more infusion it retreats into the head above the neck.

After kundalini did that consistently and lost its bearings in regards to the base chakra location, the yogi can do this advanced *agnisara* method. The mini-kundalini is a minor kundalini that is produced on the spot by the infused energy while doing the *agnisara* in a subtle body in which kundalini was drawn into the head above the neck.

The yogi does not create this mini-kundalini. It is produced by the action of infused breath. The compressed infused breath converts into a mini-kundalini at a certain point of compression, just as in static electricity, there may be a flash of lightning and no one knows where that flash will be. Once the yogi sees the flash in the psyche, he/she should intensify the infusion, while focusing at that location. Those breaths should be kept until the flash energy disappears completely.

The idea is to first pull the standard nature-created kundalini and cause it to lose its bearings in regards to the base chakra. When that is done and kundalini is kept out of the trunk below the neck, the breath infusion practice changes so that the yogi causes minor kundalinis to form (mini-kundalinis) in various parts of the trunk of the subtle body according to the degree of infusion.

Attention Inside Body

    This morning Swami Rama made an important statement about the time it takes to get success in yoga practice. He said.

Previously a yoga guru would tell a disciple that in a certain time say six months, or one year or twelve years that student would be successful, provided the person stuck to a certain method and lived at the hermitage. Usually these places were isolated. The student was cordoned from other influences.

Why is it that in the modern setting this does not happen? In fact, students who live at an ashram become disillusioned when they do not get success in whatever the yoga guru described.

The main reason for the failure is the social environment. The rigidity of the past is no longer present. Without it, the student is not supported by the disciplines and restrictions. The teachers are affected by social trends and cannot deliver what is intended.

There is a process mentioned which is conducive to yoga success. This is in the Anu Gita. *There is a period given for six months. Today that period is much longer. In fact, students may never be successful even in a life time.*

There is one key feature when practicing postures and breath infusion and when sitting to meditate. That is to keep the attention in the body.

There is a statement to that effect in the Anu Gita *in the example of a tourist in a city. Quote that at the end of this message.*

Students should keep the mind inside the body during the exercises. By mind in this case, I mean the attention. It likes to wander outside the body and go to various places during the exercises but a student should find an effective method to keep the mind inside the body during the asana postures and pranayama infusion practices.

You can practice yoga for a million years but if you fail to keep the attention inside of the psyche, you will never get the full success. You will always be falling short of the full proficiency. That will affect one's confidence in yoga and the yoga guru.

Train the attention to stay within the body during the exercises. Do not allow it to stray outside. Do not allow it to pursue thoughts which come from others during the exercises. Discipline the attention.

दृष्टपूर्वां दिशं चिन्त्य यस्मिन्संनिवसेत्पुरे

पुरस्याभ्यन्तरे तस्य मनश्चार्यं न बाह्यतः

dṛṣṭapūrvāṁ diśaṁ cintya yasminsaṁnivasetpure

purasyābhyantare tasya manaścāryaṁ na bāhyataḥ

dṛṣṭa – seen; pūrvāṁ - before; diśaṁ - place; cintya – thinking; yasmin – in which; saṁnivaset – should reside; pure – in the city; purasyābhyantare = purasya (of the city or psyche) + abhyantare (in the interior, inside); tasya – of his; manaś = manah = mind; cāryaṁ - behavior, operation; na – not; bāhyataḥ - outside

When thinking of a place which was seen before, one should reside in the city in which the incidence occurred. The mental operations are within the psyche, not outside of it. (Anu Gita 4.31)

पुरस्याभ्यन्तरे तिष्ठन्यस्मिन्नावसथे वसेत्

तस्मिन्नावसथे धार्यं सबाह्याभ्यन्तरं मनः

purasyābhyantare tiṣṭhanyasminnāvasathe vaset

tasminnāvasathe dhāryaṁ sabāhyābhyantaram manaḥ

purasyābhyantare = (purasya of the city) + abhyantare (inside); tiṣṭhany = tiṣṭhani = situated; asmin – in this; nāvasathe = na (not) + avasathe (city); vaset – should reside; tasmin – in this; nāvasathe = na

(not) + avasathe (city); dhāryaṁ - absorbed in; sa – with;
bāhyābhyantaraṁ = bāhya (exterior) + abhyantaram (interior); manaḥ
- mind

Being situated inside the city, he should reside there with his mind
absorbed in the exterior and interior features of that place. (Anu Gita 4.32)

प्रचिन्त्यावसथं कृत्स्नं यस्मिन्कायेऽवतिष्ठते

तस्मिन्काये मनश्चार्यं न कथंचन बाह्यतः

pracintyāvasathaṁ kṛtsnaṁ yasminkāye'vatiṣṭhate
tasminkāye manaścāryaṁ na kathaṁcana bāhyataḥ

pracintyāvasathaṁ = pracintya = meditating; kṛtsnaṁ - whole reality;
yasmin – in which; kāye – in the body; 'vatiṣṭhate = avatiṣṭhate =
being situated; tasmin – in that; kāye – in the body; manaś = manah =
whole; cāryaṁ - wander; na – not; kathaṁcana – any way; bāhyataḥ -
outside

Meditating in that place, the self sees the whole reality being situated in the
body. The mind should not in any way wander outside the body. (Anu Gita
4.33)

संनियम्येन्द्रियग्रामं निर्घोषे निर्जने वने

कायमभ्यन्तरं कृत्स्नमेकाग्रः परिचिन्तयेत्

saṁniyamyendriyagrāmaṁ nirghoṣe nirjane vane
kāyamabhyantaraṁ kṛtsnamekāgraḥ paricintayet

saṁniyamyendriya = saṁniyamya (completely restraining) + indriya
(sensual energies); grāmaṁ - aggregate; nirghoṣe – without noise;
nirjane – without people; vane – in the forest; kāyam – body;
abhyantaraṁ - inside; kṛtsnam – whole reality; ekāgraḥ - one object of
focus; paricintayet – deeply meditate

In an uninhabited and noiseless forest, while completely restraining the
aggregate sensual energies, he should deeply meditate within the body on
the whole reality as one object of focus. (Anu Gita 4.34)

Confidence in the Third Eye

The *agnisara* process does what Swami Rama said it would do. It affects
the operation of the third eye in reference to its potential for chit akash, sky

of consciousness perception and other supernatural means of peering into or visiting higher dimensions.

Just by doing *agnisara*, a person can, it appears, reach the supernatural and spiritual zones of existence.

There is a channel from the navel through the bottom of the trunk. At first when one does the breath infusement focusing on this area, the channel appears to be round. It appears to be filled with a dark-grey dusty subtle energy. By the infusement that changes into a light grey energy. Then suddenly it seems to catch afire and burns like burning dusty clouds in a sky.

After this the area clears and has a gold shimmer light. But then the round shape changes into an oval shaped tube. Then after more infusion, that oval shape widens. The infused energy then attacks the sex organ chakras which are in the pubic area of the body.

The progression of this development may take days, weeks or months depending on the intensity and efficient of the practice of a particular student.

After a time, the channel begins at the throat under the mouth rather than at the navel. This is when it begins to affect the operation of the third eye. During meditation what happens is this:

Initially when the student does this *agnisara*, there is no effect of it on the third eye. In fact, there is no effect in the head of the subtle body. Thus, the student may have doubts about the practice, since most students are eager to have kundalini rise into the head with its accompanying effects.

At first the yogi will be drawn into the navel area and will find the coreSelf relocated out of the head of the subtle body into the *agnisara* channel. The student may wonder what should be done there.

As the practice develops, the yogin will find that when sitting to meditate after a session, the coreSelf becomes aware of both the head of the subtle body and the *agnisara* channel which was bored and which is now filled with a gold shimmering light which sometimes has an orange hue.

Then the student will find that the third eye assumes an orange hue with small flashes of light which are like icicles shimmering a little in sunlight. The third eye will open for about three seconds or even for as much as ten seconds. It will be shimmering. It may open for less than that amount a second or third time.

Then it will not open but the student will derive from this an important confidence, that it is possible by practice to open the third eye and use it just as one could use physical vision.

The value of this is the confidence gained since a student has no confidence in the ability to use the third eye due to its resistance to the willpower of the student. It is as if the willpower is relieved to find itself operating the third eye.

This may be compared to a frustrated child who after a number of attempts to make the feet of the infant body walk, gets frustrated because of repeatedly falling due to incoordination. Then after a time, the child finds that the feet do respond to the willpower even though it does that only for a few steps and then it again ignores the commands.

Many persons think that opening of third eye is imagination of yogis or is a belief of yogis. Thus, if anyone has these experiences, faith in the practice of yoga develops. That accelerates practice.

Agnisara is one practice which helps in the development of self-confidence. Just as an infant gradually finds that the feet which were resistant and unresponsive to the willpower, eventually over time becomes more and more compliant, so the student yogi will find that the higher faculties of the subtle body which were undeveloped and even non-existent, come into focus and become usable functions. It is exactly like taking a new body having no control of it and then gradually learning how to operate it as it develops.

Raising kundalini into the head and infusing the head with fresh air, will yield the same results, but only if the infusion is thorough. That is not an easy achievement. One must have a lifestyle that is fully compliant with the stipulations of Patanjali regarding *yama* and *niyama* lifestyle. Without that compliance, raising kundalini will result in opening third eye infrequently.

When he discussed the *yama* restraint actions and the *niyama* approved behaviors, Patanjali wrote of the great commitment which is that one should not violate these, nor use awkward situations as a reason to ignore these. If one must violate these while practicing the yoga process one will get a faulty result.

Until the yogi can cease his interest in the benefits of physical existence, he cannot get the full success but that does not mean that one should not practice. One should practice with no false expectations.

Yoga has little to do with the physical body. A person can do postures and derive health benefits and even psychological benefits like relief from stress, and that same person may get absolutely zero results in the psychic sense of the subtle body.

But the *agnisara* process of Swami Rama is the hard core hatha yoga process not the Western hatha yoga process which is postures and healthy diet which results in physical beauty and health.

Ha and *tha* actually means the sun and moon influences in the body, which points to the kundalini *shakti*. It has very little to do with a physical body. The value of a physical body to an advanced yogi is that it anchors the subtle system. Besides that, the physical body is a useless limited appendage.

When the subtle body is in the subtle world, if it is not a yoga siddha form, it is a nuisance because it is fickle. It shifts from one place to the next. This makes it near impossible to have a steady practice because the subtle body acts like a squirrel, always moving and not staying steady for anything.

On the physical level, *agnisara* is a combination of kapalabhati and uddiyana bandha. The combination of pranayama and asana looks to be more similar to uddiyana bandha. The deeper emphasis is on the use of muscles in the lower abdomen and, specifically, use of the pelvic floor. When we consider *agnisara* for the subtle body, it is said that this technique activates kundalini shakti, at the navel center. *Agnisara* is a primary step toward harnessing subtle energizing air, which should result in more clarity.

My discussion concerns the subtle body even though it occurrs in the physical body as well. Swami Rama's advanced method does not involve kundalini. It involves the self using subtle energy just as kundalini would have used it. Initially a student yogi does *agnisara* with the kundalini. When this is done proficiently, the kundalini is drawn into the brain. It loses the tight hold on the base chakra, the sex chakra system and the navel chakra domain. Then that yogi practices a higher type of *agnisara* practice, in the preparation to assume a yoga siddha body.

In the subtle body we are not concerned with the muscular locks. There one deals with energy, either heavy or light weight subtle energy. The tubes I mentioned are subtle tubes and that one in particular has no corresponding one in the physical system. In the physical system we have intestines and colon in those areas. These are coiled tubing. In the subtle body there is a passage from the navel straight down (no coiling) through the body to somewhere between the anus and perineum.

The physical actions of *agnisara* are for beginners. That practice is the beginning. It is not the advanced practice which has to do with the subtle body. A point may be raised though as to why focus so much on what is subtle and abstract, why not focus on the physical and be done with it, feeling the benefits on the physical side.

This is a good argument until the time of death of the physical system, because from then onwards one must deal with the subtle part of the psyche. Yogis should be aware of the subtle before the time of death. Physical existence is not the problem. It is here because of a psychic interest in it. The problem is that psychic intention.

Part 6

Yogi with Two Bodies

Swami Rama has two bodies, one is the body he used to practice yoga. The other is an astral form which he uses to continue his yoga teacher duties. Because he was a lineage guru, he maintains an astral body in respect to that.

In the meantime, he uses another body in another dimension to continue the yoga austerities. Some students are unaware of his double life.

When the Swami showed more details of the *agnisara* practice, he transferred my perception into the dimension where he has another body. He showed how the inside of that body is constructed. That form has no spinal kundalini even though it has routes for channeling subtle energy.

Swami Rama does not have a spiritual body. He has an altered siddha yoga body. When a yogi becomes successful, his subtle body changes and is called a siddha form. That is not a spiritual body. It is a precursor to a spiritual form.

Usually yogis transfer to that siddha form but Swami Rama keeps that form and his astral form from before. The different between that siddha body and the standard astral form is this:

The standard astral form has tendencies which lead the individual back into the birth/death cycle repeatedly. It is hell-bent on gaining benefits from cultural activity in the physical world.

The siddha form has no interest in that cultural activity. It has no inclinations for rebirth or participation in human history.

To understand this, we can study our condition as helpless infants. Then we have the impulse to suck milk from the mother's body, but later this sucking tendency disappears in the toddler and juvenile stages. The body changes. It is no longer interested in sucking.

In teenaged years, my body expressed an interest in alcohol, I was with friends who had similar interest. After a time there was a disinterest. I focused on spiritual practice. Now my body has no interest in alcohol.

Many people stopped alcohol because of religious stipulations and social disapproval but I stopped because of my body lost interest. The siddha form causes a loss of interest in certain aspects of existence. That is its value.

Students Challenge the Yoga-Guru

For the last week, I worked with Swami Rama on the *agnisara* practice. Some yogis feel that if one completes this practice, one will resist having to take another body whimsically.

This practice concerns the navel and the way one took nutrients from the mother's body while being an embryo. If that system is still in place at the time of death of the physical form, it will act in the subtle body to prompt another rebirth without respect to one's spiritual needs. One will be careless in attraction to the new parents. That will be a setback when one gets the new body.

This morning Swami Rama showed how to complete that practice. He came astrally with two male students. From the appearance of the students' forms, I could tell that they still have physical bodies. The Swami has none at this time.

As he showed a technique, one of the students said this, "You never showed us that. We did not know that you do that. Since when is that part of the practice?"

With a curt smile, he replied, "What do you know about my practice? "

The student said, "But Guruji, we know this is not your practice, because we are with you every day. We never saw you practice this. It is strange that you know this. Why does this yogi do as you instruct?"

The swami replied, "You cannot see everything an accomplished yogi does. You do not know anything about my practice."

The swami showed that if the effort to perceive is totally internalized, the yogi will see in all the parts of his psyche and will, by that, get practices for the purification of the psyche.

"Kundalini, he said, "must be completely curbed"

"Then the yogi can use prana to cleared the subtle body, all parts of it, not just the spine and head. First get rid of the nuisance kundalini. Then use subtle energy to directly cleared the system. Dismiss the kundalini. Take the tasks of purification into your hands."

Kundalini & Diet

If one lives at the residence of an advanced yogi, one is duty bound to eat what is prepared. In other words, one does not have freedom in diet there. This is similar to when one assumes a new body. First of all, I was a vegetarian in many past lives. Still in this life, because of the parents I was fated to accept, I assumed a non-vegetarian diet initially. After some years, I gradually curbed that and resumed the vegetarian preference but not without a struggle because my body was designed with genes which called for a non-vegetarian diet.

People fail to understand that this is the system of how one gets these bodies, since whosoever one's mother will be, will determine what one will eat in the next life. Because you will take nutrients from the mother's blood which courses through the placenta, you will be conditioned to eat in exactly the way she does. If she eats flesh one will be conditioned to that. In her abdomen, one's body will be conditioned to eat what she eats.

We know for sure that the infant, once it is born, may not eat flesh. It will get milk. This milk is only as good as the diet of the mother. If the mother eats fish and beef, the milk was produced from that. The infant is in effect eating fish and beef when suckling the breast

When I was an infant, I stayed with my mother for the first three years. I was very attached to suckling her breast. Even though I was a yogi in the past life, still that instinct for attachment to the mother expressed itself in a forceful way even though I had no intention of being like that. Subsequently my diet in the early part of this body was non-vegetarian.

My yoga practice from previous lives was washed out through attachment to the female who happened to be my mother. We must honesty look at this and assess our lack of power over nature. Once the body becomes adult and one gets on one's own, some egotistic talk begins. The plain truth is that nature has the upper hand and will use it when one gets the next body. Even if it is raw fish, even if it is rotted matter, one will eat whatever the parents consume.

In yoga we must use intelligence and find a way to side step an outright challenge with nature because if we challenge nature, we will be the losers. Why? Because a limited being cannot be God at any stage. It is best to recognize the glory of nature. With nature it is best to stand down.

Instead of trying to establish a diet for oneself. The best thing is to practice breath infusion. The practice will stipulate the diet as one advances. Pranayama yogis have a saying:

Prana will show the way.

It means that if you practice, the purification which you gain will itself cause you to improve diet and other aspects. Instead of calculating what to eat, practice sincerely. Then the diet will be controlled by the increased purity which the psyche develops through a consistent practice.

Sometimes people wonder. "Why is this yogi eating this? Why is this yogi not enjoying food?"

The answer is that from within the yogi is told what to eat by the increased purification in the psyche.

A yogi soon learns to eat to facilitate practice but that only happens to those yogis who invest much practice. Those who play with the practice, who postpone it, do not become controlled by the purity energy in the psyche. They do not become reformed in the eating habits which deter practice.

A yogi eats to facilitate practice, which means that the time of eating must not obstruct the practice. The quantity of eating must facilitate the practice.

The key is not what should I eat and how much but when should I practice and how frequently. If one attends to that one's eating habits will be reformed. The practice itself will bring the diet under control.

When people know that I do not eat anything heavy after say about 3 pm, they sometimes become alarmed and wonder why I am such an extremist. They do not believe that such a restriction has spiritual benefit. But the point is that if I eat after that, the morning session of practice will not be as efficient and during the night my astral awareness will decrease. To facilitate the practice, I cannot eat heavy foods late in the afternoon or at night

If I want to meet yoga gurus in the astral and if I want to be aware of it, I must curb late eating which causes a decrease in subtle perception in the separated astral body during sleeping.

But it is not that I made up these rules. The rule came about from having a consistent morning practice. When I lived in Yogi Bhajan's ashram in Denver around 1973, there was a rule that we had to rise at 4 am, get cleaned and then report for bhastrika breath infusion practice. From then onwards I continued this habit. Over the years my eating habit came under the control of my practice. The practice dictates what, how and when I eat.

It is not the other way around where my eating habits dictate my practice. I practice sincerely. I take the obligation to my yoga gurus for practice seriously. One thing that gets in the way of spiritual practice is not being accountable to anyone and feeling that the yoga guru is just anybody. One gets this idea that one does not have to do what the yoga guru recommends.

Kundalini is affected by what is eaten as well as by the time it is eaten. The student should observe what takes place in the psyche when he/she eats certain foods at certain times. It is adjusted in reference to how it facilitates practice. If some food causes one to be sluggish or causes one to reduce practice, one should shift to a food which encourages practice.

Take an extreme item like alcohol, if that is ingested it has a certain effect on kundalini. If the student notices this and sees that it is undesirable, he should cease the drinking activity. If one does not live in an ashram one is on one's own regarding how one will control diet. If one does not make excuses about this, naturally and gradually one will be inspired from within the psyche to hedge the diet and reduce parts of it which are constrictive of spiritual advancement.

If the yoga guru states that the best time to practice is before sunrise around 4-6 am, obviously if one adjusts his life around that, certain things will change.

Pranotthana Kriya / Swami Rama

Last night in the astral world, I had an encounter with another person from the early part of the life of this body. This is an omen about the upcoming death of this body. This is a signpost which states: "You will soon be evicted from that form. Heed these warnings."

The person I met was an acquaintance from the early stage of this body. That person wanted to review incidences from the past. I avoided that and simply mentioned the subject of our upcoming eviction from old bodies. The person was uncertain about where we would go and whom we would meet. That person said, "Since up to now there was little or no experience of an astral heaven, my assumption is that those regions do not exist. Heaven may be there but we cannot perceive it. What is our situation? We will again come in as babies here or there at random or be wandering ghosts in the astral domains."

Soon after this, it was time to do the before-dawn session of breath infusion. I awakened to do that. On the astral side this person followed me. He did whatever I did. This person was shown these practices by me in 1974, but had left aside the practice. Now he thinks that perhaps the practice should be maintained.

About this time Swami Rama appeared. He was in a happy mood for some reason. He checked on the *agnisara* stomach pump infusion.

This is a practice which a yogi is supposed to master before leaving the body. If this is done successfully the yogi will not have to take a haphazard rebirth. Instead if the yogi must take another body, if fate decrees that as mandatory, he will select the new parents and plan a way to again skip and hop from the usual social life and continue yoga practice in the new body as soon as the body reaches maturity and the parental influence wanes.

As I practiced, Swami Rama looked into my subtle form. He made recommendations. It was like looking into a person's body using X-ray vision where one can see the organs in the body and their operation.

Swami Rama instructed that I should focus on the foot spark practice. This practice entails blasting breath infusion through the center of the leg into the foot. There is a subtle pipe which runs along the leg just as the tibia runs in the center of the physical leg. A yogi, if he reached this pipe should breath-infuse it so that the infused force blows from the knee downward into the foot. When the infused breath reaches the foot, if the yogi can push it out of the tube it will make sparks in the foot.

Agnisara practice is usually described as a navel exercise, consisting of violent rupturing turns of the abdomen, but to complete the practice, one must channel the energy from the navel downwards into the feet, even into the toes.

Kundalini yoga as it is commonly advertised concerns the spinal column, having to do with energy moving up the spine into the brain. When this is achieved the yogi will find that there is an added practice, which is infusing the lower trunk of the body with energizing energy and using the same channels or nadis which kundalini used in the past.

Kundalini is the natural supervisor of energy distribution in the body, both in the physical and astral forms. When a yogi causes kundalini to abandon its creature survival tasks, the yogi must conduct some of these routines directly by infusing breath energy into the various *hard to reach* places. He uses the same nadi channels which were designed and used by kundalini previously.

This practice is termed *pranotthana*.

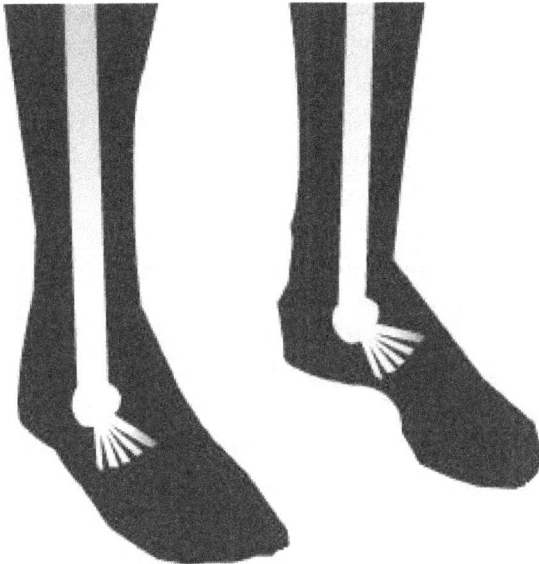

Two Yogis Curse One another

During practice this morning as I did a kriya given by a Buddha deity in South Korea and by Rishi Singh Gherwal. Muktananda came. He showed a small detail which is part of the same kriya. These are *end of life* kriyas used by yogis when they are threatened by providence with death of the body.

If the yogi ran out of time and cannot attain the siddha state before leaving the body, he must set the subtle body in such a way, that he can continue the practice after leaving the physical system. More or less right now that is my condition.

Basically, I went to Guyana around 2003 to do *end of life* austerities, but providence acted in several ways to ruin that plan. Now I roll like a stone which cannot find a place to settle as it moves downhill with a rumbling sound.

The only thing to do now is to be sure that my subtle body is not compelled to take another embryo soon after the death of the physical system. To do this, I must change the direction of the attractive force in the subtle body. Usually this force is attracted to sex facility and to hormonal energy. By that attraction one is again pulled into a mother's uterus soon after losing the physical form.

For some reason, Muktananda came this morning. He said this:

Crush the light! Compress the light there! Do not worry about getting the light to there!"

Soon after within seconds Yogi Bhajan appeared and immediately Muktananda said this, "He said he was a better yogi. He said he was a master of kundalini. Did he ever show a disciple that? He did not know of it."

Yogi Bhajan replied, "What do you know about what I know? Disciples are not shown every last detail. We leave room for others. We are not like you. We do not covet disciples."

After this they left. Regarding if this was a jest or not it, is hard to tell. Sometimes mahayogins go at it. As a disciple I am not concerned. But there may be a serious side to this.

Anyway, here is an elaboration of the instruction from Muktananda.

The infused energy which accumulates in the lower part of the body below the navel, should be crushed or pushed into the lower part of the trunk. It should be compressed there and not be permitted to rise through the spine.

This instruction is against the usual process of raising kundalini. Muktananda told me in a mental message afterwards that this is a secret kriya coming from Chaurangi a great siddha master who is long deceased.

This technique was also known to some Tibetan masters.

Once the yogi infuses the lower trunk and the energy there in the subtle form turns into light energy (light as in sunlight), he should put a downward pressure on that energy to compress it into the lower part of the trunk. As this is done the yogi will notice that the light energy is compressed and the rays of light there get shorter and shorter.

In kundalini practice, usually the effort is to raise the energy through the spine into the brain but Muktananda gave a contrary advice which is to not let the energy go up the spine but to compress it downward, forcing the light to become shorter and shorter and more intense in the lower part of the subtle body.

Muktananda spoke this into my head.

As far as kundalini is concerned getting it into the head is a basic requirement for yogis, but in the advanced stage that is not such an event. Then one should tackle the other parts of the psyche which will if not purified, cause the yogi to take another body haphazardly.

Yogi Bhajan is genuine. His system is valid. He used to criticize me. I took that opportunity to abuse him. It is nothing serious.

What is the *end of life* austerities?

The disciplines are those which would cause kundalini to leave the body through one of the head chakras. Usually kundalini leaves through base, sex or navel chakra. When it does this, the coreSelf follows it to a lower plane in the astral world.

If kundalini is trained to travel into the head before death, and if that is its habit, the yogi would go to a higher plane, avoiding a haphazard rebirth.

One person may sincerely practice pranayama and meditation and still not attain a higher realm hereafter. Whatever the yogi does, it is only good in so far as it was an effective method which upgrades his/her psyche.

A person may spend a lifetime using an inefficient method. He/she may be sincere and still that person may get a low-grade result after death. Sincerity alone is no guarantee. The method of pranayama and meditation must yield elevation, then one can vouch for it.

Kundalini's Base of Dispersal

Kundalini assumed the base chakra as its hometown. It did this soon after the sperm particle became embedded in the mother's egg.

Since it was set up it can change. We know that the placenta anchor is lost to kundalini as soon as the mother's system ceases transfusion of blood to the embryo. This happens during parturition when the fetus is delivered. To replace the mother's nourishment, kundalini switches its anchor to the lungs and to the sucking impulse in the mouth of the infant.

If there is enough infusement kundalini is forced to either rise while remaining at the base, or it may be forced to leave the base temporarily. A person is rated as a siddha when the kundalini becomes completely detached from the base and is resident in the head. Siddha means that the person is no longer in the survival business, because the psychic mechanism which runs that concern no longer operates in the subtle body.

If a yogi reduces the need for physical existence, then when doing breath infusion, kundalini will lose its interest in the survival methods. It will jump to higher chakras where it can find support from the self.

Even though a person taking a physical body, must use a subtle form which has a kundalini, still at the time of fusion into the feelings of the would-be parents, that kundalini changes in configuration to that of a sperm particle. Or stated more precisely, the entire subtle body shrinks to the size and shape of a sperm particle.

In a sense Darwin's idea about a whole line of life forms developing one into the other, occurs for each human embryo. The first form that of the sperm particle acts like a soft bodied aquatic creature. Then gradually it mutates and assumes the format of a mammal.

Kundalini's Route

Initially due to blockage in the subtle sushumna nadi channel which is the spine of the astral body, the kundalini cannot penetrate. But all the same the kundalini is not interested in making that penetration. Its default interest in the head of the subtle body is to get sensual information about what happens outside the body. It uses the faculties in the head, to get information on how best to proceed with its survival-reproduction behaviors. For these purposes it does not need a cleared spinal passage.

For a student, kundalini will rise only when something happens to force it to do so. Its interest in rising occurs in the creature existence mode by sensual excitement and sexual climax of energy. Kundalini rises during sensual excitement and especially during sexual intercourse.

The average young adult living in a modern city, raises kundalini on a daily basis by sexual indulgence. That happens. Kundalini has a passage which it takes from the base chakra to the genitals. Let us review that experience to realize that there is usually flirtation and foreplay before sexual climax. There may also be vision of pornographic scenes.

Someone looked at a video. Suddenly the scenes changed into sex scenes with a man and a man having sexual interplay. Then there was a man and woman doing the same. These sensual events and excitements came into the psyche through the eyes and then reached the emotional energy. This spread through the body. The man experienced sexual arousal. Because he was in a theatre, he could not play it out. He did not have a partner.

Later that day he met a girlfriend. He invited her to his apartment. Because he was stimulated earlier and because kundalini was struck by the sensual energy which came into the eye and spread through the psyche, kundalini encouraged him to crave sexual indulgence. While having sex with his girlfriend, he ejaculated in a rush as kundalini vented its electrical energy through my genitals.

Kundalini has a passage which it used to flow into and through the genitals but he was not aware of that passage until there is the flow of climax of energies. It was so intense that he could not determine where the passage was specifically. He experienced the rush of pleasure which overtook his objectivity.

In what I wrote above, notice that it was not clear to the man where the passage was that kundalini took. For that matter to be honest, he was not sure how kundalini created the intense sexual pleasure. Being merged into the pleasure he lost objectivity.

But he could deduce that kundalini took a certain passage because it did not feel as intense in say his arm or toe as it did in the genital area. Kundalini routes through the same passage during all sex climax experiences.

This means that kundalini bores its way through a blocked passage during the sex climax. Soon after, that passage is sealed. Kundalini gets sluggish because it loses its energy supply. If one attempts sex immediately after climax, it is difficult to engage again, unless one waits a day or two for the hormonal energy to accumulate or unless one takes a drug. In a student yogi, the spinal passage to the head is blocked just as the sexual passage is.

Experience

Physical nature provides the individual limited spirits with a range of experiences. That is the mission of nature according to Patanjali. These processes of enjoyments and the evolutionary challenges are there for the taking, but each comes with a consequence.

The consequence of having an experience is the value of the experience and not the experience itself. Primitive entities, even in modern human beings want the varied experience. They do not understand that the feature value is the consequence. In time they come to see this after repeatedly being stymied by imposed circumstances.

The reason it takes so long to understand this, is the fact that the consequences usually come in another life. In other words, because I cannot link a present fated circumstance to something I did or witnessed in a past life, I cannot reference the memory of other causes in other lives.

One of things I must deal with time and again is rampant ignorance about reincarnation. Arguments arise between me and others merely because I speak of a series of lives and the connecting actions and reactions. Others speak about this life, fitting all actions and reactions which occur within the format of this lifetime. It is actually a hellish thing to be in a world where everyone insists on seeing things fitting into this life alone.

The actions have simple value. The complexity is in the consequences. It is only by the consequences that a limited being can figure this. Since however the consequences may be sealed, packaged in one life and then unsealed and released in another life, the limited entities are at a great disadvantage. They cannot accurately gage an event.

They do however get some immediate satisfaction by their faulty equations which are compressed into this life alone. They are happy with this primitive math. Much of this is discussed in the *Anu Gita Explained*.

Sex experience is just one event. The full exploration is endless because it involves the use of the affection energies which unfortunately can be converted into many different emotions. If one converts that over and over into different kinds of relationships, there will come a time when one will lose track of morality and will not know what is serviceable in the long term.

But right and wrong has to do with the social environment and how nature reacts to various relationships. Wanting to have endless happiness, one chases after some type of pleasure which would be continuous but again and again, we see that nature frustrates that endeavor. In any case it depends on the type of life form one has. Assuming that I found a way to have continuous sexual pleasure, what will happen when the body dies.

This morning this matter was discussed by Rishi Singh Gherwal in the astral world. It was some of his disciples and myself. He blamed sexual pleasure as the main cause of student yogis getting stalled in kriya yoga practice.

Exploitation of the sexual energy will be a problem when its consequence comes in the form of resentments from disembodied ancestors who require bodies and who are deprived of such bodies by a contraception.

One must deal with the reactions which nature dished out because of feeling offended by one's decision to side step raising progeny. Even if God goes away and never comes back, still nature is there with its reactionary behavior which a limited being cannot adjust for his or her convenience.

Some effort must be made to study how kundalini operates through the sexual facilities. Those who are involved in sexual indulgence should make efforts to objectively get some understanding during the sexual acts. Those who are not involved in sex, but who were previously in this life, should reach back in memory and study the situation in retrospect.

Swami Rama and the Yogini

I repeatedly ask students to keep a journal of events having to do with meditation and astral projection. Even if I do not keep a journal, my practice and particularly my integration of progress may suffer. This means that if I cannot integrate my daily progress, my faith in practice deteriorates with a result that my practice slows because I cannot estimate how advanced I am. This leads to discouragement which terminates practice.

For those who do no astral projection, who have poor dream recall, a dream journal is vital for keeping track of dream activities, even if one is not in habit of recalling what happened while the physical system sleeps.

During this morning practice, I did not have a pen and note pad. As a result, some of what happened was forgotten. This hampers my ability to file a report. I do recall however that when I sat to meditate certain things happened which caused me to consider that students can learn much about the kundalini's alliance with other parts of the psyche.

During practice I saw two people in particular, one was Swami Rama. The other was a disciple of his who is now departed, a yogini. Swami explained that even though morality is important if one gets a chip on the shoulder about it, one will fail in practice. He made some remarks for the benefit of the yogini who was with him. She is deceased. She left her last body without sufficiently completing yoga austerities. She was a bit arrogant about her religious morality which was based on religious training during her infancy.

Swami said this:

In the West there is morality but it is differently based than in India. In India, we have morality, a very variable one at that. But it is based on what Krishna decreed or on what an ancient sage like Manu decreed. Krishna gave standards and wanted humanity to comply with his view of morality. If he is a Hindu, a yogi follows morality on that basis. If one is intellectual one may comply with what Buddha advised as the eightfold noble path. This is designed to ease the impediments which will come in the next life and impediments which come in this life from the past lives.

It is not a feather in the cap of the yogi. It is not to be used for self-righteous purposes. If one studies Bhagavad Gita, one will read how Krishna tore apart Arjuna's moral arguments in Chapter One. Why did Krishna do that? After all, Arjuna was trained in a cultured family? Arjuna was honorable. He was compassionate. He cited religious injunctions. Still, Krishna rejected Arjuna's ideas about morality.

Arjuna was self-righteous in Chapter One of the Bhagavad Gita. Krishna did not like it.

Be moral but do not let it be a feather in your cap or a chip on your shoulder. The Supreme Being wants a moral lifestyle. That is all you need to know. It is not your thing. It is his system. You comply with it. That is that. Do not try to be a moralist like Arjuna in Chapter One, because you must be insightful to know what is right or wrong in each circumstance. It varies from time to time. Consultation with the Supreme Being is essential. If left to yourself, to your judgment, miscalculations will be made because one may not be detached and may be unable to tune into the Supreme Person.

There is no system of yoga in the Western way. The Western way is designed for orderly materialistic existence without effort for spiritual upliftment as described for yogis.

The Western system of moral values are the ultimate Christian process, the so called ten commandments and the amendments and additions which Jesus put to that.

In the system of yoga, those moral standards are seen to have value in reference to this physical world but they do not necessarily apply in other dimensions. The other thing is that just as in the case of courts, the judge may change the application of a law, in morality the application varies and the past life should be considered which is impossible if one does not have mystic perception.

Therefore, the moral way used by the Western system is full of errors. That does not mean that we can live without that imperfect legal system. Despite its imperfections it is serviceable and useful. But for yogis, it is relative because a yogi has to consider what happens in other dimensions. He is aware that one cannot see all angles unless one has access to information about the past lives of the individual concerned.

Help from Muktananda

Taking help from more advanced entities, being open to their influence and ideas, knowing well that they have nothing to gain from a beginner but have much to give, serves the purpose of attaining liberation from the massive ignorance which happens to be our present existential condition.

To make advancement a person must exert himself. Unless one is willing to walk away from this social situation and get totally involved in self-reform and self-upliftment, even the Supreme Being cannot do a thing to help one but all the same if one makes the maximum effort and exerts the self to the fullest to side-step lower consciousness, one will not be successful without taking help.

Patanjali made it clear that there has to be a reliance on the Supreme Person who was the one who helped the ancient yogis, people whose attainment are legendary if we read of their existential conditions in the Puranas and elsewhere.

When giving lectures about the life of Gautama Buddha, some people stress how he rejected the teachers whom he first took when he entered into renunciation of social life. They fail to establish, that he took help from those teachers and got to a certain point. Initially he was not versed in any austerity of yoga, but from each of these teachers he learnt methods. After passing through their process and getting from it what he could, he went further. This does not mean that he took no assistance or that those teachers were useless. One must take help from teachers even if the instructors do not have the final process and even if at a certain point one must be a pioneer.

Patanjali said that there is a Supreme Person who taught the ancient yogis. They took help from someone. It is either that a particular yogi is the Supreme Being Himself or is one of the Supreme Person's parallel divinities or that yogi will have to take help from the Supreme Being either directly or indirectly, knowingly or unknowingly.

Consciousness is vast. It is outside the purview of the limited selves even when such a self attains an enlightened state which to him is everything. Thus, there is no question of doing it all by oneself.

This morning while doing exercises, at the very end of the session, near the last infusement, I saw Muktananda, a noted modern siddha who is now departed. He smiled and then sent some energy from his subtle form into mine. When I looked at it, it was an expression of some mystic processes which he perfected while he did austerities before he became a famous guru in the West.

It is possible for a yogi to send an energy into another person's psyche as a contribution to that person's spiritual progress. Sometimes such energies do not stay with the student, because he may not be proficient enough to retain the energy. Donations from great yogis are a god-sent in some situations when a yogi hustles to make progress but does not have enough forcefulness.

The energy from the Swami mixed with another energy which was in my psyche which was put in there by a Buddha deity. It concerned having the ability to infuse the subtle body even if the kundalini is dissipated out of it.

The passage of sushumna nadi spinal tube remains in the subtle system even if kundalini is dissipated. That passage is used to infuse energy into the subtle body directly with energizing force without even the kundalini charge.

If for instance a surgeon removes a man's physical heart, the physician may install an electrical pump to continue the function of plasma distribution. If the yogi is successful at wiping out the supremacy of kundalini, he must infuse the system with subtle energy and he can use the same routing or conduits which were used by kundalini.

Entities in the Subtle Body

Subtle perception gives one the ability to know when one is motivated by other entities, regardless of who those entities may be. Possession by other spirits is regarded as something negative for the most part. The situation is however that influences prevail regardless.

Escaping into a homogenous consciousness where you cannot tell where you begin and where the next guy ends, does not free anyone from such possession, even though it does free one from the sense of insecurity one may have if one senses that one is under an influence.

One molecule of water, on the bottom of the ocean is under the pressure of several hundred feet of water and is still in a confinement in an oceanic valley or plane. That is true even if that molecule has no way for accounting its time and place.

Yesterday a man called. He had domestic issues. Later during the night, I was confronted by that individual and other members of his household. Then suddenly the man jumped into my psyche and so did his spouse.

This is reminiscent of when one is in an infant body. It grows and reaches sexual maturity. At that time many entities who are ancestors or friends of ancestors may jump into one's subtle body, fuse into it on the subtle plane, and then become humbug sexual energies, which cause one to be crazed for sexual indulgence in order to generate embryos for the said entities.

During exercises this morning, those two persons were still in the subtle body. I noticed them superimposed in the body but then there was a flash of light and the Buddha deity from South Korea, said that I should do the infusion of energy into the subtle body and pretend that they were not there. He added this:

"For the deities, hundreds, thousands, millions of other entities are in their forms. This is normal. Give it no thought. Finish the session and meditate."

Kundalini Throws the Yogi to the Ground

It happens during breath infusion practice, that sometimes the yogi is thrown to the ground by kundalini. This way of looking at the fall of the body during infusion practice, is the traditional way of regarding it. Actually, when I say that the yogi is thrown to the ground, I mean that the physical body is forcibly abandoned by the -focus of the yogi.

As soon as that occurs, the physical body falls to the ground because the coreSelf is no longer in charge of it and cannot supervise it. The core loses its directive grip on the physical body.

In the subtle body something else occurs, which is that the coreSelf may or may not lose its conscious grip on that form. If it does not the yogi comes back to physical awareness with some information about what occurred, about what dimensional switch happened.

When it is broken down to what happened to the components of consciousness, as to what kundalini did to what other component, and as to what happened to the coreSelf's objective grasp on consciousness, it is an entirely different story. Here one enters no-man's land, a vague territory, a place which people usually call mergence or oneness, a place where people usually lose the sense of distinction, where they have memories of absoluteness, oneness or nothingness.

Some students questioned about the circumstances which occur when kundalini strikes and the physical body falls to the ground, with the yogi losing awareness and just finding the self to be in the body with consciousness, finding the body in a fallen position, sometimes with a slight headache, sometimes with spaced-out awareness.

This morning when after practice, I walked away with my yoga mat, to go indoors to meditate, suddenly I noticed that kundalini made a move and ascended the spine. It reached the neck and was to flare like a detonated nuclear bomb. Instinctively due to years of practice, I dropped the physical body so that the knees were on the ground, I applied locks. Then kundalini behaved itself and distributed its power evenly through the top part of the trunk, through the neck and through the head, especially to the back of the head.

Why did kundalini rise as soon as I stood up with the rug? I did the exercises. Kundalini rose more than once during the session. I used a Tibetan mantra when thoughts came to distract from the required focus. Everything went well. I picked up a cell phone which was on the ground. I folded the mat. I got up with it and walked away. After three steps suddenly I saw kundalini ascending. What did I see? I looked into the spine as I walked away physically. I saw a light-yellow mist moving up. I recognized it as kundalini and before I knew it, it moved from the base area to the heart chakra area. Then I knew that kundalini would penetrate the head. I dropped to the ground on my knees and applied some locks. Kundalini fizzed out slowly. It was unhappy because I was attentive.

I practiced this kundalini yoga since around 1971. By now kundalini should not catch me off guard. This is what happened:

Apparently, kundalini's accumulation of energy below the *small of the back,* below the navel spinal chakra, was not completely released during the session. Kundalini hesitated there. When I stooped to get the rug, kundalini was compressed more. When I straightened the spine to walk away, kundalini pushed itself passed the check valve which is behind the navel in sushumna nadi spinal passage, which is at the *small of the back.* It was determined to get into the head to hit the intellect. Due to vigilance I compressed it before it could carry out this plan.

During sexual climax, kundalini becomes so powerful, so attractive, that the intellect moves from its default position in the head all the way down to the pleasure center of the genitals. But in kundalini yoga practice, the opposite occurs where kundalini has a strong charge and it moves to the default position of the intellect.

Stated in ordinary language that would read like this:

During sex, the location where thoughts occur in the head, moves to the location where sex pleasure occurs in the public area. During rising of kundalini during breath infusion, sex pleasure location moves to the base of the spine which in turn moves with that pleasure force to the location where thoughts occurs in the subtle head.

To a normal person from just the external situation of the body, the kundalini experienced would appear to be a form of fainting. From a psychic view there is a vast difference.

In the case of kundalini rising suddenly due to breath infusion or due to bending and doing a certain posture which caused kundalini to surge into the brain in an unregulated way, the intellect would be knocked out of commission for a time, until moments or minutes after, when the power was reduced to what the intellect could handle. Then the person would be self-aware again in the physical body.

Buddha's Kriya: Ripping Away the Attention

During exercises this morning there was a flash of a location in South Korea, where earlier this year (2012), I visited three Buddha deities. After the flash there was a live connection to three deities; one being Gautama Buddha, the other being *Bhaishavya* Buddha and the other being *Amitabha* Buddha. I greeted them with the respects due to deities and spiritual masters.

I wanted to thank *Amitabha* for assistance rendered with the translation and commentary of the *Anu Gita* book. Amitabha assisted with getting the right English words to express what was written in the Sanskrit.

After these greetings which occurred simultaneously as I did breath infusion in various postures at a place in northern Alabama, Gautama Buddha said he wanted to say something about using mantras during postures and pranayama practice. The use of mantras then is different to its use during meditation practice. This was his instruction:

A yogi whose mind is obedient, whose mind is clean, whose mind does not generate thoughts, images and ideas, should not use a mantra. There is no need for it then. If during postures and breath infusement, the yogi finds that thoughts keep arising and that some attention is forcibly going to such thoughts and images, a mantra can be used.

Which mantra should it be?

The yogi should get a mantra from a senior yogi, who has used a particular mantra, and had success with it and knows when to release the self from such use of the mantra. In India, the most popular mantra used is:

Om namo Shivaya.

In Tibet it is:

Om mani padme hum.

Om *is standard as the introductory sound and is also the concluding sound as* hum *in the Tibetan* bija *mantra.*

In my time some yogis used Om *alone, which was chanted for hours during practice. Hopefully a student can get a mantra which was used by an advanced teacher to completion, so that the process was tested and proven in the progress of that teacher.*

When doing the asana postures and breath infusion, if the attention is diverted to a thought, and if the attention was hijacked by the intellect, one should confiscate it from the intellect and put it on the required focus. If one finds that when one does this the intellect again confiscates the attention in turn and takes the attention back to the thoughts and images, one should take help from a mantra. With the mantra being repeated mentally (ajapa not japa) one will have the force to cause the attention to be released from the intellect so that the attention can be on the required focus.

What is the focus?

If you do a posture to infuse breath energy into the knee for instance, that area of the subtle body is the focus. The attention should be there. It should not at that time be in the head with thoughts or images or ideas. Even if only a small part of it is with the thoughts, that is a diversion. A mantra may be used as a last resort if one finds that one does not have the power to capture the attention energy.

This is called ripping away the attention from the intellect. In time it will cause the yogi to have full success in the process of segregating the attention force from the intellect which usually commands that force and forces the self to permit the display of many ideas, images and thoughts.

Kundalini Experience

This morning during seated breathing exercises, kundalini flooded the entire body. It was felt as infusion or as a filling up. I perceived a bright white energy. The subtle body was lifted as if floating. For a split second I saw the subtle body in a seated meditation posture (as the physical one was), in the form of bright white light. This seated form was situated within a surrounding bright white light energy. It was light within light, the infused subtle body encapsulate within a circle of light. I remained seated as the energy dissipated.

Several days ago, during seated breathing exercises, I had an experience, also in which kundalini operated from the base chakra and propelled the subtle body upwards. I can only give a comparison and say that this experience is like being lifted, propelled upwards as when a rocket lifts off, vertically into space. I felt the propulsive energy, moving in waves like an upward current, beneath the subtle body, pushing it upwards.

Kundalini rose in a way in which there is a complete infusion of the subtle body and not just a part of it, or if it is a full infusion of the head of the subtle body even without any other part of that body.

One should note these dimensions, just as one would notice an important building in a faraway city during a visit as a tourist. If one reads Patanjali there is a part where he discusses various *samadhis*. If one reads that over and over one will get some idea of the locations one may reach. Then one can identify where one is in the realms of the levels of consciousness, just as a tourist can identify what is seen in some faraway place, from reading a guide book of a former traveler.

The value of these tours is this:

One gets some idea of other dimensions. One begins to have more confidence in people like Patanjali and Krishna regarding what those persons described, rather than being cynical with them or doubtful and challenging. If one reads a guide book which was written by a fiction writer, if one is informed that the person made it up, one may lose confidence in all guide books. But if one has a guide book by a reliable source, one may feel confident enough to go on a tour on the basis of that person's descriptions.

It is important to observe that even though one may reach higher places, spiritual bliss levels of existence, one is not allowed to stay there.

Muktananda's Posture for the Elderly

During practice this morning, Muktananda showed a posture which I did for five days. My assumption is that it was a posture he discovered. He did this posture before on another level in the astral world but the memory of his teaching it disappeared when I left that level. In cases like this, it seems to the student that he discovered a posture, while in fact, it was shown on a level of consciousness when he was not objective enough to realize he was inspired.

This is similar to when one is an infant and one is shown something repeatedly by a parent. One develops in the body with that skill and one does not realize that the parent spent much time training one.

It is a simply non-strenuous posture. One does not have to be a contortionist to do it. Muktananda said this relates to the posture which I show below in a few photos:

There are postures which I did when I focused primarily on breath infusion. In these postures one does not stress the complicated yoga poses. One focuses on the infusement. It works better if one mastered the postures, but one can do these even without the skill of postures. Elderly people can do some of this and get help with their introspection even if their limbs have rheumatoid arthritis.

When this posture is done, the first thing is to force the air down to the bottom of the spine. When one infused sufficient energy there, the energy spreads out into other parts of the trunk, into the groin and thighs. When that is infused sufficiently, the energy rises through the trunk into the neck. It enters the brain, particularly the bottom back of the brain.

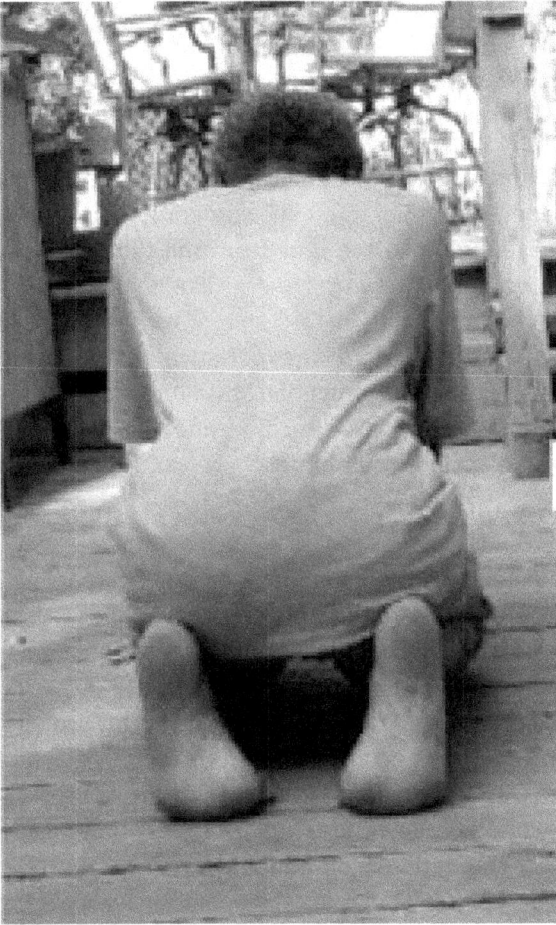

Kundalini Splits the Head

Email correspondence:

I had an interesting third eye experience.

I chanted and walked. Suddenly from the bottom my whole spine rumbled. This energy shot up. It felt like someone touched my forehead. The next sensation I felt was like the skull from the third eye to the back of my head ripped in two. What I saw was energy like heat waves bouncing around the room.

Two weeks later I had a similar experience except that it shot to top of head during kirtan. The top of my head spun intensely and then exploded. I saw the whole room get brighter in color, and everyone was ecstatic. Time was gone. I felt like a water fountain.

MiBeloved's Response:

This is an experience of kundalini rising and overcoming both the brow chakras and the brahmrandra top of head chakra.

These experiences are subjective but they give the person some idea of the kundalini and its effects in the subtle body.

In these experiences even though the subtle body remains fused into the physical one, the person becomes about 90% or more aware of the subtle body and 10% or less aware of the physical system.

This type of experience if studied in meditation will lead to an understanding of the various components of consciousness and how they interact.

Where is the coreSelf while this happened? The yogi should research that in trance states.

Head in this case refers to the subtle head but, in some experiences, the physical head may mimic the actions of the subtle one. The person in the experience will lose contact with the physical head and may not know if the physical head was involved until after the experience or until others who were present, describe what happened physically.

Usually these experiences happen when one uses mind-altering drugs, and also when there is a *flash back* effect from an earlier use of the drugs. In the Sufi tradition, this experience occurs when the person listened or danced to music. In the dervish tradition, this is a normal experience of transcendence.

In kriya yoga the outlook on such an experience, is that it is a *samadhi*. If one checks Yoga Sutras, one will find descriptions of the various *samadhis*. One can check through the descriptions to see if an experience is mentioned.

According to a person's nature, the kundalini can rise suddenly when the person is in certain environments or exposed to certain sensual conditions.

For the purpose of identifying the various levels of existence and their related advantages and disadvantages, all such states should be meticulously studied in introspection by the yogi.

Muktananda's Practice

This morning, exercises had a few incidences. First a deceased lady came. She was serious about the exercises and had the intellectual acumen to integrate yoga philosophy. She said that Rishi Singh Gherwal and some others spoke to her and instructed her in the duties involved in doing yoga. They permitted her to come and practice. A second lady was told only to learn from this first lady. A third was instructed not to come for lessons even though she could learn from other teachers. This last person was deceased over thirty years ago from a body over eighty years of age. By doing breath infusion in the astral world, her astral body which looked like the eighty years old form changed into one which was about eighteen years of age. This person was impressed with yoga but had the idea that it produces beauty and youthfulness.

During the session, Rishi Singh did not appear but I saw a few dakini angelic woman instructing the lady who was the most advanced of the three deceased persons.

Half way through the exercises, when I did a side stretch, kundalini rose on one side of the body. It went into the right eyeball and was like several micro crystals of bliss energy packed tightly in a little ball. When I stretched to the left side, kundalini rose but with less impetus.

Soon after that as I infused the subtle body, Muktananda appeared. He was glad that I advanced since I last saw him which was over one year ago. He showed inner locks but he did not mention a procedure.

He said this:

When as a youth I practiced pranayama intensively, sometimes I would do breath exercises for two hours per day. Once it increased to four hours a day.

At the time in India, some yogis did this. I learnt the technique. This practice culminated in direct perception into the chit akasha, the spiritual world.

The key to advancement is to never give up. Seek more advanced means of progression. However, there is a retardative energy which may affect a not so advanced yogi. That negative energy will keep the person down so that there is no experience of real transcendence.

The old man, our father, Nityananda Baba, assisted me considerably. He infused grace energies into my psyche but that was not all. I worked aggressively for years before he assisted me.

The neophytes are bogged by a negative energy which stipulates in their minds that they should do less yoga and that they can meditate without postures and breath infusion. This is just like when you use a jeep on a country road. If the weather is right, if it is dry, you will coast along as desired, but in the rainy season the vehicle will be stalled. I state this to bring to fore, that the yogi's endeavors alone cannot take the yogi to full success. The yogi is comparable to the jeep, the psychic environment in the mind is comparable to the road. If the road is muddy, even a new jeep that is built for the terrain will be stalled. There are external and internal forces which impede the yogi. The sooner that is realized the better it will be.

Muktananda showed some locks which are in the trunk of the body. These control the various hanging tissues which are attached to the organs in the body. These are applied when one's practice is advanced.

Yoga Guru is Annoyed

During exercises this morning, Rishi Singh Gherwal appeared on the astral side. He was annoyed because some persons came to learn the exercises. In the yoga system one is not supposed to accept students without the permission of the teacher.

In any case, these were people whom I knew from over thirty years ago. They are deceased. They found me in the astral and wanted to tone their astral forms. I did not instruct them but their subtle bodies did whatever postures and breath infusion I did. Because of getting rapid results in their subtle forms, they were encouraged. These were three women who were the age of my mother when they used physical bodies years ago.

In any case, Rishi Singh was annoyed. He said this, "What student has students?"

He waved his hands. Some dakinis, about three of them came and escorted those deceased ladies away.

Dakinis are angelic female beings who reside permanently in the astral world. They have exquisite forms but they usually associate with the siddhas.

After this I completed the exercises but I knew that Rishi was annoyed. I did not seek these persons. They found me because another person found me on the Internet. They were alerted in the astral world.

Rishi came back after a while and checked my practice. By that time, the infused energy was in the trunk and neck. He made this cutting remark, "Yoga means brahmachari. Without that everything is done. Finished! Why do you not understand this?"

Anyway, this is how these matters go with a yoga guru. Sometimes when I instruct students, they fail to understand that I have rules to follow. They feel that I impose my discipline on them. In yoga it is not like that. For success a certain austerity and isolation are required, otherwise there will be no success for the student even after years of practice.

Yogi Reaching Siddha Level

Rishi Singh Gherwal requested that I explain that the attainment of a siddha body has to do with the subjugation of kundalini. He said that no matter what the yogi attains, if kundalini is not subjugated, the siddha status is not realized and the yogi will be conveyed to whatever level of existence kundalini is compatible with. This holds true regardless of the philosophical and/or religious beliefs.

Rishi said this:

Consider that even a great professor at a university must stoop to pass stools. Even the Queen or King of England must pass urine. Even the President of the most developed country has the sex urge. Even the Pope becomes infirm in body. Even a Swami from India, must evacuate foul matter from the body.

In the world hereafter, one will have a certain type of subtle body which will manifest on a certain astral level of existence, and will function in a certain way, no matter if one professes a belief in Krishna, Rama, Jesus or whosoever is one's cherished deity, and even if one does not think there is an individual Supreme Being as Krishna professes, and one thinks that there is One Supreme Primal Energy without a supreme individual.

If one can use the physical body to bring the subtle body to a higher plane, that physical form was effectively used, not otherwise. Anyone can imagine anything and have the loftiest aspirations, but that does not mean that the subtle body was effectively curbed from lower habits. That does not guarantee that the person will not be forced to go wherever that subtle body will go in the astral world hereafter.

Kundalini yoga begins with the effort to raise up the kundalini. That entails leading the hormone energy in the body away from the sexual facilities. So long as there is a route for the hormone energies to go in the direction of the sexual facilities, kundalini will service the sex impulse and will not rise into the head.

Once the student habitually gets kundalini to go into the head, once that becomes the habit as compared to having the kundalini go to the genitals for sexual pleasure, the yogi should divest kundalini energy to every part of the body, especially in every part below the neck, even into the fingers and toes. Once this is achieved the neck should be flushed completely. Initially working on the neck means only working on sushumna passage in the central spine. Later for full subjugation of kundalini, one should flush the entire neck. When this is done the yoga siddha body becomes a reality for the yogi.

What does this mean in real terms? This makes for an astral accomplishment where the yogi can go higher than the swargaloka heavens to one of the advanced places which are listed as *janaloka, tapoloka, brahmaloka (satyaloka)*. In those places the astral body does not have the lower urges. It does not lead back to the realm of physical existence but those in the Swarga places and lower, lead back to physical existence, just as a great person with a physical body must to use a urinal.

Spiritual Cosmology

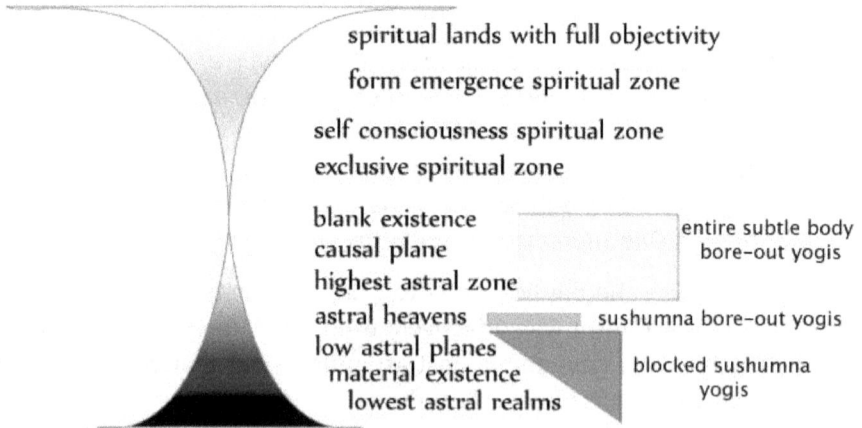

spiritual lands with full objectivity

form emergence spiritual zone

self consciousness spiritual zone
exclusive spiritual zone

blank existence
causal plane
highest astral zone
astral heavens
low astral planes
material existence
lowest astral realms

entire subtle body
bore-out yogis

sushumna bore-out yogis

blocked sushumna
yogis

Kundalini Failed

This morning during practice, I looked at how kundalini sets itself up as an embryo. I did this indirectly by seeing how kundalini made that effort during the past week to reestablish its base chakra to base area configuration in the subtle body.

It hung below the navel chakra in a grey configuration like a grey popsicle. It had only one intention which was to attach itself to the base area where the base chakra is usually attached.

I decided to track how kundalini gets the power to do this, and also what urge drives kundalini for this. I noticed a pushing force which came from one of my relatives, whom I saw recently. It appears that the adhesive force within the person's kundalini influenced my kundalini to reformulate itself and to reverse what I achieved in terms of pulling kundalini up and away from the base area.

The conclusion is that just by associating with a person whose kundalini functions in the normal materialistic way, a yogi may develop a reverse influence in kundalini which would cause it to reassert its need for physical forms. This may cause the yogi to slide downward in the mundane evolutionary cycle

Many yoga gurus from India, alerted us with the terms sadhu sanga, which is to say, "Remain in the influence of the great souls (sadhus). Be distant from others."

Kundalini Withdrawal Kriya: Rishi Singh Gherwal

This morning, Rishi Singh was there during practice. He supervised the full destruction of a stub kundalini which may hang from the subtle head into the neck of the subtle body. He did not explain much or say why he was there. My assumption was that he wanted to explain a procedure on how to deal with kundalini when it is pulled through the spine into the head.

My view is that this information is not written in plain terms even in yoga books like *Hatha Yoga Pradipika*. Rishi wants me to leave a record, for the use of others who grope in the dark in terms of what to do to retract kundalini. Usually yogis do not write or even discuss these matters except with very advanced adepts.

When kundalini withdraws from the base place, not the base chakra, the location where the base chakra adheres, it assumes a white-hot color and a diamond configuration dangling down in the center of the subtle spine. If the yogi is successful in causing kundalini to retract from the base location, then when breath infusion is done, kundalini will retreat further and further up the spine. This is provided that the yogi can infuse the bottom of the trunk and the thighs with energizing energy.

The more the trunk of the body is infused with specific areas of it being targeted, the more the kundalini will be unable to reattach to that base location. This is good and well for the yogi. This releases the psyche from the dictatorial control which kundalini held over it previously. This is total success, instead of the head success with doing trance states in the head, while kundalini continues ruling the rest of the psyche and the rest of one's activities.

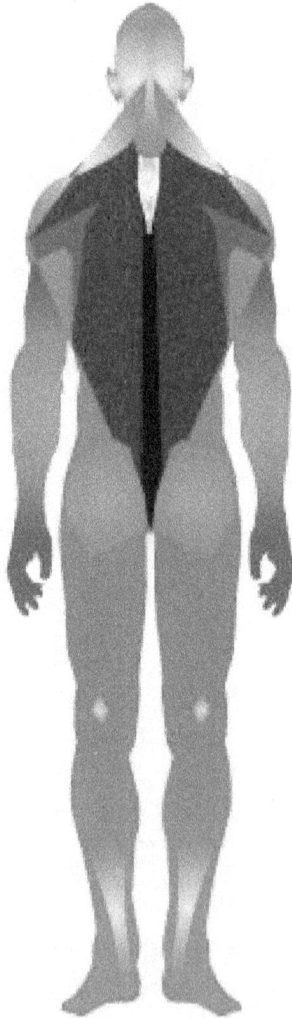

When kundalini is retracted into the neck, it loses the diamond configuration. It hangs down under the brain like a white popsicle, glowing with a white color.

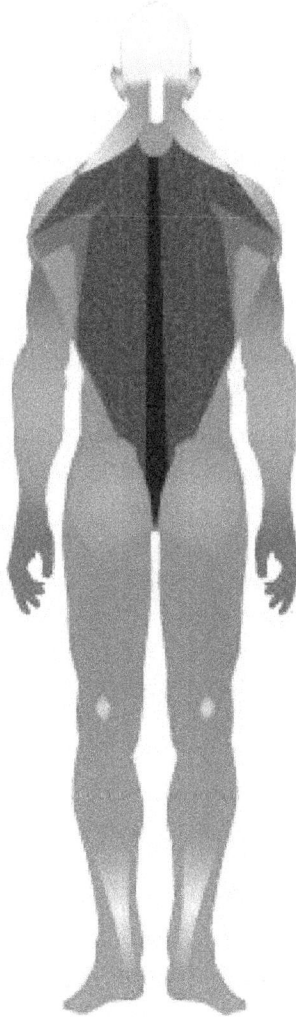

At this stage the yogi should make a deliberate effort to hold to naad, to situate the coreSelf in naad. He should do the kundalini retraction procedure, which consist of retracting the sensual energies of the kundalini into the sense of identity which surrounds the coreSelf.

Even though kundalini will be dangling like a white popsicle hanging below the brain, when the yogi tries to do the retraction practice, that white popsicle shape will seem to disappear. This happens because when the coreSelf is in naad and pulls in the kundalini sensual energies, there is only perception of these energies coming into the sense of identity. The yogi loses the vision of the kundalini hanging.

Rishi said that this is the second major pratyahar sensual energy withdrawal practice. The first one is done in reference to the sensual energy which flows through the frontal part of the head. Most yogis think that this first one is the full pratyahar practice but it is not.

The frontal sensual energies are under the control of the intellect. This is related to kundalini but it is not the kundalini's personal sensual force. The second method for retraction is for pulling in the energies which kundalini uses to run its creature-survival operations.

Kundalini Reduction and Absorption

During practice this morning Yogi Bhajan showed a kriya for kundalini reduction and then total absorption into the mind chamber which is the head of the subtle body. This process begins with the kriya which a Buddha deity in South Korea imparted to me, which is the attack of the base area to which kundalini attached itself. This is not an attack of the kundalini base chakra but the place where the base chakra attached.

There is the base chakra. There is the place where the base is attached. This is similar to a lamprey fish, which attaches itself to a rock or even to a living creature or it is like how a leech attaches itself to the body of another living creature. There are two ways to get the leech to move, which are to do something to the leech which causes it to release itself or to do something to the location where it is attached which will cause the leech to become separated from that place.

The Buddha deity's idea is for an all-out attack on the location where the base chakra is attached. This is a breath infusion attack that is so furious, so energy-forceful, that astrally the location itself becomes obliterated or vaporized. Hence kundalini is left with nothing to attach itself to and it is subdued.

It is well known that Gautama Buddha practiced yoga in India from several austere yogis in the forest in northern India. After following at least two sincere teachers, he did not achieve liberation because their methods were not penetrating enough to yield that. Thus, he practiced by himself. He meditated on his own. He did severe austerities, like living on air alone without taking food or water. Still doing all that, he could not shed physical nature. It kept clinging to his coreSelf no matter what he did. At last he shifted his attention away from reacting to matter and focused without a bias for a permanence-reality. These practices of Buddha are secret for the most part. Many monks are still at a loss to know exactly what he did.

In any case one of the kriyas which he discovered is that to deal with kundalini, if one attacks its anchor point, one can subdue it in a much quicker way than if one attacks the kundalini itself.

If one practiced sufficiently the breath infusion practice, then if one attacks the area just below the base chakra and forgets about attacking the base or even the kundalini as a whole, one will get rapid results.

First of all, one will not be able to find the base if one did not practice sufficiently. This method will not work for those yogis who began the practice recently or who have not done enough breath infusion beforehand.

What happens is this:

When one first attacks the area below the base one will find a brown-black cloudy area of mist subtle energy. This will feel like a round shaped stone, like large river stones. Above that will be the base chakra. One should ignore it. One should do the breath infusion driving the air mentally into the area below the chakra. At first nothing will happen. This may occur for days or weeks of practice. After a time, there will be a white fire energy which will surround that area. After a time, the area itself, the mist cloud, will all of a sudden ignite and burn.

At this point there may be a flash at the place. One may feel compelled to shift the focus on the base chakra. One should ignore this compulsion. As one keeps trying day after day, eventually the cloud of energy will self-consume and be no more. There will be a black space at the location. Even the base chakra will not be there but if one looks up the spine, one will see a white energy like white-hot metal.

When this first happens, one should not be over-confident. Kundalini will resume its usual configuration. The base area below the base chakra will resume Its dark cloud presence.

One should keep working at it day after day, until the cloud no longer appears. When this happens, one will find that there is no base chakra and there is no second chakra but there is a diamond shape bottom to the kundalini which hangs in the center of the spine above where the second chakra was located.

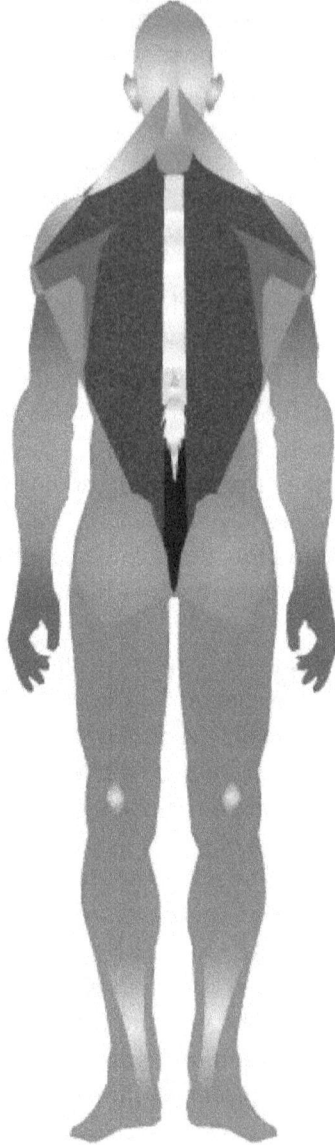

Yogi Bhajan said that one should keep infusing breath energy into that diamond until it retreats into the mind which is the head of the subtle body. That, believe it or not, is the end of kundalini for the time being. Kundalini can reestablish itself if the yogi is not careful or if the yogi is compelled against his wish to become socially involved with persons who are not siddhas.

The physical body is a pre-set time bomb which is set detonate a certain time. It will go on existing and doing what it is destined to do, even for a yogi. So long as he is in a certain environment, his karmic repercussions from past lives will find the body and deal with it accordingly. Adjusting kundalini will not stop the reactions from coming to the body.

The body is the property of physical nature. It will continue under that influence.

The destruction of kundalini does not affect the layout of time which is already coming and which is laid before us like asphalt on a superhighway.

The yogi notices a change in his perception in that it gives him more psychic insight in what nature does. But it is a mistake to think that because I know of a future event, I can change it. Nature may not accept interference.

A yogi who destroyed the base of kundalini, still has to function under time's demands. His way out is to remove his presence from certain levels of existence.

Suppose I get an idea that I will go somewhere different in order to avoid the time layout which is before me. What do you think time will do? It will not release me from everything. It will only release me from its constraints in this dimension. As soon as I arrive in another place, it will immediately assert itself and subject me to its history.

Liberation works fully if the yogi gets out of the physical energy in full. That means out of it completely, even out of its psychic reach. There is no way to escape completely from it so long as one's existence has a register in any of its gross or subtle domains. But the yogi does have the advantage of psychic insight into what kundalini does and to some extent into why it acts in specific ways. Liberated or not, it has a tag on everyone.

The only persons who will notice an advanced yogi is another such yogi. Using psychic perception these persons will notice the difference. Others will see no difference because their perception cannot acknowledge things which are psychic. There is no physical change in a yogi because of this. In fact, a yogi who is really advanced may take steps not to be discovered because discovery is costly.

If someone knows that one can read past lives or see other psychic things, others will ask about that and want the yogi to use those abilities whimsically. That will hurt the yogi. One sure sign of a foolish yogi is that he/she makes the self available for whimsical request and also for making money peddling psychic ability and the occult.

If one understands that nature does not tolerate interference in its affairs, one will not exhibit anything paranormal which would affect what nature does.

The result of this in a yogi's life is that he/she becomes more efficient in reimbursing debts incurred in physical nature. This is how a yogi reinvests his increased psychic perception into the practice and makes exponential advancement.

Yogeshwarananda gave a rule, where whosoever accepts him as a teacher should reinvest in the progress and not exhibit supernormal powers.

There should be no interference in nature's business, and prompt payment for any debts one incurred in the present or previous lives.

Sexual Adjustments of Breath Infusion

Someone inquired yesterday about the effects on the sexual energy when doing breath infusion which raises kundalini. See these diagrams.

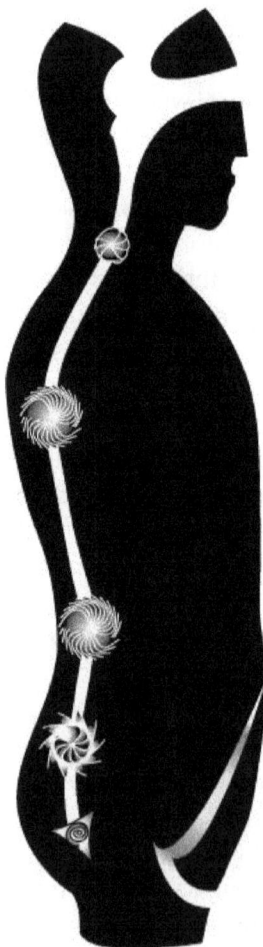

normal
sex hormone configuration

This diagram above shows that normally the sexual hormones are formed from droplets of special energy under the navel. These flow to the reproductive organs and then flow out of the body through the sexual organs. For males the flow is routed through the testes which hang outside the body, but the energy is routed back into the body through tubes. Even for males the psychic charge of the sex force is felt inside the trunk of the body as well as in the sexual organ specifically.

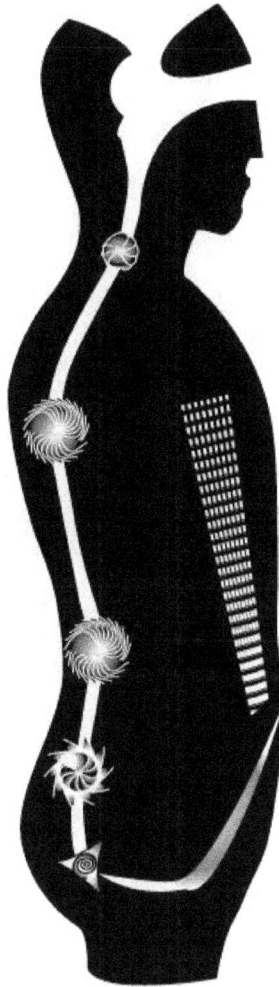

infused energy
alters path of sex hormone

In this diagram above, the infused breath energy moves from the lungs into the navel area. There it charges and mixes with the sex hormone energy. Instead of routing through the sexual organs, the infused energy forces the sex force to go to the base chakra, where when it strikes kundalini it may cause arousal.

normal sex hormone passage altered
by regular breath infusion practice

In the diagram above, the sex energy accumulates below the navel, but it does not go out of the genitals. Instead it is routed back and up into the chest. Then it falls to the navel. Even though it moves through the reproductive area of the body it avoids the sexual organs.

With this change in the subtle body, a yogi who does breath infusion attains the status of *urdhvareta* which is that of a person whose semen *(reta)* moves upwards *(urdhva)*.

If I have to resist sex in the subtle world, that means that my practice is not as proficient. The subtle body should change so that there is no sexual arousal. At nine years of age, a human body has no sexual arousal. That is not due to what the person wants but what the body is capable of. The objective in terms of subtle world sex, is that the subtle body should change so that it does not create the sexual energies and does not have the sexual attraction of an adult human body.

In my diagrams the sexual energies are reformed but they are still present. Thus, there will be problems in the subtle existence. If he wants to practice without being distracted for sex, a yogi who is not a siddha must hide in special dimensions in the subtle world.

However, if the yogi has a reformed subtle body, his sexual indulgence in the astral world will not have such a devastating effect on his psyche because only a small portion of the energy will be expended in those sexual involvements. He will not think that it is fun. He will not expand further with partners, hundreds of which are available in the subtle world without the moral constraints of physical society.

Sadly, getting liberated is not as easy as one may like it to be. The subtle body craves pleasures. I may have a great philosophy. I may say that I experienced the supreme. If my body has the sex urge and I am exposed to a sexually attractive person, then guess what will happen?

My paranoid schizophrenic kundalini

When doing breath infusion, one must check to be sure that the air is absorbed into the system. It should be absorbed by the lungs and sent to various parts of the body. It should not enter the lungs and leave without entering the blood cells. One student recently mentioned to me the ease with which he could do breath infusion in comparison to when he first started when it was not a reflexive practice.

However, be sure that the air is compressed. One may be breathing rapidly with ease and not be compressing the air into the cells. The lungs may take air and not absorb it. Or the lungs may take air, absorbing it into the lung cells and then breathing out air without distributing the absorbed fresh air.

Be sure that mentally one compresses the air into the lungs. It should be pressured into the system. First it should be forced into the navel area. When that is done to proficiency, one may force it into the groin area and beyond.

One important part of this practice is to be attentive to what happens in the psyche. This means that the mind should not be attentive to what occurs outside the body. There is an instruction in the *Anu Gita*.

दृष्टपूर्वां दिशं चिन्त्य यस्मिन्संनिवसेत्पुरे

पुरस्याभ्यन्तरे तस्य मनश्चार्यं न बाह्यतः

dṛṣṭapūrvāṁ diśaṁ cintya yasminsamnivasetpure
purasyābhyantare tasya manaścāryaṁ na bāhyataḥ

dṛṣṭa – seen; pūrvāṁ - before; diśaṁ - place; cintya – thinking; yasmin – in which; samnivaset – should reside; pure – in the city; purasyābhyantare = purasya (of the city or psyche) + abhyantare (in the interior, inside); tasya – of his; manaś = manah = mind; cāryaṁ - behavior, operation; na – not; bāhyataḥ - outside

When thinking of a place which was seen before, one should reside in the city in which the incidence occurred. The mental operations are within the psyche, not outside of it. (Anu Gita 4.31)

पुरस्याभ्यन्तरे तिष्ठन्यस्मिन्नावसथे वसेत्

तस्मिन्नावसथे धार्यं सबाह्याभ्यन्तरं मनः

purasyābhyantare tiṣṭhanyasminnāvasathe vaset
tasminnāvasathe dhāryaṁ sabāhyābhyantaraṁ manaḥ

purasyābhyantare = (purasya of the city) + abhyantare (inside); tiṣṭhany = tiṣṭhani = situated; asmin – in this; nāvasathe = na (not) + avasathe (city); vaset – should reside; tasmin – in this; nāvasathe = na (not) + avasathe (city); dhāryaṁ - absorbed in; sa – with; bāhyābhyantaraṁ = bāhya (exterior) + abhyantaram (interior); manaḥ - mind

Being situated inside the city, he should reside there with his mind absorbed in the exterior and interior features of that place. (Anu Gita 4.33)

प्रचिन्त्यावसथं कृत्स्नं यस्मिन्कायेऽवतिष्ठते

तस्मिन्काये मनश्चार्यं न कथंचन बाह्यतः

pracintyāvasathaṁ kṛtsnaṁ yasminkāye'vatiṣṭhate
tasminkāye manaścāryaṁ na kathaṁcana bāhyataḥ

pracintyāvasathaṁ = pracintya = meditating; kṛtsnaṁ - whole reality; yasmin – in which; kāye – in the body; 'vatiṣṭhate = avatiṣṭhate = being situated; tasmin – in that; kāye – in the body; manaś = manah = whole; cāryaṁ - wander; na – not; kathaṁcana – any way; bāhyataḥ - outside

Meditating in that place, the self sees the whole reality being situated in the body. The mind should not in any way wander outside the body. (Anu Gita 4.33)

Imagine that I did this infusion practice since 1972. Still, I am distracted during practice by light which enters the eyes, sounds which are heard outside the body, and mostly by the kundalini which is ever obsessed with using the senses to track events outside the body. The kundalini is crazy about keeping track of whatever is outside the body.

Even now after years of practice, I wrap a dark cloth around my eyes and head so as to keep kundalini from compelling the senses to pursue interests outside the body.

Be sure that the air is compressed and the attention is with the infusion, keeping track of where the air moves. Keep your mind inside the body during the practice. Do not allow kundalini to state the focus. It should not distract from the objective within the body.

Be sure that the air is compressed and the attention is with the breath infusion, keeping track of where the air moves. Keep the mind inside the body during the practice. Do not allow kundalini to dictate the interests. It should not distract from the objective.

Part 7

Yoga Practice Habit Failure

This morning I was with a student of kundalini yoga, who learnt the practice some ten years ago. This person studied other systems of spirituality and practiced others but it seems that he was unable to have a consistent practice.

Making a spiritual discipline a habit, is a special ability of a person who did much yoga in past lives. In the *Bhagavad Gita* there is a verse.

तत्र तं बुद्धिसंयोगं
लभते पौर्वदेहिकम् ।
यतते च ततो भूयः
संसिद्धौ कुरुनन्दन ॥६.४३॥

tatra taṁ buddhisaṁyogaṁ
labhate paurvadehikam
yatate ca tato bhūyaḥ
saṁsiddhau kurunandana

tatra — there; tam — it; buddhisaṁyogam — cumulative intellectual interest; labhate — inspired with; paurvadehikam — from a previous birth; yatate — he strives; ca — and; tato = tataḥ — from that time; bhūyaḥ — again; saṁsiddhau — to perfection; kuru-nandana — O dear son of the Kurus

In that environment, he is inspired with the cumulative intellectual interest from a previous birth. And from that time, he strives again for yoga perfection, O dear son of the Kurus. (Bhagavad Gita 6.43)

If one does not have this cumulative intellectual interest in yoga from a previous birth, one cannot instinctively strive for progress in the new body. One will not have the impetus.

When I did the exercises, five minutes after I began, Yogi Bhajan appeared on the astral side. Lucky for me this process which I teach as kundalini yoga was learnt from him. Some people I teach are his students with me as a stand-in teacher. He checked the subtle body of the student. He showed a lump of cloudy energy in the bottom part of the trunk. This was the sexual subtle force in the body.

For kundalini yoga purposes the sexual energy is compressed and sent through the spine into the head, instead of the pubic area. This student because of not practicing consistently for the past 10 years, had no compressed sexual force.

Yogi Bhajan was disgusted because here was a student who complains but who does not maintain the practice, not even ten minutes of practice per day. If the student does not practice, how can there be results from the practice?

Yogi Bhajan said this to me,

"I like you because you have no students. You have no ambition to be anybody's guru. People like you make the best students. As soon as somebody gets this idea that he is a teacher, it is over because then he no longer pays attention to his psyche. He thinks of students. He loses track of advancement.

"With you it is different you know that when you teach, it has little to do with your progression. You are not eager to have students. You realize that when teaching you neglect your advancement."

After that Yogi Bhajan left.

When the Sun Destroys the Subtle Bodies

Yogeshwarananda explained the destruction of kundalini shakti. This is a high-end kriya but since this instruction is hard to acquire from a siddha, I will repeat what he said for the record.

Basically, the idea is that to enter the causal plane one has to get rid of kundalini. Stated in another way, so long as one has a kundalini shakti, one cannot resume the existence on the causal plane. Usually one gets rid of kundalini when the cosmos collapses and the cosmic kundalini energy is no more. That will happen in many billions of years. Sometimes however there is a partial cosmic collapse. Some beings go into the causal level even though the whole universe does not break down. In that case only a segment disappears.

That may happen to us if suddenly the sun explodes. Science states that in five billion years the sun will explode. The earth will be fried. This will not only be a physical but a psychic event as well. The sun sustains us psychically as well as physically. Our astral bodies take energy from the sun for survival just as the physical forms do.

Unless a yogi can transfer his subtle body to another system or to another higher energy source if anything weird happens to the sun, say it explodes even before the scientist estimate, that is it for our kundalinis. We enter the causal plane.

One may think that would be alright but would it? For one thing if you are not advanced and you enter the causal place, it is just as if you no longer exist. Advanced entities can be objective to the causal plane but others become de-activated selves when they do so. This is because they have not mastered subjective consciousness. Their existence becomes dormant at that time. It may stay in that condition for billions of years.

Of course, there is an advantage to that, because if you are not aware for a few billion years, it would be just as if you did not go into existential dormancy in the first place. There would be no point of reference, no memory. You will not be bothered.

One experienced that in this body, when one found oneself as a baby in a crib and then as a school child and then as an adult with no memory of past existence. To oneself, life began twenty or thirty or fifty years ago. Once when I explained reincarnation to a man. he laughed at me for not seeing that reincarnation does not matter if one does not remember the past life.

Yogeshwarananda feels that a yogi must try to reach the causal plane to investigate exactly how the subtle body and the kundalini and then the physical systems come into being on the basis of the causal energy and the potency in the causal force. To do this one must eliminate kundalini. That is done by super-charging super-infusing the kundalini with energy until it burns away or vaporizes.

If you heat a metal and if you can keep increasing the temperature, it will reach a stage where it vaporizes. When yogis do this, they enter the causal plane. This is a forced entry. It is not like waiting till the cosmic situation is demolished.

What is the purpose of going into the causal level?

It is to understand how the subtle nature attracted the selves. How does it use the selves to manifest itself in various ways? If one can go into the causal plane and maintain some objective consciousness there, even a tiny amount, one could get insight into the subtle operations which control us and dictate what happens when a universe begins.

Diamond Kundalini

This morning during practice, kundalini was not in touch with the base area, which is its native anchor point. Instead it retreated up the spine right above where the 2nd chakra would be. It assumed a diamond configuration and was white hot in color. Then it was like a large diamond hanging down.

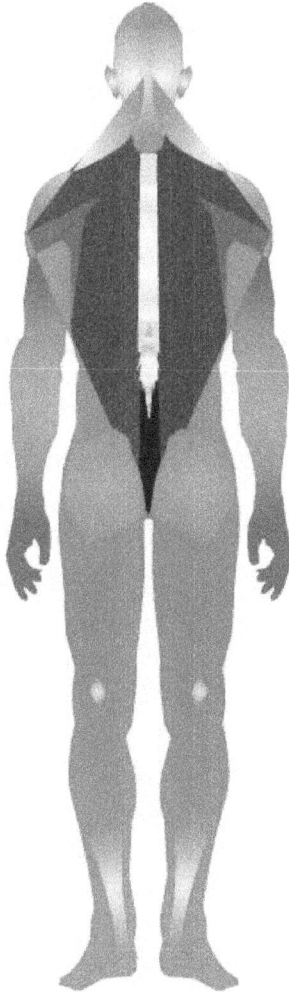

This practice began with an instruction of a Buddha deity in South Korea, who gave a kriya for attacking the base chakra anchor point instead of attacking the base chakra or even the kundalini itself.

Kundalini rose several times. One particular instance was with kundalini fired through each side of the chest and lodged in the lower jaw bones. This felt as if there was cool air in that area with a bliss aspect to it

These practices give one the opportunity to discover the various parts of the psyche which are usually getting only a low charge of energy from kundalini. Since a yogi will have to carry the whole psyche when leaving the physical body for good, it is wise to make sure that all parts of that psychic system is infused with fresh energy. Initially one focuses on getting kundalini into the head but the head is not the whole psyche.

A chain is as strong as its weakest link, so the saying goes. The psyche will go as high as its least energized portion. This is why one should seriously take a look at the various *hard to reach* parts and make sure that they are not saturated with a low grade of energy.

If only a certain part of the psyche reaches the higher planes, or the cosmic consciousness, the psyche will not go to that place hereafter. It will go to the place which the other parts of the psyche are attuned to.

Two Visitors

During exercises this morning, I had two deceased visitors. The first was Swami Rama. I did breath infusion, targetting the area below the navel. Swami Rama explained this:

> *The sperm particle heads for a particular location in the womb of the mother. At that place it crimps down to get nutrients. The same impulse one has when one is sexually attracted to someone and desires to get near to that person, operates in the sperm to find that special part of the womb where it has to extract nutrients from the mother's system.*

> *If a person passes on and does not root out that tendency of the lifeForce, he/or she will be compelled to take rebirth. When working on the navel chakra, the real problem is the expression of the chakra. This chakra is the only one which issues the energy which causes a person to seek someone for sex.*

> *At puberty, this energy becomes visible as a novel urge for romance. Usually it haunts the person from puberty onwards. It is relentless in the pursue of sex. After leaving the body that pursuit continues in the astral world. It becomes dormant there as soon as the person becomes fused into a parent's psyche.*

Near the end of the exercise session, I had a visit from Rishi Singh Gherwal. He explained that when the kundalini is infused with breath energy, it loses its struggle for survival instincts, but if the yogi's psyche is de-energized, kundalini will resume its vulgar behaviors.

When I sat to meditate, Rishi showed a level in which the self no longer has a psychic cloud of low energy surrounding it. He said this.

> *It is just as Patanjali said that the sure way to deal with this is pranayama breath infusion.*

Breathing / Rishi's Opinion

During exercises this morning Rishi Singh Gherwal mentioned a verse from Patanjali Yoga sutras. This verse is quoted in the *Anu Gita* which I translated and which more or less is Rishi Singh's book with me as a ghost writer.

Here is the verse.

तस्मिन्सति श्वासप्रश्वासयोर्गतिविच्छेदः प्राणायामः ॥४९॥

tasmin satiśvāsa praśvāsayoḥ
gativicchedaḥ prāṇāyāmaḥ

tasmin – on this; sati – being accomplished; śvāsa – inhalation; praśvāsayoḥ – of the exhalation; gati – the flow; vicchedaḥ – the separation; prāṇāyāmḥ – breath regulation.

Once this is accomplished, breath regulation, which is the separation of the flow of inhalation and exhalation, is attained. (Yoga Sutras 2.49)

Rishi said that if the body has sufficient breath energy, the breathing process will occur with a short respite between the in-breath and out-breath except that the breath will go to the very bottom of the lungs.

In normal breathing there may or may not be a respite between the in-breath and out-breath but in either case, the air never gets to the bottom of the lungs. There is only top breathing, where air reaches the top one third of the lung and the alveoli which are in the central part of that area.

Rishi claims that top breathing results in lack of access to the extremities. This causes deficient energy in many parts of the physical and subtle bodies; which result is gasping for breath or in normal shallow breathing. Since their intuition is that the body should work perfectly and should maintain itself, human beings are disinclined to helping the lung system.

Kundalini Transmigration Urge

After breath infusion, I was to make notes. Somehow, I overlooked that and went to meditate. Now I cannot recall the details. I repeatedly appealed to students to take notes and submit those periodically for review. Most students ignore this request. Some find that they do not have the inclination for this. They do not have the power or determination to thwart the disinclination. The value of notes is that if one reviews them one can gain more from the practice.

While doing exercises this morning there were subtle events, so subtle and subjective, that since I did not record it just after the practice, my objective mind has no record of it. To retrieve the information, I would have to enter the subconscious mind, which in yoga meditation is a subjective region of consciousness. Such a region is like trying to read a book in which the printer printed white ink on white paper.

Here is some of what happened.

I worked on just about everything in the lower trunk of the body, the thighs and feet, except for kundalini itself. In each thigh there was a huge cavern, like a vast cave which was filled with a misty white light. It was empty of anything except white misty energy. Once both caverns of the right and left thighs seemed to be one cavern even though they were in fact two separate zones. They seemed to be one because my observing consciousness was aware of both simultaneously.

The loop area which begins at the navel and loops around to the navel chakra on the spine, was devoid of any sexually charged energy. It seemed to be a u-shaped container which was about an inch wide. Usually this area carries a double charge, a sex charge and transmigration urge. In this experience the charge was missing.

The sex charge and the transmigration urge stay together. These are the basic identity of the kundalini chakra, which acquired a physical body through sexual means. The removal of these features of the kundalini protects the yogi from having to be attracted haphazardly to a birth opportunity.

It is a good idea, to be free of this sex charge and transmigration urge, otherwise one will not go with the siddhas after one leaves a body. It is not that one should not take rebirth. One may have to but instead of doing that immediately after the death of a body, one should get in touch with the siddhas so as to get assistance from them in determining where and when one should develop the next embryo.

Without their advice, one will be left to the means of ordinary transmigration by the usual means of attraction to the next parents through sexual attraction and the after-effects of one social activities.

Rishi Singh appeared for a split second. He looked. He made this remark:

"Get it cleared before leaving the body. Make no assumption about what you can do after departing the body. Make every effort to complete the practice before departure."

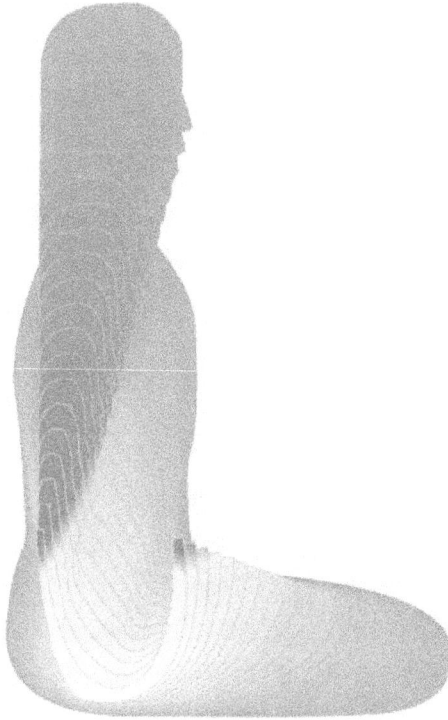

Kundalini in the Extremities

I endeavor to target the base of the base chakra. As explained previously the base chakra and the place which it is fused to are two different features. This practice is to target the base which it is fused to, which is not the base chakra.

While working on this, I got instruction from Rishi Singh Gherwal who said that I should push the air through a tube in the lower legs. When I did that, the tube was infused so much that it was full of rushing white energy, like white heat which shows on a hot piece of metal. After that the white heat spread through the feet.

The extremities of the hands and especially those of the feet are *hard to reach* places in *nadi-shodana* practice. *Nadi-shodana* is Sanskrit for purification of the nadi subtle tubes practice. *Shodana* comes from *shuda* a Sanskrit word for purification. Some yogis feel that there is only one *nadi-shodana* practice which involves alternate breathing with a count proportion but there are other procedures for *nadi-shodana*.

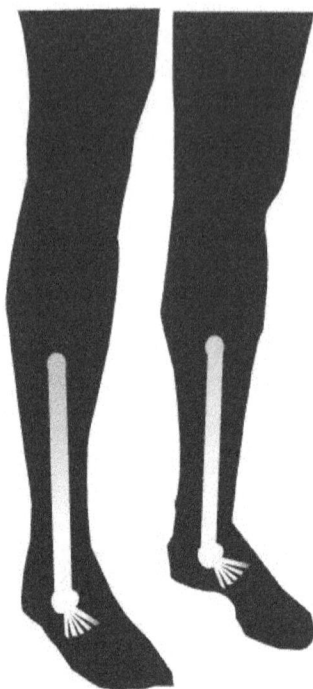

A question may be asked as to why bother with the feet if one strives for liberation which concerns the mind and not the body. The answer is that the mind is connected to the kundalini system which moves with the self at the time of exiting the body at death.

If the self could leave the body and leave with the mental chamber without kundalini, there would be no need to be concerned with kundalini. But since the self must lug both the mind chamber and the kundalini, it is necessary to take kundalini into account.

For that matter a person who is not proficient at meditation will find that at death, the kundalini leads the way out of the body with the mind and the self following like obedient tourists who happen to be in the control of an insane tour guide which is the kundalini. Where the tour guide will take them, they do not know. The only thing they know for sure is that it will take them to another body, where, when and why, is unknown.

For a student yogi, the task of reaching the extremities like the toes and fingers is a daunting one, but if one proceeds with a steady daily practice, one will over time achieve the penetration of these parts.

If you do not do it who will? Will it be the guru? Will it be Krishna or Shiva? My point is that if you do not do it, it will not be done. You will leave the physical body with a low energy kundalini and with the consequences which that entails.

Brow Chakra Opening

This morning during meditation, I had an unusual opening of the brow chakra, where it opened showing itself to be a cylindrical channel, at the end of which was an environment which was bathed in light. Instead of being like a cone-shaped tunnel or a moving energy cone-shaped tunnel, this tunnel was like a cyclinder.

I did not rush to go through it because that action usually results in the disappearance of the opening. I slowly focused on it. It lasted for the most for two minutes. Then it disappeared. Total darkness appeared where that opening was. This happened as I was focused on naad sound on the right side of the head.

Before this meditation, while I did breath infusion, kundalini rose several times, perhaps six times. Twice it rose in slow motion which gave me the opportunity to check its passage with more precision.

Breath infusion usually causes a rapid movement from kundalini, as if the infused energy strikes kundalini and puts it into a hasty mode.

The Woman, The Child, The Yogi

During exercises this morning a Buddha deity left an instruction in my psyche. During meditation that instruction read this:

Become like a nomad who has no permanent residence. If kundalini's tendencies are not directly reformed, it means that when it is time to leave the body, when it must be outside a body in the astral world after the physical body dies, it will revert to its old way of doing things.

Habits which are developed in other parts of the psyche, like in the willpower, in the desire moods or in the analytical process, will have no effect on kundalini. It will keep its posture.

This means that the other components of the psyche will be forced to go with kundalini and will experience the circumstances kundalini takes the psyche into.

Take the example of a woman with an infant. They travel. The woman does not need milk. The woman does not require toys. The woman does not require to be cleaned by someone else after evacuating.

Still, she must deal with it because of the child. Those who think that they are liberated and who are unsuccessful in reforming kundalini from its transmigration habits, must assume those habits regardless of whether they want to or not.

Therefore, one should change the features of kundalini so that it no longer requires to live in a physical body. One has to remove that tendency from it. If one fails to do this, it will not matter who one may be or who one may claim to be, one will be forced to live in the next existence on the level that is suitable to kundalini, just as the mother, even though she is liberated from infancy, must live in an accommodation that facilitates the child.

Fruits on the Sun Planet

The morning session of postures and breath infusion was for fifty minutes. It seems that the psyche took more and more air during the rapid breathing. Most of the air went to a location below the navel. Then it vanished into thin air, or so it seemed.

Arthur Beverford who was my first formal teacher of asana postures, came there in his subtle body. He was interested in seeing the effects of the breath infusion on my subtle body. During his last body he did asana postures and some pranayama methods but not the bhastrika rapid breathing.

He said that he would begin to do the bhastrika on a regular basis and would substitute it for smoking. He smoked tobacco. His main discipline in his last body was Japanese martial arts but he did have a daily meditation practice which began with a third eye focusing technique.

When I sat to meditate, there was fresh energy throughout the psyche, but particularly there was a flow of energy which ascended the spine into the head. It was a shaft of solid light, as if it were a shaft of glass.

This lasted five minutes. After this I descended to the base chakra, since that is the instruction, I have from a Buddha deity in South Korea. When I got to the base, I noticed shafts of energy positioned across diagonally. Some were crystal clear. Some had slight tints of yellow or orange. These were like thick sheets of glass passing through each other.

This experience is similar to an experience I had in 1973. While my physical body as in Denver Colorado, my subtle body was displaced from and transited in a moment to the sun planet. There I saw buildings, streets, people, vegetation, everything in a civilization which was like something from a fantasy movie. Everything was made of light energy, just as everything here is made of solid, liquid and gaseous matter.

There were trees bearing fruits which were made of light energy. These fruits were eaten by the denizens of that place.

Since the bodies used there were made of the same subtle materials, those objects were like solid stuffs to the inhabitants.

After being at the base chakra for a time, I came into the head. When I passed the right ear, I heard naad which streamed loud and clear. There are times when naad is barely heard or it is so distant like something which is light-years away. But on this occasion, it was loud and pronounced.

After hearing naad and moving to the frontal part of the brain, I noticed that the third eye (brow chakra) was open. It peered over a lady's shoulder while the woman looked through a window. An intuition flashed about this place as being an embassy building in Italy.

Third eye can open and one may not know it. If one is not focused through it, one may not know if it is opened or inoperative.

Naad sound can lead to the chit akasha, which is the sky of consciousness or which is the spiritual universe. The idea is that this creation is a shadow of that sky of consciousness. Somehow this shadow came about in the process of cosmic time. Now after many billions of years of the development of the shadow universe, somehow, we found ourselves conscious in this.

Kundalini Base Attack

The two diagrams below show how to attack the base which kundalini adheres to. This is a strategy shown to me by a Buddha deity. The motive for attacking this base pad is to uproot kundalini and to cause it to abandon its tendency for being anchored in a physical body.

This is different from the motive for a direct attack on kundalini, which is to cause kundalini to be aroused so that it moves into the brain and provides increased psychic perception of the other dimensions.

The attainment of increased perception of subtle realms does not usually interfere with kundalini's instinct for creating and taking up residence in physical bodies. But if the base is removed, kundalini may lose that transmigration tendency.

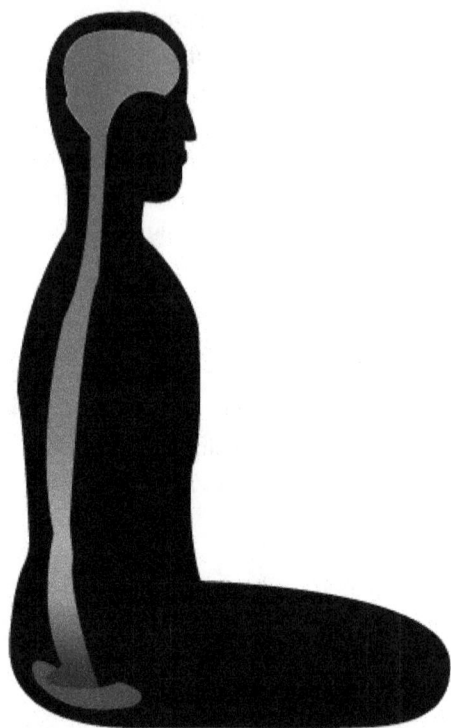

Kundalini adheres to base energy pad
which is dense due to a heavy subtle energy

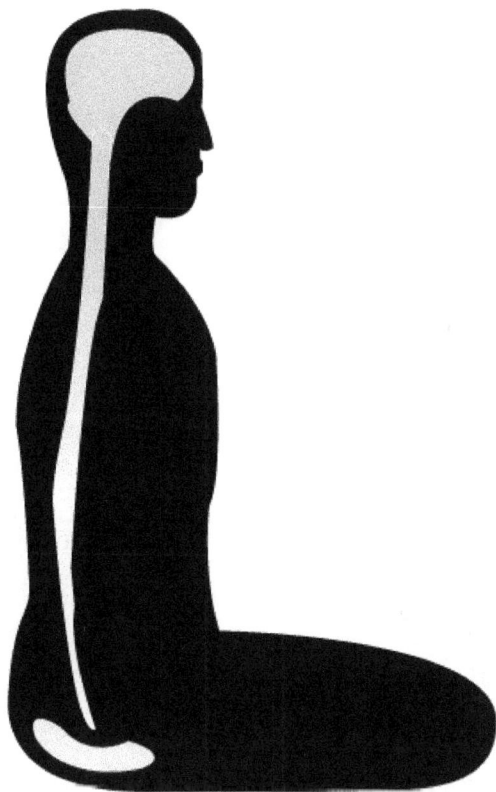

kundalini lifted from base energy pad
which is infused with breath energy

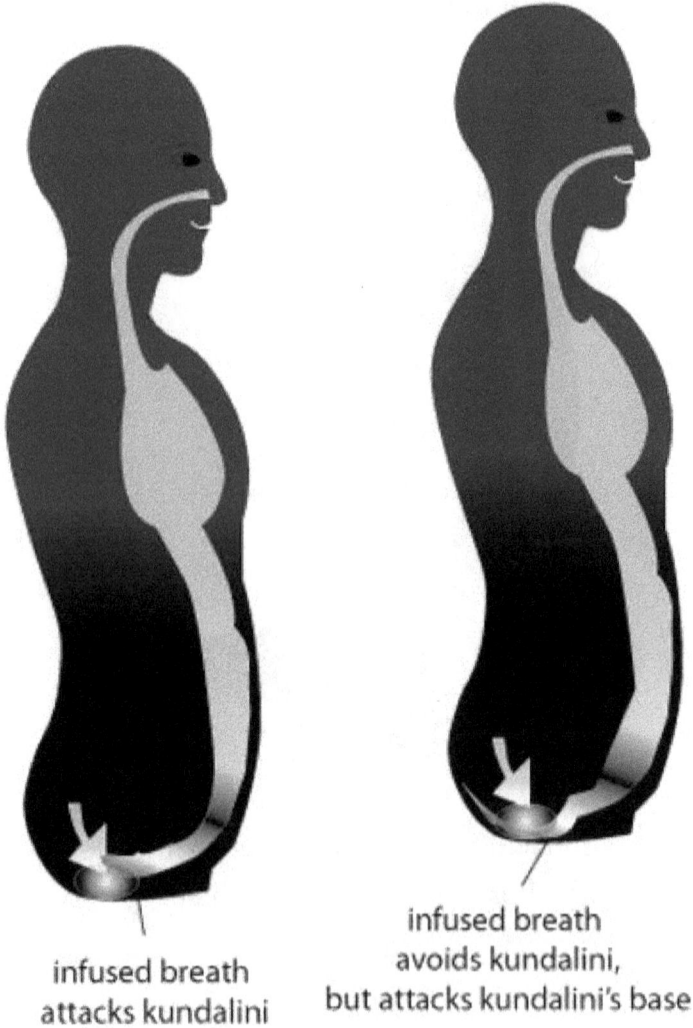

infused breath
attacks kundalini

infused breath
avoids kundalini,
but attacks kundalini's base

Kundalini Base Inspection

During the morning session of meditation, I went into the trunk of the body down to the base chakra, As I descended, I heard naad sound streaming near the right ear. It was loud but it seemed to be coming from a distant galaxy, with intentions to attract the self, as if to say, "Remain here and listen."

I traveled past it and went down. As soon as I entered the neck, I noticed that I no longer heard naad. Instead there were colors occurring as sounds. When I passed the chest area, the colors as sounds ceased.

There was light, like clear light coming through a window in the early morning. At first when I looked down there seemed to be nothing there at the base. Then there seemed to be a shaft of shadow and light mixed. This hung above the base chakra. I ignored that and went under the base.

This going under the base, was an instruction I was bestowed by a Buddha deity. His instruction was that one should attack the location of the base chakra and not so much the chakra itself. It is like if you want to move something, you can either move it or move its foundation. In either case it will be moved. If, however, it is a stubborn obsessive living something, merely moving it will not work, since it could re-attach itself. If, however, you move the location, it cannot reattach itself. It must go elsewhere.

Actually, this is exactly what happens when the body dies, that the lifeForce which is attached to the body as its residence, finds that it can no longer locate the body. It reluctantly moves about the astral world in search of another physical form. Of course, it cannot find such a form except in the body of its would-be parents. It has to use their energy to create an embryo.

The lifeForce craves a physical body. As soon as it is put out of commission in a physical body at death, getting another one becomes its obsession. Unless one can tamper with this instinct one is condemned to taking one body after another, as such bodies become available by the grace of nature.

Buddha deity's technique is to uproot kundalini by demolishing its base foundation. He said that this is something he discovered and practiced effectively in meditation. He claimed that this method did not come from any teacher whom he approached during his lifetime in India. They gave him valuable techniques but this and some others were discovered by him or inspired into his mind directly as he practiced.

He set it as my duty to develop this practice and teach it.

When I got under the base chakra, I found a light-yellow light. I was surprised because I expected brown darkness or heavy energy. Usually at this place one meets with a denseness like if one met head on with the heaviest matter there could ever be.

I realized that this light-yellow light was there because of an aggressive breath infusion practice which I did just prior to the meditation.

Kundalini Visualization

Kundalini is usually aroused through the spine during exercises for breath infusion but a yogi should know that there are nadi channels throughout the subtle body. The question arises, as to why does kundalini ascends the spine and does not travel through the nadis which are in the body even in the extremities like the fingers and toes?

The answer is that once kundalini manufactured a body in the womb of the parents it is no longer concerned with every detail of that body. Its interest shrinks to basic maintenance and to acquiring pleasures and experiences from the body.

It will not be involved in keeping every tiny nadi in order. Even physically there is the fluid pump in the body, the heart. It is not concerned with the details of how blood gets to the remote areas. It pumps the blood on the assumption that it will course through those extremities, even though as the body ages the plumbing system deteriorates.

A yogi has a chore to make certain that the kundalini flows through the extremities. That is why the postures are required as the third stage of yoga. During practice one will feel when kundalini goes to the extremities, even if that happens rarely. The postures stretch, contract and activate some nadis which are in *hard to reach* places of the subtle body. If there is no posture regiment, the yogi must depend on imagination or visualization to command kundalini to go to various remote places in the body. Of course, that would depend on how much the kundalini shows a response to such mental commands.

If you can give a mental command to raise kundalini and if kundalini will obey that urge, then obviously one has no need for postures, or even for breath infusion.

Sex Chakra Attack

This morning during exercises, I focused on the second chakra. This is not the sex organ chakra. It is the sex chakra which is on the spine. The one on the spine is the chakra of interest because it monitors the sex organ chakra.

The sex chakra on the spine is involved with changing air into liquid. The base chakra is concerned with compressing moisture to create solid materials.

Sometimes when one arrives at the base chakra one feels density. One feels a heaviness but one may see nothing. At other times at the base chakra one sees darkness or dark-brownness. There is a feeling of being at the bottom of something, as being dense and heavy.

The second chakra gives the feeling of being like a cloud or being like vapor floating over water or vapor which formed from air and is about to appear as water.

Vapor may be in the air. It may not be seen. If it condenses it is seen. This is like someone is in the astral world awaiting rebirth. During the interim period, people in the physical world do not see that astral person. As soon as an embryo is formed, people point it out and say that a woman is pregnant. Sometimes people welcome the pregnancy with smiles but in some instances, people shun the pregnancy and whisper, "Who is the father? With whom did she have a penetration? Who will raise the child? We should investigate to know when and how she had a man in bed on that night?"

When I worked on the second chakra, the sex chakra on the spine, it was unresponsive. I decided to ram some more breath infused energy into it. After a time, it assumed an airy feeling. Then there was a blank space with some light like when sunshine suddenly penetrates a dark overhead cloud.

The kundalini lifeForce is a nuisance but it must be elevated. It cannot be abandoned or ignored. Students who work on it day after day will get results from the efforts.

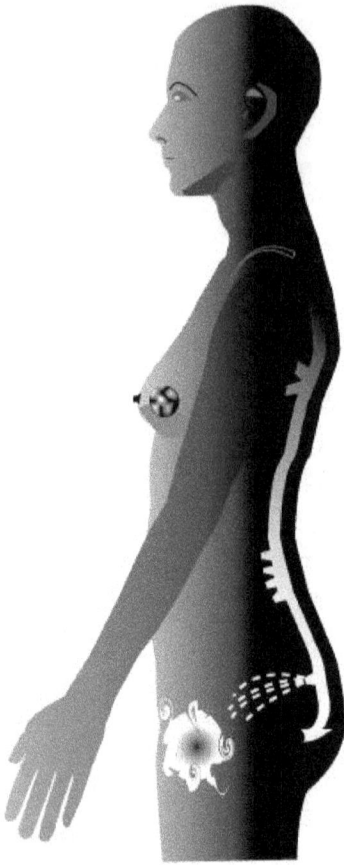

sex chakra on spine

kundalini
base chakra

sex organ chakra

Index

teaching, 126, 131
telepathic transmission, 93
Terrell, 131
tha, 170
thigh cavern, 218
thigh infusion, 57, 159
thigh extraction, 130
third eye open, 223
throat space gap, 113
Tibetan yogis, 78
tibia, 176
time bomb, 204
Timothy Leary, 153
tobacco, 222
Tobe Terrell, 131
tortoise, 99
train, 45
transmigration urge, 218
transmission zones, 93
traveler, 190
tree, 117
tree, light, 222
Trinidad, 33, 77
tug boat, 131
turkey, 100
turtle, 100

U

Uddhava, 43
up jump, 112
Upanishad, 71
upavista, 146
urdha reta, 209
Urvashee, 42

V

Vaishampayana, 91
Valmiki, 151
vapor, 229
Vatsyayana, 48
Vedas, 67
ventilateion, 154

Ventura, 144
virus, 102
Vishnu, 116
Vishnudevananda, 24-25
Vishvamitra, 93
vision, without eyeballs, 54
vortex, 62

W

well-off, 33
white flag, 158
white ink, 217
white veda, 92
wiggle method, 79
wings, 117
winos, 94
work done, 45
world class guru, 136

X, Y, Z

X-ray vision, 176
Yadus, 70
Yajnavalkya, 92
yajur veda, 92
Yoga Sutras, 48, 126
yoga,
    commercial, 126
    meditation, 8
    parts, 8
Yogananda, 128
Yogeshwarananda, 67
yogi, family life, 46
yoni clearance, 156
Zen Hostel, 133

About the Author

Michael Beloved (Yogi *Madhvāchārya)* took his current body in 1951 in Guyana. In 1965, while living in Trinidad, he instinctively began doing yoga postures and tried to make sense of the supernatural side of life.

Later in 1970, in the Philippines, he approached a Martial Arts Master named Arthur Beverford. He explained to the teacher that he was seeking a yoga instructor. Mr. Beverford identified himself as an advanced disciple of *Śrī* Rishi Singh Gherwal, an Ashtanga Yoga master.

Beverford taught the traditional Ashtanga Yoga with stress on postures, attentive breathing and brow chakra centering meditation.   In 1972, Michael entered the Denver, Colorado Ashram of *kundalini* yoga Master *Śrī* Harbhajan Singh. There he took instruction in *bhastrika* pranayama and its application to yoga postures. He was supervised mostly by Yogi Bhajan's disciple named Prem Kaur.

In 1979 Michael formally entered the discipic succession of the Brahmā - Madhava-Gaudiya Sampradaya through *Swāmī* Kirtanananda, who was a prominent sannyasi disciple of the Great Vaishnava Authority *Śrī Swāmī* Bhaktivedanta Prabhupada, the exponent of devotion to Sri Krishna.

However, yoga has a mystic side to it, thus Michael took training and teaching empowerment from several spiritual masters of different aspects of spiritual development. This is consistent with *Śrī* Krishna's advice to Arjuna in the *Bhagavad Gītā*:

Most of the instructions Michael received were given in the astral world. On that side of existence, his most prominent teachers were *Śrī Swāmī* Shivananda of Rishikesh, Yogiraj *Swāmī* Vishnudevananda, *Śrī Bābāji Mahasaya* - the master of the masters of *Kriyā* Yoga, *Śrīla* Yogeshwarananda of Gangotri - the master of the masters of *Raj* Yoga (spiritual clarity), and Siddha *Swāmī* Nityananda the Brahmā Yoga authority.

The course for kundalini yoga using pranayama breath-infusion was detailed by Michael in the book *Kundalini Hatha Yoga Pradipika*. This current book was composed from meditation and breath-infusion notes which were originally shared in staple bound booklets as Yoga Journals.

Michael's preliminary books relating to this topic are *Meditation Pictorial*, *Meditation Expertise*, and *Meditation ~ Sense Faculty* (co-author). Every technique (kriya) mentioned was tested by him during pranayama breath-infusion and *samyama* deep meditation practice.

This is a result of over forty years of meditation practice with astute subtle observations intending to share the methods and experiences. The information is published freely with no intention of forming an institution or hogtying anyone as a disciple.

Publications

English Series

Bhagavad Gita English

Anu Gita English

Markandeya Samasya English

Yoga Sutras English

Hatha Yoga Pradipika English

Uddhava Gita English

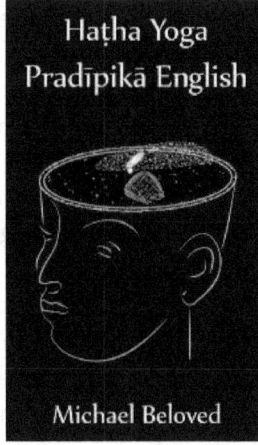

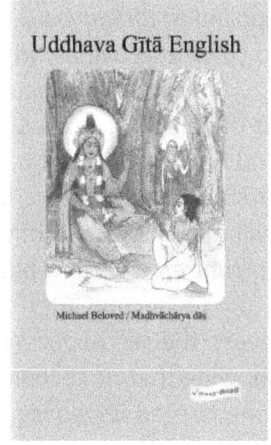

These are in 21st Century English, very precise and exacting. Many Sanskrit words which were considered untranslatable into a Western language are rendered in precise, expressive and modern English.

Three of these books are instructions from Krishna. In *Bhagavad Gita English* and **Anu Gita English**, the instructions were for Arjuna. In the **Uddhava Gita English,** it was for Uddhava. *Bhagavad Gita* and Anu Gita are extracted from the Mahabharata. Uddhava Gita was extracted from the 11th Canto of the Srimad Bhagavatam (Bhagavata Purana). One of these books, the **Markandeya Samasya English** is about Krishna, as described by Yogi Markandeya, who survived the cosmic collapse and reached a divine child in whose transcendental body, the collapsed world was existing.

Two of this series are the syllabus about yoga practice. The *Yoga Sutras* of Patañjali is elaboration about ashtanga yoga. Hatha Yoga Pradipika English, is the detailed information about asana postures, pranayama breath-infusion, energy compression, naad sound resonance and advanced meditation. The Sanskrit author is Swatmarama Mahayogin.

My suggestion is that you read *Bhagavad Gita* English, the **Anu Gita English, the Markandeya Samasya English,** the *Yoga Sutras* English, the **Hatha Yoga Pradipika** and lastly the **Uddhava Gita English**, which is complicated and detailed.

For each of these books we have at least one commentary, which is published separately. Thus one's particular interest can be researched further in the commentaries.

The smallest of these commentaries and perhaps the simplest is the one for the Anu Gita. We published its commentary as the Anu Gita Explained. The *Bhagavad Gita* explanations were published in three distinct targeted commentaries. The first is Bhagavad Gita Explained, which sheds lights on how people in the time of Krishna and Arjuna regarded the information and applied it. *Bhagavad Gita* is an exposition of the application of yoga practice to cultural activities, which is known in the Sanskrit language as karma yoga.

Interestingly, *Bhagavad Gita* was spoken on a battlefield just before one of the greatest battles in the ancient world. A warrior, Arjuna, lost his wits and had no idea that he could apply his training in yoga to political dealings. Krishna, his charioteer, lectured on the spur of the moment to give Arjuna the skill of using yoga proficiency in cultural dealings including how to deal with corrupt officials on a battlefield.

The second Gita commentary is the Kriya Yoga *Bhagavad Gita*. This clears the air about Krishna's information on the science of kriya yoga, showing that its techniques are clearly described for anyone who takes the time to read *Bhagavad Gita*. Kriya yoga concerns the battlefield which is the psyche of the living being. The internal war and the mental and emotional forces which are hostile to self-realization are dealt with in the kriya yoga practice.

The third commentary is the Brahma Yoga *Bhagavad Gita*. This shows what Krishna had to say outright and what he hinted about which concerns the brahma yoga practice, a mystic process for those who mastered kriya yoga.

There is one commentary for the **Markandeya Samasya English**. The title of that publication is Krishna Cosmic Body.

There are two commentaries to the *Yoga Sutras*. One is the *Yoga Sutras of Patañjali* and the other is the Meditation Expertise. These give detailed explanations of ashtanga Yoga.

The commentary of Hatha Yoga Pradipika is titled Kundalini Hatha Yoga Pradipika.

For the Uddhava Gita, we published the Uddhava Gita Explained. This is a large book and requires concentration and study for integration of the information. Of the books which deal with transcendental topics, my opinion is that the discourse between Krishna and Uddhava has the complete information about the realities in existence. This book is the one which removes massive existential ignorance.

Meditation Series

Meditation Pictorial

Meditation Expertise

CoreSelf Discovery

Meditation Sense Faculty

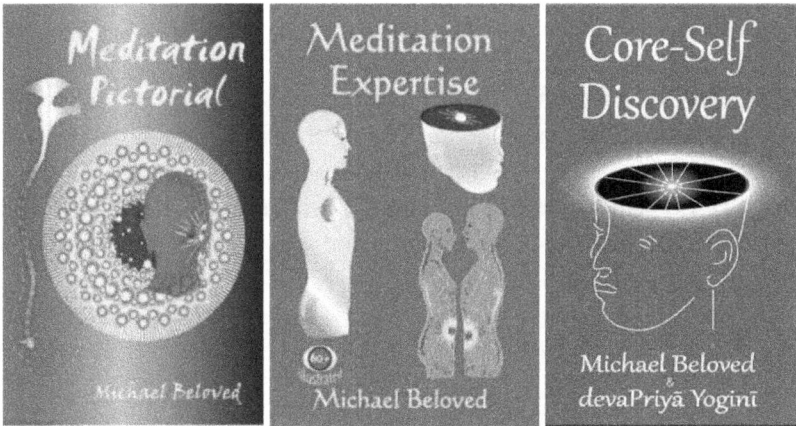

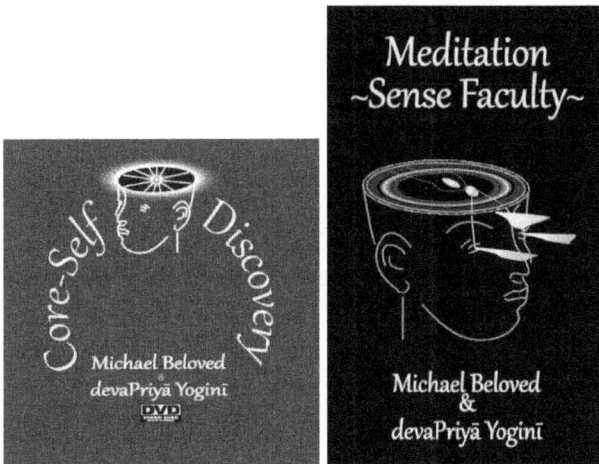

The specialty of these books is the mind diagrams which profusely illustrate what is written. This shows exactly what one has to do mentally to develop and then sustain a meditation practice.

In the **Meditation Pictorial,** one is shown how to develop psychic insight, a feature without which meditation is imagination and visualization, without any mystic experience per se.

In the **Meditation Expertise,** one is shown how to corral one's practice to bring it in line with the classic syllabus of yoga which Patañjali lays out as the ashtanga yoga eight-staged practice.

In **CoreSelf Discovery,** (co-authored with *devaPriya Yogini*) one is taken though the course of *pratyahar* sensual energy withdrawal which is the 5th stage of yoga in the Patañjali ashtanga eight-process complete system of yoga practice. These events lead to the discovery of a coreSelf which is surrounded by psychic organs in the head of the subtle body. This product has a DVD component.

Meditation ~ Sense Faculty (co-authored with *devaPriya Yogini*) is a detailed tutorial with profuse diagrams showing what actions to take in the subtle body to investigate the senses faculties. The meditator must first establish the location and function of the observing self. That self must be screened from the thoughts and ideas which usually hypnotize it.

These books are profusely illustrated with mind diagrams showing the components of psychic consciousness and the inner design of the subtle body.

Explained Series

Bhagavad Gita Explained

Uddhava Gita Explained

Anu Gita Explained

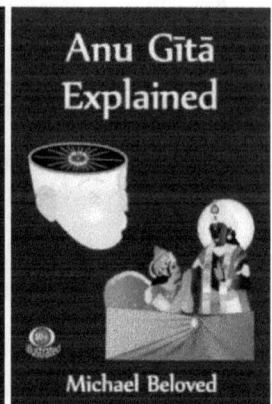

The specialty of these books is that they are free of missionary intentions, cult tactics and philosophical distortion. Instead of using these books to add credence to a philosophy, meditation process, belief or plea for followers, I spread the information out so that a reader can look through this literature and freely take or leave anything as desired.

When Krishna stressed himself as God, I stated that. When Krishna laid no claims for supremacy, I showed that. The reader is left to form an independent opinion about the validity of the information and the credibility of Krishna.

There is a difference in the discourse with Arjuna in the *Bhagavad Gita* and the one with Uddhava in the Uddhava Gita. In fact, these two books may appear to contradict each other. In the *Bhagavad Gita*, Krishna pressured Arjuna to complete social duties. In the Uddhava Gita, Krishna insisted that Uddhava should abandon the same.

The Anu Gita is not as popular as the *Bhagavad Gita* but it is the conclusion of that text. Anu means what is to follow, what proceeds. In this discourse, an anxious Arjuna request that Krishna should repeat the *Bhagavad Gita* and again show His supernatural and divine forms.

However, Krishna refuses to do so and chastises Arjuna for being a disappointment in forgetting what was revealed. Krishna then cited a celestial yogi, a near-perfected being, who explained the process of transmigration in vivid detail.

Commentaries

Yoga Sutras of Patañjali

Meditation Expertise

Krishna Cosmic Body

Anu Gita Explained

Bhagavad Gita Explained

Kriya Yoga Bhagavad Gita

Brahma Yoga Bhagavad Gita

Uddhava Gita Explained

Kundalini Hatha Yoga Pradipika

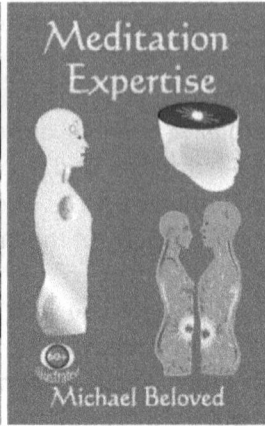

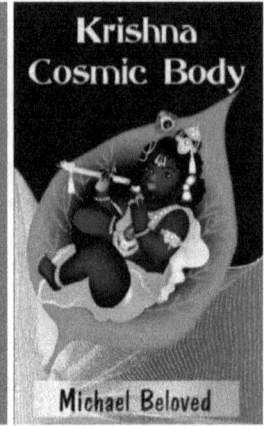

***Yoga Sutras* of Patañjali is** the globally acclaimed text book of yoga. This has detailed expositions of yoga techniques. Many kriya techniques are vividly described in the commentary.

Meditation Expertise is an analysis and application of the *Yoga Sutras*. This book is loaded with illustrations and has detailed explanations of secretive advanced meditation techniques which are called kriyas in the Sanskrit language.

Krishna Cosmic Body is a narrative commentary on the Markandeya Samasya portion of the Aranyaka Parva of the Mahabharata. This is the detailed description of the dissolution of the world, as experienced by the great yogin Markandeya who transcended the cosmic deity, Brahma, and reached Brahma's source who is the divine infant, Krishna.

Anu Gita Explained is a detailed explanation of how we endure many material bodies in the course of transmigrating through various life-forms. This is a discourse between Krishna and Arjuna. Arjuna requested of Krishna a display of the Universal Form and a repeat narration of the *Bhagavad Gita* but Krishna declined and explained what a siddha perfected being told the Yadu family about the sequence of existences one endures and the systematic flow of those lives at the convenience of material nature.

Bhagavad Gita **Explained** shows what was said in the Gita without religious overtones and sectarian biases.

Kriya Yoga *Bhagavad Gita* shows the instructions for those who are doing kriya yoga.

Brahma Yoga *Bhagavad Gita* shows the instructions for those who are doing brahma yoga.

Uddhava Gita Explained shows the instructions to Uddhava which are more advanced than the ones given to Arjuna.

Bhagavad Gita is an instruction for applying the expertise of yoga in the cultural field. This is why the process taught to Arjuna is called karma yoga which means karma + yoga or cultural activities done with yogic insight.

Uddhava Gita is an instruction for apply the expertise of yoga to attaining spiritual status. This is why it explains jnana yoga and bhakti yoga in detail. Jnana yoga is using mystic skill for knowing the spiritual part of existence. Bhakti yoga is for developing affectionate relationships with divine beings.

Karma yoga is for negotiating the social concerns in the material world. It is inferior to bhakti yoga which concerns negotiating the social concerns in the spiritual world.

This world has a social environment. The spiritual world has one too.

Currently, Uddhava Gita is the most advanced and informative spiritual book on the planet. There is nothing anywhere which is superior to it or which goes into so much detail as it. It verified that historically Krishna is the most advanced human being to ever have left literary instructions on this planet.

Even Patañjali *Yoga Sutras* which I translated and gave an application for in my book, **Meditation Expertise**, does not go as far as the Uddhava Gita.

Some of the information of these two books is identical but while the *Yoga Sutras* are concerned with the personal spiritual emancipation (kaivalyam) of the individual spirits, the Uddhava Gita explains that and also explains the situations in the spiritual universes.

Bhagavad Gita is from the *Mahabharata* which is the history of the Pandavas. Arjuna, the student of the Gita, is one of the Pandavas brothers. He was in a social hassle and did not know how to apply yoga expertise to solve it. On the battlefield, Krishna gave him a crash-course on yogic social interactions.

Uddhava Gita is from the *Srimad Bhagavatam (Bhagavata Purana)*, which is a history of the incarnations of Krishna. Uddhava was a relative of Krishna. He was concerned about the situation of the deaths of many of his relatives but Krishna diverted Uddhava's attention to the practice of yoga for the purpose of successfully migrating to the spiritual environment.

Kundalini Hatha Yoga Pradipika is the commentary for the Hatha Yoga Pradipika of Swatmarama Mahayogin. This is the detailed process about asana posture, pranayama breath-infusion, complex compressions of energy, naad sound resonance intonement and advanced meditation practice.

This is the singular book with all the techniques of how to reform and redesign the subtle body so that it does not have the tendency for physical life forms and for it to attain the status of a siddha.

These books are based on the author's experiences in meditation, yoga practice and participation in spiritual groups:

Specialty

Spiritual Master

sex you!

Sleep Paralysis

Astral Projection

Masturbation Psychic Details

Spiritual Master

sex you!

Sleep Paralysis

Michael Beloved

michael beloved

Michael Beloved

Astral Projection

Masturbation Psychic Details

Michael Beloved

Michael Beloved

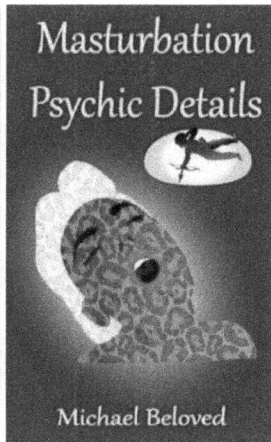

In **Spiritual Master**, Michael draws from experience with gurus or with their senior students. His contact with astral gurus is rated. He walks you through the avenue of gurus showing what you should do and what you should not do, so as to gain proficiency in whatever area of spirituality the guru has proficiency.

sex you! is a masterpiece about the adventures of an individual spirit's passage through the parents' psyches. The conversion of a departed soul into a sexual urge is described. The transit from the afterlife to residency in the emotions of the parents is detailed. This is about sex and you. Learn about how much of you comprises the romantic energy of one's would-be parents!

Sleep Paralysis clears misconceptions so that one can see what sleep paralysis is and what frightening astral experience occurs while the paralysis is being experienced. This disempowerment has great value in giving you confidence that you can and do exist even if one is unable to operate the physical body. The implication is that one can exist apart from and will survive the loss of the material form.

Astral Projection details experiences Michael had even in childhood, where he assumed incorrectly that everyone was astrally conversant. He discusses the lifeForce psychic mechanism which operates the sleep-wake cycle of the physical form, and which budgets energy into the separated astral form which determines if the individual will have dream recall or no objective awareness during the projections. Astral travel happens on every occasion when the physical body sleeps. What is missing in awareness is the observer status while the astral body is separated.

Masturbation Psychic Details is a surprise presentation which relates what happens on the psychic plane during a masturbation event. This does not tackle moral issues or even addictions but shows the involvement of memory and the sure but hidden subconscious mind which operates many features of the psyche irrespective of the desire or approval of the self-conscious personality.

inVision Series

Yoga inVision 1

Yoga inVision 2

Yoga inVision 3

Yoga inVision 4

Yoga inVision 5

Yoga inVision 6

Yoga inVision 7

Yoga inVision 8

Yoga inVision 9

Yoga inVision 10

Yoga inVision 11

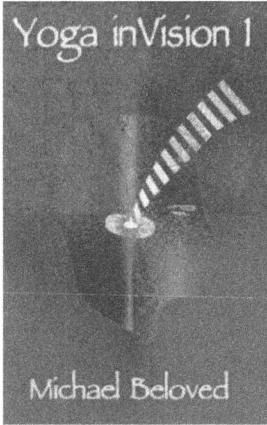
Yoga inVision 1 — Michael Beloved

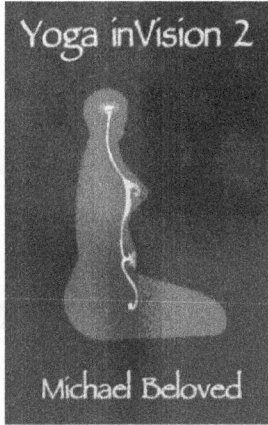
Yoga inVision 2 — Michael Beloved

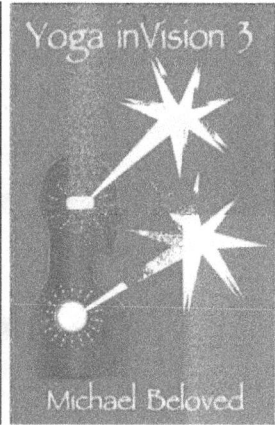
Yoga inVision 3 — Michael Beloved

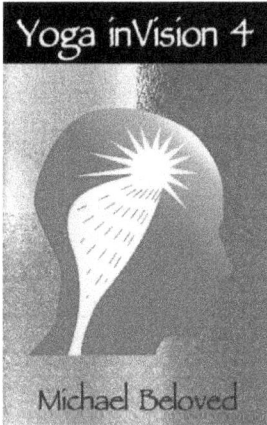
Yoga inVision 4 — Michael Beloved

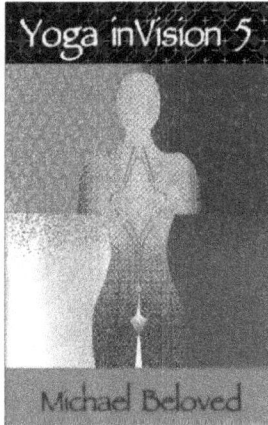
Yoga inVision 5 — Michael Beloved

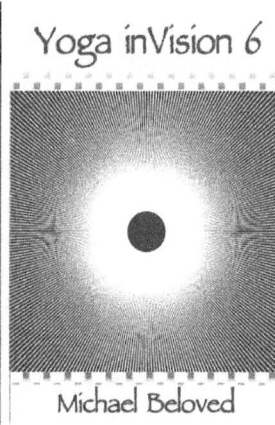
Yoga inVision 6 — Michael Beloved

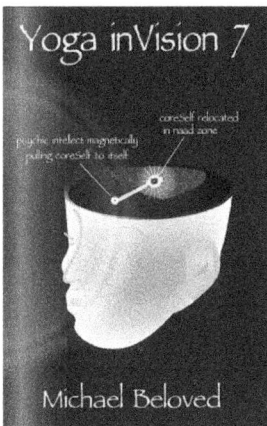
Yoga inVision 7 — Michael Beloved

Yoga inVision 8 — Michael Beloved

Yoga inVision 9 — Michael Beloved

Yoga inVision 10

Yoga inVision 11

Michael Beloved

Michael Beloved

Yoga inVision 1, the first in this series, describes the breath-infusion and meditation practices during the years of 1998 and 1999. There are unique, once in a lifetime as well as recurring insights which are elaborated. inFocus during breath-infusion and the meditation which follows is an adventure for any yogi. This gives what happened to this particular ascetic.

Yoga inVision 2 reports on the author's experiences from 1999 to 2001. Each day the experience is unique, illustrating the vibrancy of practice. Many rare once-in-a-lifetime perceptions are described.

Yoga inVision 3 reports on the author's experiences from 2001 to 2003.
Yoga inVision 4 reports on the author's experiences from 2006 to 2009.
Yoga inVision 5 reports on the author's experiences from 2006 to 2008.
Yoga inVision 6 reports on the author's experiences in 2010.
Yoga inVision 7 reports on the author's experiences in 2011.
Yoga inVision 8 reports on the author's experiences in 2011.
Yoga inVision 9 reports on the author's experiences in 2012.
Yoga inVision 10 reports on the author's experiences in 2012.
Yoga inVision 11 reports on the author's experiences in 2012.

Online Resources

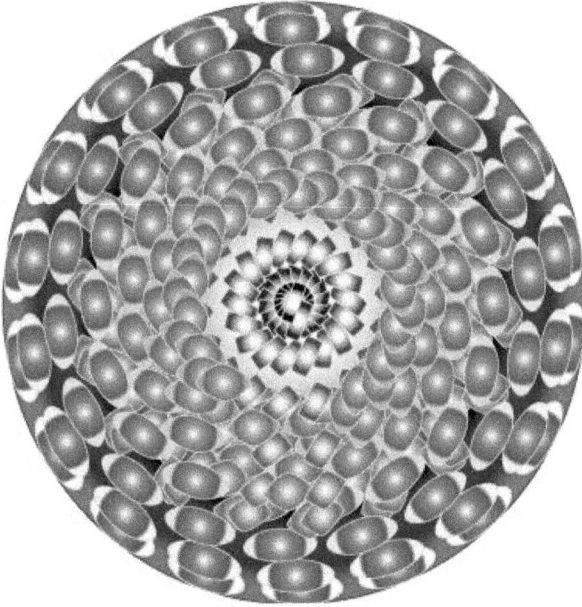

Email: michaelbelovedbooks@gmail.com
                axisnexus@gmail.com

Website: michaelbeloved.com

Forum: inselfyoga.com

Posters: zazzle.com/inself

www.ingramcontent.com/pod-product-compliance
Lightning Source LLC
Chambersburg PA
CBHW072342090426
42741CB00012B/2882